OURS TO FIGHT FOR

American Jewish Voices from the Second World War

OURS TO FIGHT FOR

American Jewish Voices from the Second World War

Introduction
Robert M. Morgenthau

Essays
Jay M. Eidelman
Bonnie Gurewitsch
William L. O'Neill

Afterword
Tom Brokaw

General Editor, Jay M. Eidelman

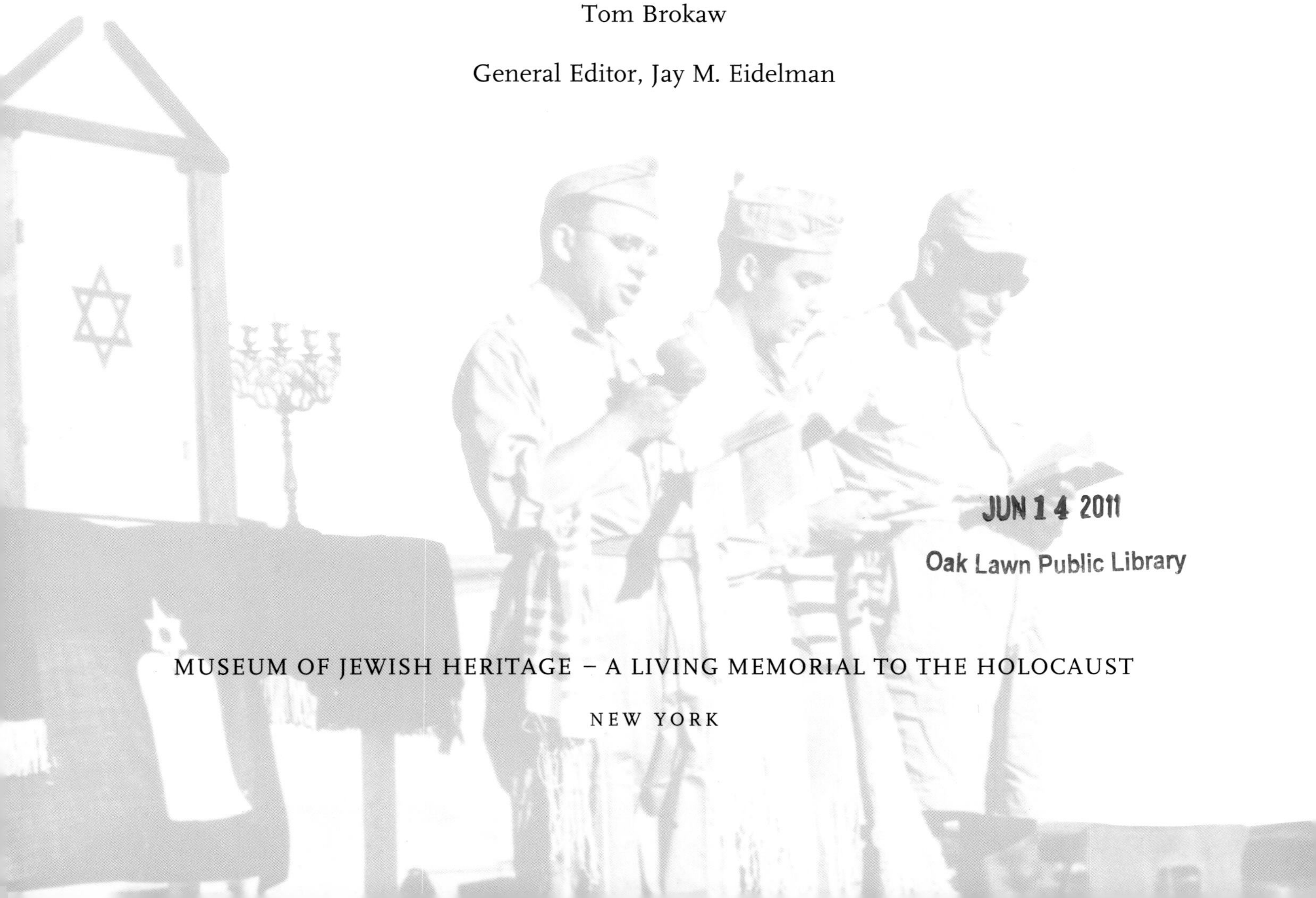

MUSEUM OF JEWISH HERITAGE – A LIVING MEMORIAL TO THE HOLOCAUST

NEW YORK

Published on the occasion of the exhibition *Ours to Fight For: American Jews in the Second World War*, organized by the Museum of Jewish Heritage – A Living Memorial to the Holocaust, New York, October 21, 2003–September 5, 2004.

Major funding for this exhibition has been generously provided by Jack and Susan Rudin and Family in memory of Lewis Rudin; by Irving Schneider in memory of his friend Lewis Rudin; and by Irving and June Paler in memory of June's father, Duncan Robertson, who fought for justice in both world wars.

Project director: Louis D. Levine
Project coordinator: Bryan J. Kessler
Publishing consultant: Osa Brown
Manuscript editor: Gillian Belnap
Designer: Russell Hassell
Printed by The Studley Press, Inc.

Library of Congress Control Number: 2003111552
ISBN 0-9716859-1-6 (clothbound)
ISBN 0-9716859-0-8 (paperbound)

Produced and published by the
Museum of Jewish Heritage – A
Living Memorial to the Holocaust
36 Battery Place
New York, New York 10280
www.mjhnyc.org

Cover: Chaplain Samson Goldstein with the 20th Combat Engineers, Battle of the Bulge, 1944–45
Frontispiece: Chaplains in the Marianas, 1944
Page 4–5: Dog tags and mezuzah worn by Lawrence Luskin
Back cover: Chaplains in the Marianas, 1944

Manufactured in the United States of America

CONTENTS

Preface and Acknowledgments

David G. Marwell
Director

Many question the value of oral history as a discipline, citing a lack of clarity and objectivity inherent in the information gathered. Those who make this judgment expect both too much and too little from an essential tool for understanding the past. It would be risky indeed to rely solely on oral testimony—especially testimony taken after nearly six decades—to determine the history of the Second World War. Historians must mine the archives and analyze a broad range of material to be able to make confident judgments about what happened during this monumental event and why. There are, however, precious few documents or other kinds of material that can help us understand the impact of the war on the men and women who participated in it. Oral history provides the means, perhaps the only means, to achieve this most important goal. Furthermore, oral history can provide a glimpse of the quotidian details of history that are absent from more traditional sources. The resourceful uses of a soldier's helmet, for instance, would not be described in a training manual, or any other military document for that matter.

It would be unwise to expect that any narrative of World War II woven by oral testimony would be seamless. Instead, it is like the story of the six blind men who try to describe an elephant; each can only recount the part he himself experiences. Taken together, however, oral testimonies can portray in words a compelling record of the war—not the only record, but one that would be lost to us otherwise. What is remarkable about these personal histories is not what might be missing in terms of clarity and objectivity, but what is present. What we find sixty-odd years after the fact are the indelible impressions left on memory by extraordinary events.

This book and the exhibition, *Ours to Fight For: American Jews in the Second World War,* represent the culmination of over four years of fascinating research, collecting, and planning by the Museum of Jewish Heritage – A Living Memorial to the Holocaust. The twelve narratives presented here were chosen from an exceptional collection of oral histories. One comes from the collection of more than 3,000 oral histories taken from survivors and liberators by the Center for Holocaust Studies, which began collecting this material before it was fashionable and widespread. The Museum is fortunate to have joined with the Center and is now the repository of this collection. The remaining eleven narratives were selected from the Museum's more than 400 videotaped interviews with men and women who served during the war. These recordings constituted the first phase of the *Ours to Fight For* project. All of the narratives have been edited for length and clarity but remain as true to the original testimony as possible.

Arthur Coren at Tarawa Island, 1944

Coren served with the U.S. Army in the Pacific theater, where he fought at Tarawa, Saipan, Guam, and Tinea.

These narratives are extraordinary in many ways, but what marks them most is their honesty. As the title *Ours To Fight For: American Jewish Voices from the Second World War* implies, there is a spoken quality to these stories. While it is not possible to reproduce the experience of watching and listening to the narrators' interviews, their words and the accompanying photographs are powerful and transport the reader into another time and place. These stories are filled with a deep emotion that comes across on every page.

The Museum is grateful to all of those who made the exhibition and the book possible. Museum Chairman and District Attorney of New York County, Robert M. Morgenthau, provided the inspiration for the project and vigorously advocated for its realization. His heartfelt introduction to this volume demonstrates both the wisdom and the modesty of his generation of veterans. Irving and June Paler were quick to realize the potential such an exhibition held and generously agreed to fund the oral history project. They were kind enough to provide further funding for the exhibition and publication in memory of June's father, Duncan Robertson. We received essential and significant support in the form of two gifts in memory of Lewis Rudin, who served in the army during World War II. One came from his brother, Jack Rudin, himself a combat infantryman, and the other from his friend Irving Schneider, who served in the U.S. Army Air Corps during the war. We appreciate that Lew Rudin's memory inspires such devotion and generosity.

I would like to thank Tom Brokaw for contributing the afterword for this volume. Writing from the perspective of the generation that came after, he defines for us the legacy of those who fought for their country in World War II. Special thanks are also due to Kate Medina. Distinguished historian and Rutgers University professor William L. O'Neill joined two of the Museum's staff, historian Jay M. Eidelman and archivist Bonnie Gurewitsch, in contributing the essays that provide context for the veterans' narratives.

An extraordinary staff contributed to all aspects of the exhibition and this accompanying book. Louis D. Levine, Director of Collections and Exhibitions, directed the project since its inception and provided the overall leadership to both the exhibition and publication teams. Bonnie Gurewitsch served as exhibition curator, and Frieda Wald as project manager. Jay M. Eidelman managed the collection of oral histories, was general editor of this volume, and served as curator for a part of the exhibition. Ivy Barsky, Deputy Director for Programs, contributed to both the exhibition and book and coordinated the contributions of all the Museum's departments, ensuring that the project moved forward smoothly. Deborah Dash Moore, Professor of Religion, Vassar College, was the principal academic advisor to the project. Osa Brown, publishing consultant, expertly managed all phases of the book's publication. Russell Hassell provided a distinctive design for the volume that visually complements the book's subject matter. Gillian Belnap edited the text with skill, sensitivity, and insight. Peter Goldberg photographed the artifacts and scanned all original photographs.

The list of those who worked on the *Ours to Fight For* project is a very long one, but without the contributions of all of these people, neither the exhibition nor the book would have become a reality. We are grateful to Dr. Alfred Gottschalk for his commitment to this endeavor. We also extend particular thanks to members of the Museum staff: Ilana Abramovitch, Courtney Aison, Brad Alter, Lindsay Artwick, Rosa Berland, Lisa Brahms, Esther Brumberg, Elizabeth Edelstein, Svetlana Emery, Ezra Davidson, Tracy Figueroa, Aaron Greenwald, Emina Hadzic, Jamie Hardis, Inbar Kerper-Saranovitz, Ronit Frenkel Kornbluth, Igor Kotler, Indra Mahabir, Joshua Perelman, Matthew Peverly, Andrew Piedilato, Meredith Quinn, Adam Rosenthal, Andi Rosenthal, Elissa Schein, Nili Schiffman, Michael Spielholz, Abby Spilka, Jason Steinhauer, Timothy Stewart-Winter, Deborah Tropp, Rachel Weinstein, and Daniel Wool. Bryan Kessler's assistance with the book ensured its timely publication.

Finally, we extend our greatest thanks to the 415 veterans who participated in our oral history project and to the thirty-five interviewers and many videographers who captured their testimony. Their contributions made this book possible. To the veterans whose testimonies appear in this volume, thank you for the honor of publishing your compelling stories.

INTRODUCTION

Robert M. Morgenthau
Chairman

Four years ago, I suggested that the Museum of Jewish Heritage – A Living Memorial to the Holocaust begin a liberators project, interviewing veterans of World War II. We defined liberator as anyone who participated in liberating the world from the Nazis and their Axis partners. Ultimately the Museum interviewed more than 400 people, representing a broad spectrum of experiences. Just as Holocaust survivors did not begin to tell their horror stories until decades after the war ended, veterans, too, were unable to articulate fully the darkness that dwelled deep within.

The *New York Times* once referred to these stories as "stories from silence," because the experience was so difficult to put into words. The inexpressible nature of the experience is a quality that many of these testimonies share with those of Holocaust survivors collected by the Museum over the years. As with survivors, World War II memory becomes more precious as it becomes more scarce. It is humbling to note that the Department of Veterans Affairs predicts that two-thirds of the approximately 300,000 World War II veterans living in New York State will be gone by 2005. Beyond these similarities, however, is the intimate connection between the history conveyed in these pages and the history that is conveyed in the Museum's core exhibition; those who survived the Holocaust would not be able to tell their story if it had not been for the men and women who served.

My own naval career began in the summer of 1940 when I enlisted in the U.S. Naval Reserve Force. Just about a year later, on June 6, 1941, I graduated from Amherst College with my fellow classmates at a graduation ceremony held a few days early to accommodate the schedules of those of us who were shipping out. Five years earlier, on a summer day in Philadelphia in 1936, President Franklin Delano Roosevelt predicted that my generation would have a "rendezvous with destiny." He was right of course, but I think most of us felt differently at the time. We simply had orders to carry out, a mission to fulfill. In the fullness of time, I realize now how unprepared we were as individuals and as a nation.

My father, Henry Morgenthau Jr., was Secretary of the Treasury under President Roosevelt. Through fact-finding missions of his own, he knew what was taking place along the perimeters of Nazi Germany and what might be in store for Europe. Yet this country was still in the depths of economic depression and getting America back to work was a major priority for the Roosevelt administration. I was certainly aware of what was being done to prepare a reluctant nation for a war, which by 1940 looked impossible to avoid. And it is because we did not avoid that war that the world is a better place today.

Now more than half a century later, it is hard to imagine that the United States entered the war politically and militarily unprepared. When people think of that war—if they think of it at all—they see it only from the end point: America and her allies victorious over genocidal tyrants bent on world domination. In World War II America certainly showed its mettle. The war brought this nation together through common purpose and forever changed it for the better. Before America entered the war, Hitler's armies and their allies, having already gobbled up most of Europe, had now turned east to invade the Soviet Union. The British, who were overrun at Dunkirk, had faced aerial bombardment in the Blitz, were bogged down in North Africa, and about to be expelled from the Far East. The Japanese controlled large areas of China, enslaving and oppressing its people with terrible cruelty. The prospects for an Allied victory were anything but certain.

Despite any military preparations made by the United States, the surprise attack on Pearl Harbor—brought again into stark relief by the events of September 11, 2001—quite literally shocked this nation into action. Even then, the Axis powers continued their advances in Africa, Eastern Europe, and Asia. Thousands and thousands of men were lost at sea in attacks that were stinging and embarrassing defeats for the United States, many of which have only come to light a half century after the fact. Two ships on which I served as Executive Officer, the USS *Lansdale* and the USS *Harry F. Bauer,* were attacked by the enemy. The former was torpedoed and sank along with two troop transports in the convoy, resulting in great loss of life; the latter was the victim of both a torpedo attack and a kamikaze raid—one of more than 1,900 such suicide attacks in Okinawa. It is nothing short of a miracle that we lost no one on that ship. Before the tide of the war turned in 1943, Hitler's reach extended to the gates of Moscow, Leningrad (now St. Petersburg), and Stalingrad (now Volgograd). The Japanese took Burma, Hong Kong, the Dutch East Indies (now Indonesia), Singapore, and the Philippines and were threatening India, Australia, and New Zealand. And as the United States entered the war, the Nazis unleashed the full fury of their "final solution" to obliterate the Jewish population of Germany and conquered Europe.

In 1939 the United States had a standing army of only 190,000 men. By the end of World War II, more than 16 million American men and women had been inducted into the nation's military. The war itself was the largest and most brutal confrontation in history. The United States spent the equivalent in today's terms of almost $4.7 trillion in fighting World War II. To supply the war effort, American business added 17 million new jobs between 1941 and 1945, almost doubling industrial production and eliminating the privations of the Great Depression.

The cost of World War II to the United States in human terms was immense. More than 400,000 Americans lost their lives in the war, another 600,000 were wounded, and tens of thousands more were traumatized. About three-quarters of American deaths were a direct result of combat, the rest from accidents, disease, and privation in POW camps. On average 6,600 Americans were killed in action every month of the war—in the last six months alone there were over 53,000 casualties. That is just about the same number of Americans who lost their lives in combat during all of World War I. Worldwide, military and civilian deaths attributable to the war tallied between 50 and 60 million people. Approximately one-third of the world's Jewish population lay among the dead, murdered by the Nazis. How many more people would have suffered had America not entered the war when she did? How great might our own suffering have been had the war come any closer to our shores?

But America's collective contribution to World War II is only part of the story. In many ways as extraordinary as this collective history are the individual stories of the participants, stories of men and women who left their homes, left all that was familiar to them, in order to heed their nation's call, many paying the ultimate sacrifice. These people were our brothers and sisters, cousins, schoolmates, and friends. Some volunteered, compelled by religious or ideological beliefs; others were drafted. Among them were the soldiers, sailors, marines, and airmen who died too young, while many of those who returned are now the senior citizens we greet at reunions. But all share in the honor of having helped rid the world of a monstrous evil. Their stories are our stories.

Along with an archive of memory, the Museum has crafted a major special exhibition on the Jewish experience in the United States military during World War II. *Ours to Fight For: American Jews in the Second World War* looks at how American Jews came together with other Americans to help win the war. As in the Museum's core exhibition, this history is told from the perspective of those who lived it, using their stories and their words. Narrated almost entirely by the words of the veterans themselves, the exhibition relies upon quotations to describe the hundreds of artifacts drawn from the Museum's collection, from material borrowed from veterans and their families, and through loans from sister institutions. The exhibition includes eight original films, a variety of audio-visual presentations, and an interactive presentation created primarily from interviews with veterans. A web site and new curricula and tours for students and their teachers complement the exhibition. In addition the Museum's Speakers Bureau has added veterans to its roster to provide another opportunity for the public to hear personal testimony.

In reviewing the testimonies in preparation for *Ours to Fight For*, the exhibition team was amazed by their richness and poignancy. They wanted a place where longer narratives could reside, and this book is the result. It is more a book by veterans and less a book about them, with the main content consisting of the veterans' own words, with brief introductory essays written by distinguished historians to give the stories a larger context. The book is divided into three thematic sections, each accompanied by narratives. Jay M. Eidelman's "Jewish GIs and the War Against the Nazis" examines Jewish motivations for fighting and the Jewish experience of military life. Bonnie Gurewitsch's "American Soldiers Confront the Holocaust" describes the shock and horror that swept through United States forces upon discovery of the concentration and death camps. Finally William L. O'Neill's "Race, Ethnicity, and Religion in World War II" compares the state of American racial, religious, and ethnic relations in the pre- and postwar periods. Tom Brokaw, to whom veterans owe an enormous vote of thanks for helping rekindle interest in World War II memory, contributed the afterword.

Reading through the book I was touched by the depth of the narratives. They are human, familiar, and sometimes shocking all at the same time. I recognized much in these stories from my own service during the war, but there was much that I learned. The book is a tribute not only to the veterans featured here; it is a testament to all the men and women whose heroic service in World War II helped win the war—a war whose outcome was far from certain.

Jewish GIs and the War Against the Nazis

Jay M. Eidelman

The United States came of age in World War II. Entering the war on the heels of the Great Depression, Americans struggled to equip themselves for the conflict, and the country was radically changed in the process. For American Jews the experience of serving in the armed forces was no less profound. Jews had served before— Jews have served in all of America's conflicts from the Revolution to the present—but never in such numbers and never in such diverse locations, both at home and abroad. The war years introduced Jews to America and America to its Jews. Jews learned to fight, and they learned to see themselves in new ways, holding their own with non-Jewish comrades. Indeed, the war transformed almost every aspect of American Jewish society, from where Jews lived to how they earned their living. Anti-Semitic feeling in the United States, which according to one poll reached its apex during the war years, was greatly reduced by the war's end. World War II also made American Jews witnesses to the Holocaust and conferred upon them new responsibilities as the world's leading Jewish community.

In the years preceding World War II, American Jewish life was played out for the most part on the streets of big cities. Together, New York City and Chicago were home to more than half of the Jewish population of the United States. Jews nevertheless remained provincial. Most American Jews, whether immigrant or American born, lived among themselves or with other immigrant groups, removed from America's acknowledged political and cultural elite. By the 1940s some

Jews had made inroads into politics and the arts; others had made names for themselves in business and industry. On the whole Jews remained marginalized in an America whose "core" was almost exclusively wealthy, white, and Protestant. Contrary to the myth of Jewish wealth that prevailed, most Jews were of middling economic status at best, earning their livings as industrial and clerical workers, as small-scale merchants, and to a lesser extent, as professionals. By the start of the war many Jews remained traumatized by the Great Depression and skeptical about their prospects.[1]

As a consequence of their economic status and immigrant origins, many Jews differed politically from the so-called American mainstream, involving themselves with leftist and in some cases radical movements. The election of Franklin D. Roosevelt in 1932 and the introduction of his New Deal put Jews squarely among the Democrats, where they would stay for the next five decades. Support for the Zionist cause of a Jewish state in Palestine was popular among American Jews, though hardly universal. On the immigration issue, which continued to gain urgency in the 1930s, most Jews opposed American restrictions. As a group Jews were also more inclined to support intervention in the war in Europe, although Jewish communists, for instance, reversed their previous interventionist stance after the conclusion of the Hitler-Stalin nonaggression pact between Germany and the Soviet Union in 1939.

Jews entering the military in World War II faced several obstacles. The United States was rife with anti-

Meyer Birnbaum at his brother's grave,
Blosville, France, June 26, 1944

Albert Birnbaum died in battle after
the D-Day invasion at Utah Beach.

Semitism in the 1940s, which ranged from physical attacks to the "polite," exclusionary social anti-Semitism of the elite. Theories based on the same racist logic that animated Nazi ideology were widespread in America and pointed to American Jews as a racial and economic threat. Even during the war, pollsters found that Americans considered Jews a greater danger to America than Germany.[2] This kind of thinking was commonplace among America's military leadership, whose obdurate anti-Semitism mixed Social Darwinism, eugenics, and a deep-seated fear of radical insurgency. In the years preceding the war, the army was so concerned about the threat from Jewish subversives that it devoted tremendous energies to surveillance of Jews. Communism and miscegenation were feared more than Nazi Germany, whose warmongering and racial policies were excused if not admired by many high-ranking officers. Americans, both in and out of the military, saw Jews as the driving force behind the Roosevelt administration's desire to enter into a conflict with Nazi Germany that was not, according to the isolationists, in America's best interests.[3]

In the service Jews faced the age-old charge of not being able to pull their own weight or of being physically unfit to serve. Claims persisted that Jews were draft dodgers. The stereotype that Jews had a talent for working with numbers pigeonholed some Jews into particular military occupations such as clerks, quartermasters, and navigators. The same prejudices that kept Jews out of elite colleges before the war sometimes made it difficult for Jews seeking military commissions. Name-calling and bigoted remarks led to fistfights as Jews stepped up to defend their honor. Ignorance, however, was the greatest hurdle for Jews to overcome. Outside of major centers, most Americans were unfamiliar with Jewish people.[4] Many of the Jewish veterans interviewed for the Museum's oral history project recall non-Jews in the service who were surprised to discover that Jews did not have horns or tails. By living with non-Jews in the close quarters of military life and by risking their lives for non-Jewish comrades, Jews demonstrated that in essential ways they were not different from others.

For the more than 550,000 Jews who served in the United States military, World War II was an all-encompassing experience. Jews in service represented 11 percent of the total U.S. Jewish population. Half of the Jewish men between the ages of eighteen and forty-four were under arms during the war.[5] Young men and women who had seen little outside their neighborhoods now found themselves traveling to distant parts of the country and the globe. Jewish communities around the country did their part, taking in Jews stationed far from home on the Sabbath and on holidays. The Jewish Welfare Board, working through chaplains and the USO (United Service Organizations), provided for Jewish spiritual health in these far-flung locales with everything from prayer books to Passover matzohs. After the war many Jews chose to relocate to new communities. Postwar growth of the Jewish communities in Los Angeles and Miami is directly attributable to the numbers of Jews who spent time there during World War II.[6]

Jewish motivations for fighting in World War II were clear. The shock and anger wrought by the Japanese surprise attack on Pearl Harbor reverberated in the Jewish community. Patriotism, feelings of duty to their community, and a sense of adventure stirred Jews to action. A complete understanding of Hitler's intention toward the Jewish population of Europe would not be realized until the liberation of the concentration and death camps, but American Jews knew enough to know that Hitler had to be stopped. Like Bernard Branson they were eager and proud to fight the Nazis. Jewish refugees who had fled Europe before the start of the war were also keen to avenge themselves on Nazi Germany by serving in the military. Jews on the left may have questioned the imperialist nature of the war, but most saw the war for what it was—an unjust and brutal assault by the Axis powers on freedom. Contrary to the claims of draft dodging, Jews enlisted in equal or higher numbers than the general population.[7] Once in, Jews served, fought, were wounded, and died in similar ratios to all other Americans.

Despite the less than warm welcome experienced by many, the military did take certain steps to integrate Jews. The Chaplain Corps instituted a kind of ecumenism that, in theory, called on all chaplains to serve all faiths. Recognizing that their ranks were not monolithically Christian, the military also promoted the new concept of Judeo-Christianity. While these high-minded ideas did not always play out in practice, the fact that Jews were permitted, if not encouraged, to express their religion in public was heartening for Jews in service. The shared experience of combat was another important factor in diminishing anti-Jewish animosity.[8] Many Jews found that like atheists, anti-Semites were hard to find in foxholes.

Capture at the hands of the enemy was a matter of special significance for Jews serving in the European theater of operations. Information was fuzzy, but the word in military circles was that captured Jews would be summarily executed or sent to concentration camps. These were not baseless fears. The full extent of the Holocaust was still unclear, but Nazi persecution of Jews was well known. In accordance with Hitler's Commissar Order to eliminate Soviet leadership, Jewish POWs on the eastern front were murdered in July of 1941. Four thousand Jewish POWs from the Red Army were sent to Majdanek in 1942, where few survived. An additional 20,000 Soviet Jewish POWs were murdered at Auschwitz between the spring of 1940 and the end of 1943. The Germans did not issue similar orders for Jewish POWs from western forces because of fear of reprisals against German POWs in Allied hands.[9]

The *H* for Hebrew on their dog tags, there to assure proper religious burial, could also identify Jews to their captors. American Jews in danger of being taken prisoner had to decide whether to hide or discard their dog tags to avoid the fate of European Jews. Many chose to keep them. On the whole American Jews were treated like other American POWs, but that did not ease the fear that accompanied being a Jewish prisoner in Germany. After the bombing of Dresden in 1945, Jewish prisoners at Stalagluft I, a POW camp near the Black Sea, were segregated from non-Jews but suffered no other negative consequences; a threatened deportation kept getting postponed. At Stalag IX B in Bad Orb, 350 prisoners, most of them Jewish, were separated and sent as slave laborers to the town of Berga, where they worked in the Schwalbe 5 mines run by the SS. The loss of life in Berga alone accounted for 6 percent of all American POW deaths.[10]

Returning from the war was a mixed experience for American Jews. They had helped to win a monumental victory, and now they stood to benefit from all the fruits of wartime economic expansion. For the first time this generation of American Jews, having lived through the Great Depression, could aspire to the solidly middle-class American dream put in place by the GI Bill of Rights. Serving in the military had integrated American Jews into white American society in ways that were unimaginable just five years earlier. The economic and social benefits that resulted from the war are still being felt in the American Jewish community. At the same time American Jews came face-to-face with the truth of Nazi brutality. They understood that Hitler's threats were not threats at all but a plan for worldwide Jewish annihilation. American Jews took these lessons to heart, working tirelessly for Zionist and Jewish causes. Imbued with fighting spirit instilled in them by the military, American Jews returned to the fight for social justice with renewed vigor.

NOTES
1. Deborah Dash Moore, "When Jews Were GIs: How World War II Changed a Generation and Remade American Jewry," Fourth David W. Belin Lecture at the Jean and Samuel Frankel Center for Judaic Studies, The University of Michigan (Ann Arbor: Jean and Samuel Frankel Center for Judaic Studies, The University of Michigan), 2–3. On the effects of the Great Depression, see Beth Wenger, *New York Jews and the Great Depression: Uncertain Promise* (Syracuse, N.Y.: Syracuse University Press, 1999).

2. Edward S. Shapiro, *A Time for Healing: American Jewry Since World War II* (Baltimore: Johns Hopkins University Press, 1992), 6–7. See also Leonard Dinnerstein, *Antisemitism in America* (N.Y.: Oxford University Press, 1994), 129–49.

3. Joseph W. Bendersky, *The "Jewish Threat": Anti-Semitic Politics of the U.S. Army* (New York: Basic Books, 2000), 259–306.

4. Deborah Dash Moore, "When Jews Were GIs," 6–9.

5. Ibid, 7; I. Kaufman, *American Jews in World War II: The Story of 550,000 Fighters for Freedom* (New York: Dial Press, 1947), 1: 349; Samuel C. Kohs, "Jewish War Records of World War II," *American Jewish Year Book* 47 (1946): 167.

6. On postwar migration to Miami and Los Angeles, see Deborah Dash Moore, *To the Golden Cities: Pursuing the American Jewish Dream in Miami and L.A.* (Cambridge: Harvard University Press, 1996).

7. Bendersky, 296.

8. Deborah Dash Moore, "Worshipping Together in Uniform: Christians and Jews in World War II," The 2001 Swig Lecture, The Swig Judaic Studies Program at the University of San Francisco (San Francisco: The Swig Judaic Studies Program at the University of San Francisco, 2001), 1–12; idem, "When Jews Were GIs," 9–11. On the emergence of the concept of Judeo-Christianity, see Mark Silk, *Spiritual Politics: Religion and American Since World War II* (New York: Simon & Schuster, Inc., 1988), 40–53.

9. Mitchell G. Bard, *Forgotten Victims: The Abandonment of Americans in Hitler's Camps* (Boulder, Colo.: Westview Press, 1994), 36–37.

10. Ibid, 35, 77–90.

"I Wanted Those Sons of Bitches to Know"

Bernard Branson U.S. ARMY AIR CORPS

I graduated at sixteen, in 1941. There was a war on, so what you did was you waited to get old enough to go into the army. I was working as a Western Union messenger. I used to work down at the Brooklyn Navy Yard delivering telegrams. I remember seeing the HMS *Barham* come in. It was a British battleship, which had been pretty shot up, and I would go down there and look at it and I couldn't wait to get into the service.

There was a course in Quoddy, Maine, for about four or five months. I got to Maine and then I worked my way out to St. John in Canada. And I walked into the RCAF and I said, "Oh, here I am. I'm ready to fly." And they just sent me home. They laughed. I must have been seventeen, just about seventeen. And they said, "We're not taking Americans. You're not Canadian, you can't go in. You've got to go back and you've got to tell the Americans to take you in." So I went back and I had to wait until I hit eighteen to get into the air corps because there were no enlistments any more. And at eighteen, as soon as I hit eighteen, I said, "Take me in. I'm ready." My brother was already in by then.

I was a very thin little kid. The marines wanted me. And the airborne wanted me. And I'm looking, and I said, "I don't want them. I want the Army Air Corps." That's all I knew, was the Army Air Corps. And the marines said, "Well, you're going into the marines," when I was getting my physical. I said, "My mother's going to hate you for this. I want to be an air corps man." And he stamped the thing and I looked. It said "Army." And I'm like, *Oy!*, that's what I wanted. I'd always wanted the army ever since I was a kid. And I went from there, I went to Camp Upton, and the first day they get us our uniforms, you know, all the shots and stuff like that. To make a long story short, I went down to Miami Beach. That's how I found out I was in the air force. As the train went out and the officer came through, I noticed he had the air force badge. And I went, "Oh! Everything is working out." And then my mother made me swear—and that was the only thing—on my father's grave that I would not fly as a pilot. I would not try to be a pilot.

She had a thing about the military. She had a son in the military. He was already in, my older brother. He was a radar man when it was still top secret. And she knew what I wanted to do, but she made me swear. So when I took the exam and they wanted to send me to pilot school, I couldn't really tell them that I couldn't do it. It was like, you know, I had sworn on my father's grave. I don't know how you describe it but it was a . . . it was a real promise. I made the promise and didn't really realize it. I'm like that. If I give you my word, I'm, I'm a dead man. I don't change it. She thought I'd be on the ground. I never told her that there were gunners. So the guy said, "Well, then you're going to gunnery school." I said, "I'll take it."

You stay about two or three weeks in tents waiting to go to class, and then it's about a six-week course of gunnery. First week is sitting and practicing. The second week is shooting skeet on trucks. I was a good skeet shooter. I never shot a gun in my life, but I was a marksman. Don't ask me how. I was good. Till one time I was so good that one guy who had been a corporal in 1938—George Ostamulow was his name—said, "Boy, look at that Abie shoot. Look at that. He, that Abie, he can't miss. He can't miss." He said, "Jesus, that fucking Jew boy, he can't miss. Don't you miss, Jew boy?" And then I missed. I missed two and I turned around. I just nicely said, "Oh, fuck you," and turned around and I got the rest of them. That was about the extent of any anti-Semitism I had till one other time. But it wasn't really anti-Semitism. You couldn't really call it that, because when I came back from overseas I met him, and this guy couldn't . . . he was so thrilled to see another guy alive that he just hugged me. We were friends.

The crews' names were put together. And then what they did, you went and you met each other and you were given three months to either get together and get close or drop out of the crew. No questions asked. And we, we just hit it off. Joe and I were in the same crew, and we met Irving Simon, who was another Jewish boy—most of the crews had a Jew somewhere in there, you know. And very luckily, my pilot . . . I think I'm here because I had a good pilot. Calvin Hall. He had flown with RCAF, flown dive-bombers, and then switched over and became an instructor on B-24s. And so when he came to us, he had 500 hours on B-24s, and that's a lot of hours. He was one of the few guys who could stall a B-24 and bring it out of a stall. Nobody could do that. That's how wonderful this guy was. And that's why I can talk about one of the worst experiences I had in my life.

Don Gray was my copilot. He didn't make it through. They took him away because he started to see enemy fighters all over the sky. He couldn't, he couldn't even control the plane. And we had an engineer. He had an appendectomy and we got another engineer, a guy named Johnny Murphy who was an old man and an alcoholic. He became a problem. They took him off the crew. And then there was Bob Polk, who had been a lumberjack. He was a front-turret gunner. And Bob Polk was a very good Catholic. He would go out and sleep with anything that walked, and then he would go to confession. He didn't care what age. We, most of us, got disgusted with him. And Earl Everett, who was the shortest man in the air force. He was four feet eleven and a half inches tall. You had to be five feet. He just got in. He was our bombardier. Our navigator we had for a very short time, and then when we were over there we received another navigator, a flying officer called Bill Fidraki. And he was hit over a target where the nose gunner was killed—his eye was shot out—but he had a choice to pull the nose gunner in and try to save him or try to save his eye. He tried to save the nose gunner, so he went home with a decoration. But thank God he lived. He wanted to be a doctor. And that was us.

The gunner's job was never to shoot enemy planes down. You only fired at the planes as they were firing at you because you only had just so much ammo. You had to fire in three-second bursts. If you held it long, you were finished with your ammo. So your job was really to make sure to throw them off, because they were just as scared, I realize now, to come in at you. But your job was to basically shoot and make sure they don't get your plane. And that was basically your job.

We were up at Westover Field, Massachusetts. We'd spent a few days there talking and learning to be together and what about you and what about you? And of course as soon as I said the name Abramson, they gave me the Abie name—I didn't change my name till later. And we just got along well. We liked each other. We got along—it was all first-name basis. There were no officers, no enlisted men. It was just a bunch of guys who liked each other. We all learned in phase training how to fly the plane, how to do every other person's part, because it was important if anybody got hit

somebody should be able to do what you had to do. And so we practiced. We went down to Chatham Field, Georgia. This was still in 1943, around the end of 1943. We went to Chatham Field, Georgia, where we spent months in training. Then one time we went down to Cuba and flew for ten days out of Cuba, a ten-day antisubmarine patrol, just to keep the crew knowing how the crew works.

I think most crews got along. Most crews, because that's what the air force wanted. If you got along together, you worked as a team. And if you were hit, you went down as a team. I mean, there was no, no safe place to hide. And I can just say for myself, I left with thirty-nine crews. That's 390 men. And 7 men came home when I came home. You'd make friends with a crew, and they were gone the next day. And all you knew was that every day you would check to see if you were flying.

B-24 *Flak Happy* and its
crew, tail gunner Bernard
Branson front row, second
from right

We went overseas around April 1944. My group, I realized, started in February. So I got there in April and started to fly my missions in May. The group we were assigned to had already been there in February. We were like a replacement crew at the time. To make a long story short, we were a lead crew after five missions. That was it. And when I was shot down, they made us come back and fly because they had no lead crews.

Nobody was prepared to fly. You knew you had to do it so you did it. I mean, that was all. There was always a fear, a terror inside. When we got there, before we got there, a colonel spoke to us and he told us, "Look to the right of you, look to the left of you. Take a good look, because two out of three of you are not coming back." I remember saying to myself, "I'm going to miss you guys." Don't ask me why I said it. And that was what happened basically. In fact, worse. You get the idea—I think there was a feeling that I wouldn't get through, I wouldn't make fifty. Now I honestly had that feeling. I can't even describe it. You know it's going to happen and you know you have to do your job, so you do your job and that's what happened.

When we got to the base, they asked all the Jewish fliers to stay behind. And there were quite a few of us, officers and enlisted men. And this Lieutenant Levine came out, he was the Intelligence officer, and he asked all of us to give him our dog tags so he can change the *H* on the dog tag from Hebrew to either *P* or *C* for Protestant or Catholic. Because he told us point-blank that if we're shot down and they find the *H* on our dog tags, we will not live, we will not be put in a stalag. We will either be tortured to death or beaten to death or killed right away or sent, if we're lucky, to a concentration camp. And at that point none of us would do it. None of us. Oh, I knew what the Nazis were doing. "Nobody knew," that's bullcrap. We knew what they were doing to the Jews. We knew what they were doing to the Jews in 1941 and even in 1940. Come on. I have a lot of very strong feelings about that. No, we knew it. And I knew that if I was going up there, I'd be in deep water if I got shot down. But my feeling was I wanted those sons of bitches to know that the bombs that are dropping, that there's a Jew up there doing it. That was my feeling. Nineteen years old, didn't know any better. I always had the feeling, you know, if we get hit I'll probably blow up anyway, so let them know it's a Jew. And that was the feeling. We didn't even question, there wasn't a guy that said, "Yeah, I'll do it." We just said, "Fine," and we walked out. I think he was proud of us. More than anything else, I think he was proud of us. And I'm proud of us when I think about it.

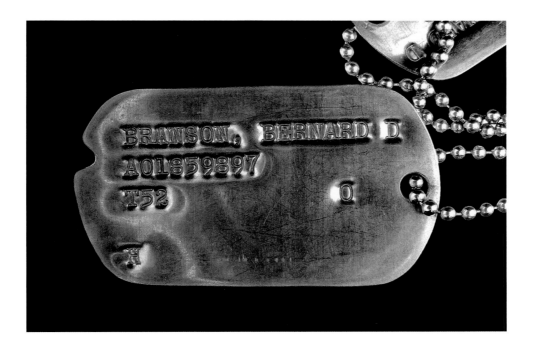

The first few missions, they gave us what we called milk runs. They wanted us to learn how to fly, how to fly in formation, when to clear your guns. That means no flak, not too much, no fighters. By my fifth mission, I realized a *mensch ken derharget veren*—a man can get himself killed. Because what happened is . . . it happens to others. They crash. They get shot down. And, you know, you reach a point, and people don't talk about it because they don't like to, but when a plane blows up next to you in the air, you don't say, "Oh, poor Joe." You say, "Boy, was that close! Thank God it wasn't us."

Another feeling which I don't think people talk about, and this is a general feeling, is that when you fly and it's a big expanse of sky and you see enemy planes, you don't get that involved as in, "Oh, they're after me." You actually feel like you're almost in a movie. It's that kind of a feeling. You're in a movie. When you can shoot your guns, oh, it's a relief. You feel so much better you could do something. But when they're shooting flak and you see the puffs and you see planes get hit and you see guys bail out, you just sit there because you can't move; the only way you can handle that is you . . . you just make it unreal. It's like you're in a big movie. And when you land and you get your coffee and you sit down, then you realize what you went through. Then the terror starts. And that's when guys would usually break down if they broke down. So by the fifth mission, we had lost enough planes so that we were a lead crew already. They were glad my pilot had 500 hours so he could be a lead pilot. And that was basically it. And we flew, and we had some pretty rough ones.

One of the most miserable feelings you had was when you landed and were taxiing to your hard stand and the chief, the crew chief and the mechanics, were waiting for the planes that didn't make it, and you'd have to signal to them to let them know they went down. And you could just see them wilt, just like that. And that, that was a terrible feeling. After that a lot of things happened.

You know, guys got drunk and guys would do a lot of things they shouldn't have done, and that was the way they handled the pressure. Some of the guys—I was not a drinker and I didn't smoke, you know. I was what Mama would say "a good Jewish boy"—they would get big, big barrels—glass barrels—and they would make stills. You'd have guys drunk all the time. Murphy, who was my engineer, broke down. He couldn't take it beyond about thirty-something missions and he broke down. He had a fourteen-year-old daughter. He was about thirty-seven. To me that was an old man in those days. My pilot was twenty-five. I was a big nineteen. And Murphy, he just couldn't handle it. He would urinate in his pants all the time. If we were off one night, he'd be brought in by someone. "Is this Murphy's tent?" And he'd be drunk, and they'd throw him into the tent. He just couldn't take it.

Just before the invasion of southern France, we were given supposedly a target in Toulon, and for days we were attacking the beaches at Toulon. And we went over the target. They told us there'd be no flak and no fighters, that this was a milk run. Well, they didn't tell us that that's where the Abbeville Kids were stationed. They were a German group that was Goering's personal group. In order to be a pilot in the Abbeville Kids, the "Yellow Noses," you had to have five Allied planes to your credit. Then you could transfer to them to fly. Well, nobody told us that that's where they were stationed. I have never seen such accurate flak. I saw four puffs of flak and four planes go down. You know, the majors are firing and the sergeants are loading, because they had fantastic flak. And we were hit by the Abbeville Kids. We got over the target and one of our engines was knocked out, and as we pulled out, they jumped us and they hit another engine. So we lost two engines. And we were then hit by six 109s and three 210s. They were twin engine. And they chased us because we couldn't stay with the group. They chased us back over Corsica where some of our planes came from. But we couldn't maintain the altitude because our number three engine, which everything works off, started to shoot black oil out the tail. And we just didn't know what . . . we tried and tried to get the plane back, but it was really going down, down, down. You couldn't keep the altitude. Finally the pilot said, "Who wants to bail out? You better bail out now." Well, you don't tell that to guys like us because if you're told, "Bail out," none of us will do it, because everybody knows we had a twenty-four-foot chute, and bailing out is like jumping from two stories. You don't walk away too well. But heroic Bernie said, "I'll stick with the plane." That's all the rest of the crew needed to hear. If Abie sticks, they're all sticking. The pilot brought her down. He belly-whopped her in, and every one of us was okay.

We were outside of Rome. Marcigliana Air Base, it was called. Marcigliana was the Rome airport. But there was nothing there when we came down. And here's where it's fuzzy. I don't remember everything, but I know we got out and we ran and the partisans helped us, but I can't remember exactly where. And we came out of hiding and this Italian man yells, "Hey, Joe." I look, "Yeah?" He says, *"Sholom aleichem."* I said, "What?" So my friend Irv hits me, he says, "Tell him, *'Aleichem sholom.'"* I didn't know what to do. So I said, *"Aleichem sholom,"* and we talked a little bit in Yiddish, a little bit of English. He had hid out, he was hiding out in the Vatican. And he hid out till the Americans came. Rome had fallen. So right away we go back to the air base because Rome fell. We were the first Americans into Rome that came from an airplane.

Most of the missions were over Europe, over Romania, Hungary, Poland, parts of Germany, Bulgaria, all of that whole area. In fact, my group was also one of the first ones to bomb an area and land in Russia. The Ploesti oil fields were probably the most important oil fields in all of Romania and all of Europe. It took care of most of the oil that the whole Axis powers used. And we . . . I hit that six times. We really had to give it a pounding. It also was one of the most heavily defended. They used to shoot red, white, and blue flak. Nobody ever knew why, but the flak was red, white, and blue. And you knew when you went there you were going to lose planes. It was just one of those things.

Their fighters would come in under their own flak to shoot you down. And many times we would be hit. It depended on where you were. There was always a couple of what they called dead man's corners, and you always hoped you didn't get that corner. One of the most frightening things is to be the last guy in the last plane in the last group over a target, because everything out there is not yours. I remember that once in Greece, we bombed

Athens, and I remember we came through a gap and they had the guns in the mountains and they were shooting. And I'm sitting there and watching the flak blow up. They got our altitude and they'd send up flak and we'd keep moving, and I'm watching it get closer and closer and I can't move. And that was scary. That was horrible because you . . . you think the next one's going to get you. We were lucky. We got through. We bombed and went home.

We were sent to bomb the Moosbierbaum oil refinery in Vienna. We got there and it was the most brutal flak and fighters we'd ever seen. It was loaded. The smoke from the fire and the oil was over thirty thousand feet high. We were flying at twenty thousand feet. And we had blasted it. And I'm sitting there going over the target when all of a sudden just below me the guy blows up. I start to press my button when my pilot says, "The guy in front of us just blew up." I turn around. This guy starts getting flames, it starts to spin down, and this guy just turns on his back and falls all the way down in less time than I'm telling you. Like boom, boom, boom, boom, and it's over. And we are alone, because from being in the number seven spot, we're now all by ourselves. Stragglers are dead meat. My nose gunner calls in, "Fighters coming in twelve o'clock high." So we get prepared for twelve o'clock. I'm at six o'clock, if you look at it. They start coming. My . . . my tail gunner . . . my nose gunner, my ball-turret gunner yells, "Fighters at six o'clock low." And I look and I see fighters coming up six o'clock high, six o'clock level, and six o'clock low. And we're alone. So I yell, "Fighters at six o'clock high, level, and low." They came around and they lined up and they started to make a pursuit curve at me and I started to shoot. I didn't think my bullets were going out fast enough. They were three-second bursts, and I felt I wanted it more than three seconds but I knew I couldn't afford to. They got so close that the first plane . . . peeled off. I saw him hunched over in his plane. He had come in and then he went just like that, and they all broke up. I had killed . . . I got them. I got them. Don't ask me how or why. I think God watched me because I couldn't aim. They were coming in like crazy, but he was the lead. And I realize now, you know, years later, if I was a pilot and the guy in front of me got hit, I'd pull away. How do I know I got him? Because my ball-turret gunner and my waist gunner said he went straight into the ground. My pilot had pushed the RPM to fifty-three inches, which on a B-24 is like you blow your gaskets, and he pushed it so we, we pulled into what was left of the group. And that was probably the most frightening time I had of all. To see those four guys go down so fast, it was mind-boggling. And

I don't care what anybody says, you see a bunch of fighters like that, it's not like one comes and you're shooting and another one comes in like in the movies. They were lined up. There were twenty of them. It was scary. And we got home, we got home with thirty-five holes in the plane, but we got home.

Once I started shooting, boy, I was right there. That was the difference. When you could do something, you were there. I felt I could get them back. It was that kind of a feeling. And there was no fear. They said I saved the plane. I don't know if I saved the plane. I think everybody saved the plane. Everybody shot. Everybody was doing it. And we got in under the group so that the other people could shoot also. And they put me in for the decoration and, of course, there were no pictures. If you don't have pictures . . . the fighter pilots, they get credit because they have a picture. They took our cameras away. They used to do that. They took the bombsight away. Our bombardiers, we used to call "targetiers" . . . we only had a bombsight in number one, number two, and number five.

It was never "bombs away." We go to the target, and the engineer would start to pull the pins out of the bombs that were ready to be dropped, and he'd go back and he'd watch. And when the first lead plane dropped the bombs, he would drop the bombs. Nobody ever said, "Bombs away." He would say, "Let's get the hell out of here," and the word wasn't "hell." That's how we knew he dropped the bombs. "Let's get . . . get the fuck out of here." Yeah. "Let's get the fuck out of here." And that's what we would do. And we'd just pick ourselves up and just move. And that was my . . . my roughest time, I think, was that time. It was the most scary thing.

Interestingly, I met a man who was a prisoner in the concentration camps. They took the Jews in Vienna and made them clean up where we had dropped bombs, and he remembers my group—he didn't know who it was—but he remembers that day. And he said, "I hope you dropped the bomb on me." He told me that. He had a cleaning store here in America. And I said, "I'm glad I didn't get you." But interestingly, when I became a psychoanalyst, I was interviewed by this woman and she had a real accent. They were all Viennese, but I didn't know they were all Jewish, you know. And she said, "What did you do in the war?" and I told her. "Did you ever bomb Vienna?" I said, "Oh, yes, I bombed Vienna." And she says, "I hope you got my house." And I just felt so good.

You have to understand, we're a bunch of kids. We were kids. I wouldn't do that today. I got to be meshuga. But a bunch of kids? We would take a watermelon up there so it would be ice cold when we landed, you know.

Three gunnery
instructors
after the war in
Apalachicola,
Florida, Bernard
Branson on right

We'd wrap it in a towel. It was that kind of thinking. And we would land and of course we got priority, because if you had wounded aboard or something you landed first. And then we got down and we got to the base and then we went to the Red Cross where they gave us coffee and donuts. My missions were so terrifying, between you and me, that for years I couldn't take donuts. I could never take . . . eat a donut and have coffee together because that was the first thing they gave you was coffee and donuts. And I remember coming back from a mission over Ploesti. We couldn't make Ploesti because we'd lost an engine—half my missions were on three engines—and that's why I say my pilot was good. And we landed. We got . . . I don't know how many holes in the plane. We're miserable. Unshaven. We fell out and we dropped our bombs. We didn't know where, but we dropped them somewhere in a farmland somewhere because I saw them go. And we're going down and my bombardier is saying, "Oh, we're crossing the Blue Danube. We're crossing the Danube." I looked down and said, "Oh, Shorty, that's not the Danube." He says, "Come on, what are you talking about?" I'm doing dead reckoning. We didn't have a navigator. I said, "Shorty, that's not the Danube. The Danube is dirty brown. That's got blue water. That's not the Danube." It was a river near Sofia, which was right over a thirty-five-fighter base for the enemy. What do I have to say? I'm sitting there listening to Bing Crosby, because we would always be able to fool around with the radio. We could listen. The Germans loved to play Bing Crosby records. But then I hear, *"B-vier und zwanzig vierzehntausend füsse."* I said, "Oh, shit, that's us." We're down to fourteen thousand feet. So I yelled to my pilot, "They have us. The B-24 at fourteen thousand feet." Well, he pulled up. They took off, and we got into the clouds and we flew in the clouds. And thank God they got so bollixed up they never . . . they never shot us down.

I came home September 1944. When I came home they sent me for three weeks to Atlantic City for a break, and then they offered me another stripe if I would go out on a B-29 or become a gunnery instructor. At that point I felt I had pushed my luck a little too far. I said, "I'll take the gunnery school." And so I ended up being a teacher anyway when you think about it. And I went through gunnery school, gunnery instructor school quite well. I had no problems with it, learned it, learned it cold. And that's when I had the only anti-Semitic thing I had in the service.

It was in Laredo, Texas. I was friends with a Greek guy named Gabby. We were friends. Palled around, did everything. And toward the end of the

school—all of us hated physical ed, you know, because the guy who was running the phys ed could keep you there as long as he wanted until you did it the way he wanted—and everybody was making fun and so on. So I turned to Gabby, and I said, "Gabby, we want to get the hell out of here. Let's do the thing and get it over with." And he says, "Shut up, Jew." I'm dumbfounded, "What?" He said, "You heard me, you fucking Jew." I said, "Gabby, you know what you're saying?" He says, "Yeah. You're a fucking Jew." My feeling was that if I hit this son of a bitch, and he was bigger than me, I will never become commissioned. That'll go on my record. Yeah, I'll get off but they'll never . . . I'll never be commissioned. So I just said, fuck him. I didn't say a word. I turned away. And he kept yelling, "Jew," and I acted like he didn't exist. He must have been the most frustrated guy in the world. And you know why I say that? Because I had a fight with one guy on our thirty-fifth mission.

We used to have what we called two eggs, three eggs, and how-many-eggs-do-you-want missions. You knew if they said how many eggs do you want, it meant Vienna, Munich, or Ploesti. You just knew that. They get you up at four o'clock in the morning to fly a mission. You're out, you're off the ground at seven, you're over the target at twelve, you're home by three. And I'm standing there and it's pitch black, and we're shuffling and shuffling. So I said, "I wonder how many eggs they're going to give us this time?" And Bob Polk said, "What do you care?" I said, "Bob, I'm just talking." Bob was my nose gunner. And he gives me a push. And I said, "Bob, leave me alone." He says, "I don't want to leave you alone." Now, I know years later, we were all tense. We were all . . . you know, about every eighth or ninth mission, somebody would refuse to fly, and you'd ignore him and he'd get up and he'd fly. I remember my ninth mission. I wouldn't get out of the bunk, out of the cot. I said, "I'm not going to die. Go ahead. If you want to go, go ahead." And they don't say a word. They get dressed, and then you get up and follow them. That's what everybody did. But he kept hitting me. I said, "Bob, leave me alone." He said, "I don't want to leave you alone." And I just made a scream! And I jumped him. The guy was a lumberjack, remember? And I got him in a neck lock and I was going to kill him. Realize, I was also nervous. To make a long story short, they pulled us off. He was mad, I was mad. But when I shot the guy down, because that was the same mission that I shot the guy down, he said, "Oh, Abie, I love you. I love you. You're wonderful." But this Gabby was a son of a bitch. We were buddies! We, we did everything together. Never once said a word. We were pals at gunnery school.

I don't know whatever happened to him. I was shipped to a good place. I became a gunnery instructor. I did that from 1944 all through till October 12, 1945, and then I came home. And that was good duty. I had two lovely friends. We were buddies. Johnny Barrell and Franklin Benjamin. Just nice guys. We all did the same thing. Never a thing about Judaism.

I wanted to join and help Israel during the war of 1948. They told me they didn't need me. I walked over. They didn't need me. They had three airplanes. What could I give them? A tail gunner? But I wanted to do what I could. By then I was married and my wife said, "You can't do it." They told me I'd be about three thousand on the list to get to be a tail gunner, so I never bothered.

I want my kids to feel proud. I want my kids to appreciate it. Proud, because if it wasn't for guys like me, there wouldn't be any Jews around. That's my honest feeling. I'm one little tiny cog in the whole wheel, but there were enough of us that to me that's what's important. What does it mean? If it wasn't for us, there wouldn't be an Israel. If it wasn't for us, there wouldn't be a Jew. I could cry half the time when I think of it. That's really what it's about. And if the goyim read this or the *antisemitin*, good for them. Let them know. And I want also the Jews who say, "*Oy*, military is no good and the Jews should try to hide and never go . . . " You know, hey, there were Jews that fought and we fought the same as everybody else, and we did the same job and we got the world safe, safe for however long it's going to be.

"I'm Not Going to Stand By and Let Him Do It"

Jeanne Zamaloff Dworkin U.S. WOMEN'S ARMY CORPS

I was a good student. I read a lot. I was reading rather ambitious books at an early age, like *Don Quixote* and French authors—I really went for the more exotic stuff. I don't recall reading Nancy Drew at any time or any popular kids' books. I used to cut high school once a month to go down to 42nd Street to watch French movies at the Apollo, and I remember going down to the Metropolitan Opera House and sneaking into the Ballet Russe during the intermission. I had become in my early teens very conscious of the higher cultural scene, and I became very enamored of it.

I wanted to be a ballet dancer and a research scientist—oh, and a writer. The ballet lessons had to be cut short because we didn't have the money for it. What happened to my career was that at the age of sixteen and a half I graduated high school and had to immediately get a job so the family could eat. I got a job for twelve dollars a week, telling them I was twenty-one when I was only sixteen and a half. I got fired in two weeks and then went and took a job for eight dollars a week.

I became political at age sixteen. I met a group of people who were politically aware. It was an informal organization. I just absorbed the ideas. I would have found it myself anyway because I was conscious of social injustice, economic injustice. When I was a child, we saw people getting evicted from their homes, and then we saw neighbors putting the furniture back into the houses. At an impressionable age you pick up what you have to know about the world. I used to go to May Day parades, but I was not what you call an activist; I never liked that kind of activism. I was more interested in the cultural artistic life around me. But I was aware of what was going on in Europe. I was aware of the Spanish Civil War because a lot of the students in the high school were talking about it at that time, and I was certainly aware of Hitler. I think the relatives were all gone, except the ones in Russia. My father's family in Russia was, I think, untouched. My mother's family in Poland, I think, was wiped out.

Jeanne Zamaloff
[Dworkin], 1944

When Pearl Harbor was bombed, I was up at City College with a new boyfriend by the name of Philip Dworkin, who later became my husband. I met him through the political circles that we were in. Left, definitely left-wing organizations. Anyone with a conscience and consciousness was in the left wing at that time. He was a student at City College, and I was his new girlfriend. We went to a production of *Pens and Pencils,* which was being put on at City College, and somebody said Pearl Harbor is being—has been—bombed. I was about sixteen or sixteen and a half, and I said, What's the significance of that? And I . . . I found out—it was the beginning of the war. My boyfriend was inducted later that year. I stayed here on the home front for about two years. Then I joined the army at the age of nineteen.

I always had a sense of adventure and restlessness—intellectual restlessness—and I really wanted to see for myself; I wanted to be part of it. The home front had become boring for me. Two years in a secretarial job—it was too boring. My mother said, "You can't go." I said, "All your relatives are in danger there." She said it again, "You can't go." And I said, "'Well, if you don't sign me in, I'll sign myself in." I had to be signed in or else change my birth certificate. I changed my birth certificate. I had to be twenty so I only changed it by about six months. My brother was already in the navy. My sister was five years younger than me, and I don't recall if she had any opinion. I've always done things pretty much on my own. I don't wait for family or friends' opinions about what I should do next.

I think I always felt that I was not like the kids that I used to play jump rope with on the street. I always knew that I wanted to break out more than they did. I didn't consider myself a pioneer in the world, but I did consider myself a little different. Not only did I want to get away from the home front, which was a little boring at the time, I really did want to participate in the war and I wanted to see the world. I knew there was a women's division in the army, which was available to me to participate in. The politics of it was that Hitler was conquering the world and I'm not going to stand by and let him do it.

The women lived in barracks by themselves. They were totally surrounded by the rest of the army—the men, the officers—this whole army structure. I was a T-5. T-5 is a technician fifth grade, which is equivalent to a corporal, about the lowest grade you can be in a specialty like mine, that is, secretarial. I don't think you would call it privilege. A corporal outranks a private, but a T-5 is a technical specialist. So I don't think you outrank anybody.

Did the GIs take the women seriously? I don't know what the sociological attitude toward them was. I do know that when women appeared on the scene, the GIs were very grateful. They enhanced the scene. The women did not have the same jobs as the men. The women came in with secretarial and office skills. There weren't many men that had those skills. There was a Women's Auxiliary Army Corps before there was a Women's Army Corps, so they had been on the scene long enough during the conduct of the war that I don't think any attitudes were established about their replacing anybody.

We had skirts and jackets and we had pants and jackets. I think we wore pants as fatigues for off-duty time and skirts. When I was in New Guinea, you did wear pants all the time also as a uniform. They were attractive. Ah, one guy used to make fun of my name Zamaloff. I don't know why, but I wouldn't call that anti-Semitic. I would call that part of the nastiness of small-minded people.

Women were permitted to go to the canteen, to drink beer, to sit around with the girls and drink beer, but it wasn't anything I was ever interested in. If I had time off, I would either find a friend or two to talk to or get a book to read. I did not join the beer-drinking group.

The soldiers that we were exposed to were in the lower ranks. We could not consort with officers. Lower-ranking soldiers are, by and large, simple, unassuming people, and they respected other people and they respected the women. You have to understand that part of their perception of the women was not coming from the view that they were an intrusion on the war scene. They were just glad to see women. They were always delighted and were always hanging around the women's camp waiting for someone to notice them or asking someone for a date. Once I made two dates for the same time and they both called me and I realized that I had made a mistake. They were always there.

I remember some very cruel women in the barracks. I remember the first day that I came into the barracks—I picked out a bed and I had a nap because I had been on the go all day. Two burly women came in and stood over me and said, "What is she doing in that bed?" And I said, "I'm sleep-

ing." They started to get a little rough, and I just found myself standing up to them. I said, "This is my bed and I'm sleeping in it—leave me alone." I was a gutsy kid. Until about the age of fifteen or sixteen, I was very shy. Then I looked around and I saw that the world was not my fault, and I got a lot of courage from that.

I had secretarial and office skills, so they assigned me first to the Medical Corps in Fort Dix, New Jersey, to do secretarial work. That's where I got disillusioned. I found people callous and ignorant; I just didn't want to be with them. I told my CO, my commanding officer, after about six months in the army when I was totally disillusioned with the brutality of army life, I told her, "You know I'm underage." She said, "Well, if you don't tell anybody, I won't tell anybody." So I was stuck. I said, "In that case, send me overseas." So she did; she immediately sent me overseas.

When I went to overseas training, I met quite a number of Jewish women who were going also. I met a young woman from Brooklyn—a Jewish girl from Brooklyn—and she became my closest friend. She had a boyfriend in the army, she was politically aware, and she had a sense of adventure. I think she was a student before she went into the army.

I was in overseas training about six weeks. Climbing up ropes and down ropes, taking long hikes, strengthening, strengthening the body—I think that was the primary thing. The primary purpose was to strengthen the body. No weapons at all.

Well, it was fun. I always liked a bit of physical challenge. I was athletic without the opportunity to engage in athletics. That's why I enjoyed ballet dancing for a while. So I enjoyed the overseas training, but I had no expectations of what it was going to be. I just knew you had to go through this three- or six-week training period before you were sent overseas.

I went overseas in 1944. We were boarded on a big troop ship full of men and women. They had converted a luxury liner into a troop ship, and each stateroom that would have held two people now held sixteen to twenty people, bunks one on top of the other. So there were thousands and thousands of soldiers and WACs on that ship, and they dropped people off along the Pacific route in various places.

I remember one incident particularly. Previous to assignment to a locale in the Pacific, we were asked to present ourselves to a particular room, and in that room there was an officer who was assigning positions. All you had to do was stand in the doorway, and he would take one look at you and would say, "Thank you," and that was it. By the time everybody had gotten off the ship, we realized that he had selected the more attractive women to send to MacArthur's headquarters in Australia—the other women went to New Guinea. They had your record in front of you. They knew what you were capable of doing, and I concluded that they wanted to make sure that if you were a secretary or a clerk and they were sending you to the headquarters in Australia, that you were going to be easy to look at. The generals there would invite some of the women out, but most of them didn't go. But it wasn't hard to know that. I went to Australia. I went to Australia, others went to New Guinea.

Brisbane, Australia. It was MacArthur's headquarters, the general headquarters of the U.S. Armed Forces in the Far East, and I had clerical

Ft. oglethorpe Georgia 1944

Hollandia New Guinea 1944

assignments, stenographic assignments, things like that. I was attached to the adjutant general's office, and in the Philippines I was attached to personnel, troop movements, etc.

As MacArthur took over Japanese territory, or the territories that the Japanese had conquered, and as we regained those territories, his headquarters moved from Australia to New Guinea to Leyte then to Manila. The war ended while I was in Manila. We followed with his headquarters while there were still battle zones, so I got battle stars for those zones. There's a certain cutoff date when a zone is no longer a battle zone, and I always was sent in before that cutoff date, which gave me three battle zone medals.

We were bombed a few times. It was interesting, very frightening. We had to go out to trenches or holes that they dug for safety, but it only happened once or twice. So I really never felt in danger. In fact, I think I courted danger in a way because I used to hitchhike down from Manila to Batangas, and I knew that there were Japanese soldiers still isolated in the hills not two miles away, and I'm standing there in the road and holding out my thumb. I don't think I had any imminent sense of danger.

I did not know too much about the Japanese atrocities that came out later. So I did not have any particular impressions. No, I just knew they were the enemy and to be defeated. Oh, I did know what they had done in China. Yes, I did have that piece of history in my consciousness.

I found everything interesting. Everything was fascinating. New Guinea was very, very beautiful. We were in very wild territory. Hollandia is in the mountains, and you would be sitting in your tent and a cloud would come floating through. The cloud was coming in over the ocean, floating through your tent.

I didn't, but some of the women got in touch with the resistance movement in Manila. They were on a higher political consciousness than I was. I know that they tried to get in touch with them and talk to them. The only civilians that I came in contact with were women who came to sell services to the army. They would either come to do laundry—take your laundry away—or they would bring mangoes from their backyards and sell them for two cents. Mangoes became my favorite fruit, possibly my only fruit. The food in Manila was not a balanced diet.

There were some rapes in the army. I was never subjected to that, but what would happen was the generals would send messages to an office where there was somebody that they wanted to go out with, and they would ask if that woman would go out with them. And they did or they didn't, as

they wished. But when I got those invitations, I looked very innocently at my superior officer, the officer in charge of the department and asked, "Why would I want to go out with him?" And he would say, "Oh you don't have to, you don't have to." And I would say," Well I don't want to, that's it." You know, totally innocent.

But there was another side of the coin—women who did—and I don't say that there were a lot. I knew one woman who did, who danced around all the officers and was promoted to warrant officer very quickly so she could consort with them—in a passive sense—not so she could be part of their group. It was very obvious to all the other women that if you wanted to become a warrant officer, you had to do what she did, and nobody wanted to. A lot of the women who were in the army were politically conscious. Very intelligent women; they wouldn't have been in MacArthur's headquarters if they weren't.

I got stuck at a T-5 designation and part of that, I think, was being a Jew. The other was that I had a colonel, commanding officer, in the office who would never give me what I asked for. If I asked for a three-day pass, he would pretend it got lost under the papers. Then one day I asked him for a three-day pass and I waited and waited, and I didn't get it. Finally, I went over to him and said, "Did you make up my three-day pass yet? And he said, "Oh, no, I forgot." I said, "Well don't bother, I got it." So I got it from somebody else, you know. He was very nonplussed.

Now, what was remarkable about this colonel was that he was a southerner. He couldn't put three words together, he couldn't spell; he depended on his secretary. I used to write out his letters for him. He was a totally ignorant man, and he had reached the level of colonel. We were all outraged that this was the caliber of officer we had. Officers could climb on more than merit. Naturally, there were ways of climbing in the army.

I was working in an office—a small office building in Manila—when the announcement about the bomb came through. Again, I didn't understand what an atom bomb was. You know, they said atom bomb, atom bomb, and I, well, I figured it's a bomb, but I didn't know what the atom bomb was at that time. But it soon dawned on us what it was. When we found out the extent of the damage, we knew. I was not as outraged as I was a few years later when I saw the total world picture and the way they used the bomb and why they used the bomb. At that particular moment, I was still green, unaware—didn't know the scientific definition of an A-bomb, didn't know how many people it could kill, didn't know it could flatten a city, didn't know any of that. So I had no immediate reaction.

I do not remember V-J Day. I think the older people did. The officers did. It was not as carved out a day in my memory as the dropping of the A-bomb. The A-bomb . . . I can see the people standing there . . . I can see the car that we were getting into, I can see everything.

After the war ended, you stayed overseas until you were sent home, and I was sent home in August, maybe September, about three months later. There was still a lot of paperwork. We were all paper pushers. There was decommissioning, there was demobilization, there was sending home, there was as much or more paperwork than before.

Des Moines, Iowa, was the disembarkation point, where we landed. Then I was sent home in November and was discharged on November 26. My future husband was discharged on November 27.

When I was headed overseas, we were in a troop train in the United States, and my friend and I were taking bets. If we went to the Pacific, she would be with her boyfriend. If we went to the European theater of war, I'd be with my boyfriend. We ended up in the Pacific theater of war, where she met her boyfriend again and they got married in New Guinea. When I came home to New York from Des Moines, it took one day, so I got home a half hour after my boyfriend, after four years of separation. I called his mother to tell her that I was home, and she said, "Phil is here. He's drinking a bottle of milk." And he came downtown to meet me at Grand Central Station.

We were married later in New York on a three-day Washington's Birthday weekend because we immediately got very busy resuming our schooling, our education. I used a four-year benefit from the GI bill. Where all my friends had been going to City College, I was given $350 a semester to go to an Ivy League college, which I did. I went to Barnard and Columbia. The cost was $700 a year.

"THE GREATEST ADVENTURE OF MY LIFE"

Franklin Mellion   U.S. NAVY

I joined the navy in May 1943. I was drafted. My father would not sign for
me when I was seventeen, so I joined when I was eighteen. I had completed
three years of high school.

The way it worked was that we all gathered in Suffern, New York. They
took all us local boys and sent us down to New York City. Then they shipped
us up to Samson, New York, which is up near Utica, and then I think it was,
maybe, eight weeks to boot camp, which was in Pensacola, Florida.

My dad was in the food business; I was in the food business. In Pensacola they sent me through cooks and bakers school—today I guess they'd
call it culinary school. I think I got out of Florida in November '43. Three
drafts came up: submarines, PT boats, and amphibians. I tried for the submarines, but I was six feet two and weighed 196 pounds. I thought I was in
pretty good shape, but I weighed 10 percent more than they would accept
for submarine duty. The next draft was for PT boats. The difference was
that you could be 10 percent higher in weight than they would accept for
submarines. I qualified and went up to Melba, Rhode Island.

You could not ride a PT boat unless you went through school because
you had to hold down three rates. In other words, I was a cook, but I also had
to know how to launch a torpedo and how to change the gun barrels aboard
the boat. I had to know how to send a message and plot a course. If some-

Franklin Mellion, 1944

PT torpedo boat
speeds away from
an exploding ship

U.S. War Department,
Public Relations
Bureau poster, 1943

body gets hit, and you have only twelve men and two officers, you had to put another person in to take his place. That's the reason you had to go to school.

The PT boat had fourteen men, twelve enlisted men and two officers. I was on the 151 PT boat. All together, we had approximately 500 boats in World War II—some of them were given to the Russians and some were sent to England on lend-lease. I was in Squadron 12, which they called Ron 12. So I was on 151 Ron 12. The original crew spent just so much time—one hundred combat patrols—and then they were shipped home for thirty days. Then the second crew went aboard; I was the first replacement of the second crew. I was the "oldest man" on the boat because I had more time in than anyone else. The man who went aboard with me became the skipper. I didn't even know he was an officer because there was no rank. Everybody wore the same clothes and did the same things. In the South Pacific you'd have a pair of shorts and a pair of sandals, and that's what you wore until you went on patrol. Then you had to wear dungarees and a cranberry shirt with a helmet.

There was no armor plating on a PT boat. They were made out of one-inch thick mahogany planks. They say they were made out of plywood, but actually they were made out of mahogany planking. One plank went this way and one plank went that way. And that's all you had. You had two

PT boat at a jungle
river base in the
South Pacific

inches between the inside of the boat and the sea on the outside. That's all we had—there was no armor at all aboard the boat. I was the lead gunner. I shot the 37mm on the bow. In other words, when I opened up, the rest of the boys would follow suit. When the old man—the skipper, that is—would holler "Fire," that's when I would open up and lay out what I had. I think I had nineteen rounds on the 37mm. They actually came out of an army air corps plane—they had a round belt on them that fit in the nose cone of an airplane. It was put together, jury-rigged, by some ship fitters.

It's documented that PT boats and crews spent more time in contact with the enemy than any other force afloat. We had more firepower per square inch than the battleships had per square foot. When the boats opened up and we'd make a run on either a Japanese logger or a barge, we had eighty feet of flame. Every man aboard shot a gun except the engineer, who was down in the engine room running the engines. The engines were 1500-horsepower Packard V8s that burned 100-octane gasoline.

Being the oldest man on the boat, I had the choicest bunk, and my bunk was in between three 1,000-gallon tanks of gasoline. I slept right in the middle of all of that, because it didn't matter where you were if you got a direct hit on 3,000 gallons—the whole boat would go up. But it was the coolest spot on the boat—I had a couple of windows next to my bunk so I had ventilation, and that's the reason I took that bunk.

When we would go on patrol at night, four boats would leave and go out, and if we were going to attack an island, we would try to hit that island in the center. Two boats would go north and two boats would go south. The way we found out where the Japanese were trying to resupply personnel or material or guns was to pick it up on radar. And then we would make two runs. The first boat would go in and strafe and try to kill anything that was alongside of them and then go out to sea and then come back. As we were coming out, the second boat would make a run, and then we'd come back behind the second boat and make another run. We actually made two passes. We were maybe thirty, forty, fifty feet from them. We were there to stop them—we didn't play with them. If there was anything we could to do to stop them resupplying their personnel or weapons, we did it.

The Japanese had their barges and loggers, and they had guns on board—we were shooting at them and they were shooting at us. What we had was speed. We could turn up fifty knots. We had three 1500-horse-power engines, and in flank speed we would burn 180 gallons per hour per engine. Now we only had 3,000 gallons of gasoline, so we had to get in,

make our runs, and get out fast, because quite often as we were making runs on their boats, the shore batteries would open up and try to hit us. That's what we did.

We had a tender, a seaplane tender. It was our mother ship. There were two squadrons. That means there were between twenty-two and twenty-four boats on each tender, and as they moved the tenders up the coast, we would go with them. They would supply the food and the torpedoes and also the fuel. We would work off that tender.

We had to resupply our boats. We ate off the tenders while we were tied up for twenty-four hours. We slept. We were out all night on patrol, so you couldn't sleep then. You had to sleep when you could. Another reason we had these tenders was because there were doctors on board and also a dentist. It was this little city in itself actually. They took care of us. Sometimes we didn't see capital ships—big ships—for months on end. And that's how it was.

The only thing I lost is the hearing in my right ear. I used to shove cotton in my ears, but one night the vibrations of the gun shook so much that the cotton came out of this ear, and I had a set of twin 50s going off over my shoulder. I couldn't hear for three days. In fact I have hearing aids today. We had boys aboard the boat who got hit, but that's part of being in the service I guess. We took them back to the tender to the doctor. If they were alive, we tried to keep them alive and get them to the sick bay and have the doctor take care of them. That's what they were there for.

When you're in combat and you're a small group as we were, you think more of your fellow crew members than you do your family because they're watching your rear end and you're watching theirs. That's the way it is in a small combat unit. I don't care what service you're in, you bond like a family because you have to depend on each other. There was no such thing as picking on one or the other. You're just very glad that you were there and that you took care of each other. That was the important thing.

It was the greatest adventure of my life. I would not take a million dollars for it, and I wouldn't sell it for a million dollars. Everybody had to be some place, because if you were a red-blooded American, you wanted to protect your flag, your country, and your family. And when I saw what was going on with the Germans and with the families over in Europe and what was going on with the Japanese, I was very happy to try to stop it. I originally volunteered to go to Europe, but they said, "No, we have enough over there." They thought the war was winding down, so they shipped us to the

South Pacific. And that's the way it went. Everybody had to be some place, and I was just lucky that I picked out the branch of service that I always wanted and enjoyed and that I did what I wanted to do. I was grateful that I could ride a PT boat and be in a tight-knit group. I loved those boys like brothers, believe me.

In the battle of the Surigao Straits, we snuck in. There were three boats going up and down the straits. One was on the right side, one was on the left, and the Japanese went up the center. The first group and the second group tried to make torpedo runs on the Japanese, but the Japanese drove them off before they could get close enough. While the Japanese were firing on these two groups, we snuck in with a third group and got 800 yards off a heavy cruiser and hit it with a torpedo. Then the Japanese destroyers jumped on us, and those big guns sounded like freight trains going by in the night. They made an awful racket. The skipper—John Ladd—got us through, he got us out. His quick thinking is what did it. Otherwise, we'd all be dead today. He was a wonderful man. He always gave us the opportunity to get off the boat. The fact that we were a volunteer group meant that you could get off the boat any time you thought you'd had enough. If you wanted off, they would put you on the beach. In other words they could not keep you on board that boat.

He was a wonderful, wonderful man, John Ladd. He took us into his confidence. He had drilled us and drilled us and drilled us. When you're in the service, the reason that you're drilled so much is the fact that you must react to the command that's given. You can't stop and talk about it. You must do it and do it right away. That's what the service is all about. On the night when we were sneaking in between those Japanese destroyers to make a run on their heavy cruiser, I was on the bow and the skipper hollered "Fire One," which meant the first torpedo should leave. The only thing I heard was "Fire," and I opened up with my 37mm, and just at that moment the Japanese put their lights on us—you could have read a *New York Times*. It was an awful, awful night—squally, rainy, you name it, it came at us—but when the skipper hollered "Fire," every gun on that boat opened up, not that we could do anything. I mean, it's a little piece of cork out in the middle of nowhere, but we certainly tried. We were sent out to stop them or to get intelligence, and that's just what we did.

It's not a question of how you cope—it's how you're trained. An eighteen year old . . . there were 14 million of us under arms in World War II. How did we cope? You did what you were trained to do. Of course, we were civilians. The war was won not by this army elite or that navy elite. It was won by guys like me who were taken off the streets of New York and Spring Valley and Suffern and Niagara and Newark. We were taken off the streets and trained, and we did what we were trained to do. Things happened so quickly that you could not think about it. It was automatic. After it was over, then you could stop and think about it. You get a little dry in the mouth and sometimes start to shake. But that's what happens. It's past tense what you went through. When I first came home, if you touched me when I was sleeping, I would come up fighting. There was no teenage time—you went from a child to a soldier. There was no in between. My wife says that when she married me, she married an old man. I was twenty-four or twenty-five and she was nineteen. There was none of that period of being a teen in World War II.

My father's family all perished in the Holocaust, except one nephew who got out and went to England and a niece who got to Canada. My mother died from breast cancer—both breasts were removed—and my father wanted to bring her into the shul for a service, but he was turned away at the door of the shul because she was not a whole person. He stood there with the funeral entourage behind him, and he got turned away. Not only did he get turned away, he got turned off. We were brought up in the Christian Science church until World War II.

When I was in the South Pacific and we were going into a battle, I saw boys take out rosary beads and sing Hail Marys. The kid right next to me who shot the 20mm gun took off his helmet—he had a yarmulke on and was asking God's blessing. I said to myself, if I ever get out of here alive, I'm going back to my religion. When I came home after the war, I was twenty-one, and I was the first bar mitzvah of Temple Beth El, which became the largest organized Jewish group in Rockland County. My dad was a charter member of that group. I raised all my children in the Jewish faith. They have all received religious instruction, both girls and my son, who was bar mitzvahed. All my children married Jews. I feel that I did what God sent me to do on this earth. I tried to honor the religion and work at it as hard as I could. What else can I say?

"OH, THE GREAT SPECKLED BIRD"

Burton Roberts U.S. ARMY

When I was very young I had two conflicting ambitions: I didn't know whether I wanted to play second base for the New York Giants or be a mayor like Fiorello LaGuardia. I didn't know which I was going to do. And then I decided that I would play second base on the New York Giants and then become the mayor. Neither ambition was realized. Now, I did play baseball. I played baseball at New York University, but I also was pre-law and I matriculated at NYU at the Heights. I was in my senior year—I think I enlisted before that—but I stayed in college and tried to finish. By enlisting they let you have some extra time in school.

I recall the people who had come here from Germany talking about the Nuremberg Laws and that Jews couldn't own property, but the newspapers didn't seem to be playing it up too much, which was puzzling to me. And I think I remember my grandmother reading a newspaper, sitting there on the sofa reading the Yiddish newspaper, dealing with *Kristallnacht*. And she said, "This is a terrible thing that's happening to the Jews in Germany."

I was called into service on April 23, 1943. It was infantry and I went to Camp Wheeler, Georgia. The enlistees from NYU all envisioned that after basic training we would go into the Army Specialized Training Program, ASTP. We were going to study languages; we were going into military government. That was what was supposed to happen. But what, as Robert Burns would say, the best-laid plans of mice and men oft go, how does he say it, go awry. No ASTP. They needed combat soldiers. So we all were sent as replacements, either to the Pacific or to the European theater. I was sent to North Africa, Casablanca, as a replacement.

I remember getting a bayonet—first time we got the bayonet—and I remember sitting on the steps of the barracks in Georgia and looking at it. I kept pulling out the knife from the scabbard and saying to myself, "My God, not only do I have a bayonet, but the guy I have to bayonet with this also has a bayonet, and he's going to try to bayonet me." You know, it sort of caused you to believe that no one was kidding around any more, that this was for real. And even on the ship across, the liberty ships to North Africa, one or two of the ships were hit. We saw the flames go up. We were all summoned on deck— some of the ships didn't get through to North Africa.

I had no concept that there was any organized anti-Semitism. There would be fights in line, you know, if somebody tried to sneak on the mess line, you would say something and sometimes the retort would be, you know, some vile language. It was street language, some street language plus some anti-Semitic remark to me which resulted, whenever I heard it, in a fight. But that was a rare occurrence.

Well, you're put in no unit. You became a replacement. I was a replacement in North Africa, in Casablanca, and then in Algiers. We heard mattress covers were to be used as body bags. In other words, that's what you'd be buried in. So I says, "I don't need to be buried in a mattress cover. They can bury me without a mattress cover." You got twenty bucks for a mattress cover in Casablanca. So we went into Casablanca to sell mattress covers and cartons of cigarettes. And while we were there I saw an elderly gentleman with a skullcap, a yarmulke, with his grandson. This old man was being kicked off the trolley car, or maybe it was a bus, and I heard the driver, he kept calling this elderly gentleman a *sale juif*, which in my limited French meant "dirty Jew." I excused myself from my friends and said to the old man, "Here, here's some cigarettes." I gave him about, out of the carton, gave him four or five packs. And I rejoined my colleagues. Then I said, "What the hell am I going to sell these cigarettes for?" And I remember the old man and his grandson were out of sight. Running like hell, I said, "Wait for me." I ran like hell, caught up, and gave him the whole carton of cigarettes. I remember that. That was my experience in Casablanca.

Again, in Oran, I was just there as a replacement, waiting to be assigned somewhere. And there, as I recall, I went to one service in a Sephardic synagogue where the *bima* was in the middle of the synagogue.

And after we davened we were invited to someone's home for dinner. And I remember my embarrassment, because the young daughter of the people who invited me to dinner stayed by the door of the bathroom with a towel in her hand while I had to go and urinate—she wouldn't move.

While we were in Oran, I remember there was an airplane crash, and we were all recruited to go up Lion Mountain and retrieve, you know, the bodies. It was very sad because it was around Christmastime and people were coming back with gifts. A military plane, it was carrying servicemen back. We saw gifts and arms and legs. It was very sad.

But after that, it was real business. I was shipped to Italy. I was in Naples and I remember seeing Naples and seeing Pompeii and then being assigned, it was in April 1944 I'm quite sure, being assigned to the 3rd Infantry Division in Anzio.

When I arrived in Anzio the commanding officer of the Fifth Army was Gen Mark Clark. The corps commander was Gen Lucian K. Truscott, and the division commander was Gen Michael "Iron Mike" O'Daniel. Truscott saw us in Anzio. He had on these riding boots with a riding crop. And he informed us how fortunate we were to be joining a division that had 200 percent casualties. So I was trying to figure out, oh, that means that you get wounded once or you get wounded twice or you get killed, and then you get killed a second time. It didn't make us too happy about this whole thing. And I remember we were in a big shed, like a lean-to, only a few miles from the coast. And people came, it was like a market, you know, different regiments, different battalions, etcetera. And I remember a first sergeant by the name of Andrews coming over to me and asking, "How many of you have any college?" I raised my hand. I had some college. And I became a member of Headquarters Company, 1st Battalion, 7th Infantry Regiment. I would sit and take notes of calls to and from the battalion command post and also be in the intelligence and reconnaissance platoon. I remember some of my friends went to a heavy weapons company in the 15th Regiment, and others went to rifle companies. And off we went.

A jeep took me to the command post of the 1st Battalion where the Headquarters Company was located. And it was in the basement of a destroyed castle. As we were going there, somebody from the German observation post—they had all the high ground and the mountain range—they started firing at the jeep and the jeep was zigzagging. And finally we got out of the jeep and the mortar shells or artillery shells kept coming at us. And finally I felt a pain in my left arm and hand. I had been cut by some

Helmet issued to
Burton Roberts

Nazi propaganda
leaflet dropped
to soldiers of
the U.S. Army

shrapnel. Bloodied, I entered the command post. So that was my introduction to joining the 3rd Division.

The battalion surgeon was there and he just, you know, he cleaned the wound and bandaged my arm and hand and that was it. And you stay. There's nowhere to go. They would send you back from the hospital. The hospital was being shelled in Anzio. And there was a need for manpower, so there I was. We had a great many casualties. Compared to others, mine was a superficial wound. And when we finally moved out of Anzio . . . well, we didn't ever secure it. We moved out of Anzio, I believe, sometime around May 21, and we moved toward Rome, and we had a series of battles. They were holding battles—we were fighting to cut off Highway 6 and Highway 7. We had to go about thirty kilometers to reach Rome from Anzio. And we finally . . . we were successful.

We were with the whole 1st Battalion, A Company, B Company, Charlie Company, Dog Company. Well, we were among the first to come into Rome. And Rome was quiet. We didn't have any battles in Rome because they had evacuated Rome. We had plenty of fighting to get to Rome, plenty of fighting to capture Cisterna di Littoria, which was the village on the foothills of a mountain range, which we did as we broke out of Anzio.

Well, it always seemed to be raining. Always raining. And mud. And if you were moving, you would dig a hole. You were in a foxhole. And if your position got hit with artillery while you were in a foxhole, you know, you would stay in that foxhole. The helmet was a fully equipped bathroom. That helmet was used for bathing purposes, it was used as a urinal while you were in the hole, used as a commode in an emergency while you were in the hole. It was used for water to brush your teeth while you were in the hole. The helmet was an infantryman's bathroom if you were stuck in a foxhole.

Now, there were times before we broke out of Anzio, when they would send over shells with propaganda pamphlets before an artillery bombardment. And that's God-awful, by the way, to be bombarded by artillery, mortar, or 88s. But in any event, they would sometimes send over shells which would have pamphlets with a propaganda theme. The villain of the piece was a fellow by the name of Levy. And it was a caricature of . . . you know the Nazi propaganda, the way they made all people of Jewish faith look. And he was always perspiring, this particular cartoon character, and smoking a cigar. And this fellow Levy was making a fortune in these cartoons, these strips, making a fortune. "And are you going to let this happen to you?" All in English. And an ex-soldier—you—would be on a corner

The Girl You Left Behind

It was a rude awakening for her.......

selling pencils on crutches, one leg, and this Levy character would be coming out of a restaurant, a fancy restaurant with the soldier's girlfriend. She's now bedecked in minks and jewels, and the crippled ex-soldier would see his girlfriend with this Levy guy. And that caused, you know, that really did not make for an air of harmony.

There were Jewish soldiers from the northeast in my battalion, but most of the soldiers came from southern states or the west and a lot of them were farmers. I remember one guy only shaved with cold water. He never, never wanted to shave with hot water. And if you were pulled back off the line and went to get a meal sometimes, let's say you wanted some pancakes. It was cold and raining and you wanted pancakes. He wouldn't even use the mess kit. Not that you could, it would fill up with water it was raining so hard. The cook would just put it in your hand and you smeared it with the marmalade. And it's like, it was like Bill Maulden's GI Joe.

Well, you get used to living like that. You think that's the only way you're going to live. I mean I was never repulsed by the fact that I was doing it. When we were walking, you know, fighting and walking and going toward Rome and we'd go through a field, I would pick onions. I would eat onions. I'd rather just eat onions than have those damn franks and beans, or the K rations or the C rations or whatever they were giving us.

This was everyone's way of life. But coming back to the anti-Jewish propaganda. After that, for example, I remember Charlie Company, which was a good company, good rifle company with a very good company commander and good noncoms. But I remember that after one of these barrages, I heard that some soldiers in Charlie Company were singing in their fox holes, "Oh, the great speckled bird, oh, the great speckled bird . . . the Jews are the cause of it all." Over and over again. Couldn't believe it happened, but that existed. But I think that changed. It changed for me, as you will see, as we went on.

Now, after we took Rome, they put us, the infantry, in I think it's known as Borghese Park. Big park. We slept in that park. We did more to take Rome than any other outfit in the United States Army, including the air force. And we suffered more than any other outfit. And they put us in the park, to sleep, in pup tents. We were like animals. And there was great bitterness. And if an infantryman saw somebody from the air force, there might be a fistfight. We weren't in Rome too long before they took the 3rd Infantry Division out of Rome. Oh, we were able to see Rome. I remember we went to St. Peter's. I remember we had an audience with the Pope. And I remember Augie Barber, who was a real nice guy, told the Pope he was getting mistreated because he would get every heavy duty. He was right, if we ever were to stay somewhere, he'd be the one to dig the latrine. I told him later he was going to have a profession gained in the army. He was going to be a latrine digger for the rest of his life.

Every time you get down during an artillery bombardment or a mortar bombardment or get a concentration of 88s and it continues and it goes on and on and you get hit with the rocks and the pebbles from the earth and, you know, you think any minute one's going to land right on top of you, what did you do? I didn't pray to God—I figured everybody's praying to God—I used to pray to my grandmother, who had died. And I figured that God is looking out for so many people, one could, you know, slip through. But if I prayed to my grandmother . . . there's only one person out there that was going to pray to my grandmother. And if there was a God and there was a heaven, she was up there. And I figured that she would help me more than anyone or anything. There was no question in my mind about that. So that's who I would pray to when I would run out of courage.

From Rome, after training for an invasion, we went to southern France. We went in on the invasion on August 15, 1944. I received two medals in France. I believe it was on September 14, we were coming into the foothills of the Vosges mountains. I recall we had open terrain ahead and then we had to cross a road.

And what happened was, on that road there was a high embankment then another open field and mountains ahead of that. And I remember praying to my grandmother, because they were bombarding us with artillery in that first open field and there were casualties. This was a whole battalion—Able Company, Baker Company, Charlie Company, Dog Company and Headquarters Company.

A battalion has 700 people, 800 people, who knows what our full complement was then. And it was difficult to move through that field to the embankment. Shells would be landing in front of us, shells behind us on the field, but once you reached the embankment you're pretty safe. It was not bad. It wasn't great but it wasn't bad. And there were guys that were out there in that second field beyond the embankment that were wounded. One that I knew was calling for help. And there was a medic who asked me to help him, you know, pull this guy back. And, I remember, we went out crawling on our bellies under heavy shelling. There was approximately 30 yards of open terrain ahead of us and we heard him hollering. Now we dragged and carried this fellow back. We took him to where the battalion surgeon was. The wounded soldier was from Charlie Company, and that's why after this I could do no wrong as far as the captain of Charlie Company was concerned, because he knew this guy that we pulled back. And we pulled him back while the artillery was hitting around us. We're carrying him. Then we'd hit the deck and he would fall—it wasn't the greatest thing for this guy. The battalion surgeon asked me to go across the first open field to the forest where the medics were located—I thought it was about 1,000 yards but it was really about 200 yards. So I ran as fast as I could run into this open field, about 200 yards, you know, running about 20 or 30 yards and hitting the deck, and I'm running and I'm hitting the deck trying to avoid being hit. And finally I reached this place where the medics were, and I told them what was happening and they, God bless them, they grabbed a couple of stretchers and they ran with me up to the embankment. By then the shelling had stopped and didn't resume.

And I went out on three different occasions with them to carry people back. I was exhausted. I know there's one guy that I brought back that couldn't have survived because his stomach was open from around his chest down to his belly button. This was September of '44, and I was just twenty-two. That was my first Bronze Star.

I got my second Bronze Star for action on October 7, 1944, in Vagney. Our command post was set up in a house in Vagney. The intelligence and reconnaissance platoon and the ammunition and provisions platoon were quartered across the street. At that time, the German and American lines were fluid and shifting. Our position was not secure. At around 9:00 or 10:00 P.M. a German tank with German infantrymen riding on board rumbled down the narrow roadway. The German commander was calling for us to surrender. He was saying, "American *Soldaten* surrender. American *Soldaten* surrender." Before we took any action an American tank situated at the town square rumbled to the road where we were quartered. Lt James Harris of the 756th Tank Battalion, which was a support battalion for the 3rd Infantry, having heard the noise came from the square to the road where our command post was. The German tank and the German infantrymen moved off the road to a place where they could not be seen. Apparently they also heard the American tank coming. Lieutenant Harris selected six men, including me and my buddy George Rebovich, to accompany him on a patrol. As we moved toward the German tank, Rebovich and two guys were on the left side of the street, myself and two others were on the right. Lieutenant Harris moved five or ten yards ahead of us when all hell broke loose. In the middle of the road, the German tank and the American tank fired at each other from about 75 yards apart. As that was happening, the German tank started firing at us with a machine gun. I hit the ground and fell into a pile of copper telephone wire that had fallen. I got untangled and climbed over a white stucco wall about four to five feet high. I saw a box of grenades that Rebovich had shown me earlier that evening. I grabbed two grenades and crawled closer to the German tank.

The American tank was hit by a German tank shell and was on fire. I heard someone calling from the tank, "Mama mia, I'm burning." I heard the rumble of a tank. I tossed the two grenades toward the German tank. It was dark and foggy, I couldn't see whether it did any damage. The Germans must have heard something too because they took off. Shortly after, I went back to the road and I saw Lieutenant Harris. His leg had been severed at the hip. He asked me to apply a tourniquet. I told him that I wasn't able to. I was thinking to myself there was nowhere to put the thing, but I assured him that the medics would soon be on the scene to take care of him. I climbed on

TM 30-606

RESTRICTED

GERMAN
PHRASE BOOK
NOVEMBER 30, 1943

Dissemination of restricted matter.—The information contained in restricted documents and the essential characteristics of restricted material may be given to any person known to be in the service of the United States and to persons of undoubted loyalty and discretion who are cooperating in Government work, but will not be communicated to the public or to the press except by authorized military public relations agencies. (See also par. 18b, AR 380–5, 28 Sep 1942.)

top of the tank and looked inside; it appeared that no one was alive. Lieutenant Harris died before the medics got there. Without him, the battalion command post would have been destroyed and most of us would have been killed or taken prisoner. He provided the leadership and courage which prevented this from happening. Lieutenant Harris was a real hero. He got a posthumous Congressional Medal of Honor, which he very much deserved.

I remember Lure. I remember the town because I remember seeing the German writing on the windows of the stores. And I felt as if the war would end some day. It was a medieval town with, you know, the narrow roads and the small distance between buildings on either side of the road. The I & R platoon were all sitting on the sidewalk and we had German dictionaries that the army had given us. I remember Curtis James from my outfit seeing some kids and saying with a Southern accent, "*Kinders, choko-lade.*" They all came—he had some chocolate from a K ration—and he said, "*Kinders, choko-lade, choko-lade.*" They took the chocolate. Then he said, "*Kinders*"—he didn't know how to pronounce *Jude* in German—pointing to the group of us he said, "Jew-deh, all Jews." It was France, it wasn't Germany, but he said that. And he turned to me and said, "Red, how am I doing?" And I remember turning my head away because I had tears in my eyes, because it was like . . . it not only indicated to me my acceptance but the acceptance of anybody, you know, who was Jewish. And I'll tell you, I don't remember after that hearing about anybody ever singing, "Oh, the great speckled bird, oh, the great speckled bird . . . the Jews are the cause of it all." Never, never heard it, nor do I know anyone else who heard it.

Burton Roberts, Strasbourg, France, December 1944

Army-issued German phrase book

American Soldiers Confront the Holocaust

Bonnie Gurewitsch

On March 31, 1945, Lt Col Lewis Weinstein, chief of the Liaison Section of General Eisenhower's staff, made his daily visit to the Situation Room in Paris. He noticed a red X crayoned on one of the maps that covered the walls, marking a spot near the town of Gotha, Germany, with the words "Death-Camp." It was the first time he had ever seen these words on a map or a report. He reacted instinctively. "Death-camp? It can't be a cemetery; it must be a murder camp and the victims must be Jews; a death-camp to murder Jews."[1]

The head of Intelligence told him that a million, or perhaps two million, Jews had been murdered at Auschwitz. As the Intelligence officer provided details about Ohrdruf, the camp near Gotha, Weinstein could hardly comprehend what he heard. He rushed back to the office and tried to persuade General Eisenhower to be present at the liberation of Ohrdruf, but Eisenhower insisted, "I just can't be at Ohrdruf on the fourth. I know that it's specially important to you personally, but I just can't." Weinstein knew what Eisenhower meant by "personally." He responded, "It's not so much that it's important to me as a Jew, but it's important the world know the Nazis are deliberately, scientifically annihilating Jews in enormous numbers. The Allied liberation of the first Nazi death-camp is one of the most important events of the war. . . ." Weinstein lost the argument; Eisenhower turned his attention to the documents on his desk.

Intelligence estimated that the camp would be liberated on April 4. Weinstein entered Ohrdruf that day in an ambulance with the medical teams. What he saw he could not have imagined even in a nightmare; he knew Eisenhower had to see it. Before Weinstein left for Paris, Col Hayden Sears, commander of the 4th Armored Division troops who liberated the camp, begged him,

"Don't let this death-camp remain a secret." Weinstein convinced Eisenhower, and he and Generals Bradley and Patton visited the camp on April 12, 1945, in a carefully documented visit that was photographed and reported on extensively. Eisenhower thanked Weinstein for his persistence, "You were right. I never would have believed that this was possible."

American troops reacted to the encounter with the concentration camps with universal shock, revulsion, anger, and disbelief. This was partly because they were totally unprepared. Officers were not told what to expect, and certainly enlisted men were totally ignorant of what awaited them. Lt Col Walter Fellenz describes Dachau as a "complete surprise to all of us."[2] Gen James Gavin says that the camps "hit us like an avalanche." Even soldiers who were German Jewish émigrés, like Maximilian Lerner, who knew about Dachau before they arrived in the United States, were horrified when they saw it after liberation. But most Jewish soldiers had a reaction that reflected their Jewish identities: "But for the grace of God, had not my parents left Europe in the early 1900s, I would be dead, or in a place like Dachau."[3]

For soldiers there was a pattern to the experience of liberating a concentration camp. First there was the smell, the stench of decaying human corpses, unwashed bodies, and open latrines. Some veterans still smelled it decades later, whenever they remembered. Sometimes there was the sound of gunfire, as retreating Nazis killed surviving prisoners. Sometimes a last-minute attempt to burn the evidence left the smoldering remains of charred bodies. Nazi guards often fled prior to the arrival of American troops, leaving emaciated, sick prisoners wandering among the corpses or lying in the barracks in their own filth. GIs recoiled physically, vomiting, cursing, or stupefied into silence. Some left very quickly, either because they were ordered to move on to the next target or because they could not tolerate the scene. Some Jewish soldiers simply couldn't go in. They were ashamed: "We didn't want our buddies to see how cheap Jewish life is . . . we didn't want to be there when the goyim see it."

Another universal reaction goes to the heart of the military frame of mind. What soldiers encountered in the camps was contrary to the values that the military had taught them. Battle-hardened soldiers, veterans of difficult fighting, who had seen death and destruction on the battlefield, were shocked and revolted by German brutality. Lt Col Walter Fellenz was a West Point graduate, a career soldier. The Nazi genocide violated the basic tenets of his moral code. "You got a gun, I got a gun, if we have to do this, let's get with it. But this kind of death, this was something against my heritage . . . how could people do this? This was an organized scheme of destruction of a whole race of people!" Pfc Joseph Wright, a Jew, put it simply: "the [victims] were human beings who were defenseless." This was not war; this was much worse.

There was no manual of operations for liberating a concentration camp, and none for what to do once the area was secure. Because of this, American responses were improvised at first. After the liberation of Ohrdruf, Colonel Sears had the *Bürgermeister* of the nearby town tour the camp with his wife and ordered him to bring the townspeople the following day to see the camp. The townspeople came, but without the mayor and his wife; they had hanged themselves. After Eisenhower visited Ohrdruf, he ordered all American soldiers who were in the vicinity to visit recently liberated concentration camps: "We are told that the American soldier does not know what he is fighting for. Now, at least, he will know what he is fighting against."[4]

Many GIs offered their own rations to the starving survivors. GIs were horrified to see survivors die because they could not tolerate the rich protein and fats in the K rations and learned to wait until medical teams could come in to provide suitable nourishment. Another immediate need was to separate the living from the dead. Gen Terry Allen ordered his infantry units to stop their rush through Germany for a few days "to clean up Nordhausen first," and the mayor of the town was ordered to draft every able-bodied man to help the GIs bury the dead, send the survivors behind the lines for medical attention, and then dynamite the camp site, "because it was an abomination." American troops set up evacuation hospitals in former SS barracks, requisitioned housing from civilians, opened warehouses of provisions stockpiled by Germans, and distributed food and clothing to survivors.

The response to the physical needs of the survivors was universal among GIs, without regard to background. Jewish GIs, however, recognized that Jewish survivors needed to be recognized as Jews. Wherever possible, there was a Jewish component to burial services for concentration camp victims. Jewish chaplains and enlisted men, like Victor Geller, organized religious services for survivors, so they could begin to feel human again as they began to function as Jews. As survivors recited the mourner's prayer, the kaddish, they took the first step in a mourning process that had been forbidden to them until then.

Concentration camps were not military targets, and the military had no real interest in them beyond basic control. Jewish chaplains and enlisted men stepped into the vacuum, responding to survivors' needs. Those who spoke Yiddish, the language of Eastern European Jews, had instant credibility with the survivors. At Buchenwald, Chaplain Herschel Schacter entered a prisoner barrack. "Impulsively, instinctively, I shouted out in Yiddish, '*Sholom aleichem yidn, ihr zeit frei!* The war is over, I am an American rabbi, you are free!'" And the survivors responded in Yiddish, "Is it true? Is the war really over? What happens now? Where do we go from here?" Schacter realized that he had found the purpose for which he enlisted in the army. His work with the Jewish survivors superseded his military duties; he became chaplain to the survivors of Buchenwald, helping them not only with their physical needs but with their rehabilitation as human beings.

Victor Geller, Herschel Schacter, and other Jewish GIs who spoke Yiddish and could communicate with Jewish survivors realized that the army could not respond to crucial survivor needs. Survivors wanted to contact their families, to inform them that they were alive, to ask for help. GIs made lists of names of survivors and their American relatives and sent this information to the United States, where Yiddish newspapers published the lists. They sent letters home requesting material assistance for the survivors. American Jews began to send packages of food, clothing, and other necessities to Germany, addressed to Jewish chaplains. These activities were completely voluntary and, in some cases, contrary to military policy, which forbade fraternization with civilians.

United States Army policy regarding liberated prisoners was to provide essential medical care, food, clothing, and temporary shelter. Civilians were supposed to be repatriated to the countries of their origin, but most Jews could not be repatriated. Their former communities were destroyed, their homes and possessions looted. Jews who had found refuge in the Soviet Union did not want to live there permanently. Joined by those who had survived the Holocaust in the war zone, Jewish survivors flooded into the American Zone of Occupation, where they were confined to displaced persons camps, waiting for permission to emigrate. The DP camps were organized by nationality. American policy defined Jews as a religious group, not a nationality, so they were assigned to camps together with non-Jews, who were often collaborators or indifferent bystanders to the Holocaust. This situation became volatile as anti-Semitic incidents occurred.

Meanwhile, the volume of mail and packages that began to pour into Germany in response to efforts by Jewish soldiers looked like a massive black market operation to the American authorities.[5] When President Truman saw one of the letters begging for help for survivors, he realized that the situation was not under control. In the summer of 1945, Truman sent Earl G. Harrison as a special envoy to investigate the situation.[6] Rabbi Klausner was a member of the group that toured the DP camps with Harrison, and he pointed out the problems that Jewish survivors were experiencing. As a result of Harrison's report, American policy towards Jewish survivors changed. Separate camps were established for Jews, where they had a measure of autonomy, and efforts were made to increase their rations of food and basic necessities. Jewish relief organizations such as the American Jewish Joint Distribution Committee did not participate in the rehabilitation of Holocaust survivors for months after liberation. When the International Refugee Organization, an agency of the United Nations, took over responsibility for the DP camps in 1946, conditions for Jewish survivors were still grim.

"Where shall we go?" became a crucial question for the survivors. Years of Jewish powerlessness had taught Jews the need for self-determination. They wanted a homeland, where they could shape their own lives and determine their own futures. Britain was limiting Jewish immigration to Palestine to 1,500 a month, a ludicrously inadequate number for the tens of thousands of homeless Jewish survivors. Some American soldiers, Jews and non-Jews, became involved with the Zionist-led Brichah, a clandestine effort to transport Jews from Europe to Palestine "illegally," without waiting for British immigration certificates. Some provided trucks for transportation to port cities while others forged orders that permitted the travel; some provided food for the émigrés, and others facilitated the work of the Palestinian Jewish emissaries who organized this transport effort in the DP camps.

Participating in these relief activities was against army regulations. The GIs who did so were sometimes court-martialed; many were sent back to the United States by sympathetic higher-ranking officers in order to avoid court-martial. For the GIs who assisted Holocaust survivors, it was a simple question of right and wrong, and the GIs were on the side of the underdog. "I was interested in justice, life, dignity, and I was going to do everything I could to give them what they deserved," explained Rabbi Abraham Klausner. Survivors of the camps deserved no less.

NOTES

1. Lewis H. Weinstein, "The Liberation of the Death Camps," *Midstream* (April 1986): 20–24.

2. Unless otherwise noted, all subsequent personal recollections are in oral history interviews in the collection of the Museum of Jewish Heritage – A Living Memorial to the Holocaust.

3. Cpl Eli Heimberg, chaplains assistant, quoted in Dann, Sam, ed. *Dachau 29 April 1945: The Rainbow Liberation Memoirs.* Lubbock, Tex.: Texas Tech University Press, 1998, 162.

4. Quoted in Gerald Parshall, "Freeing the Survivors," *U.S. News and World Report*, 3 April 1995, 61.

5. Displaced persons were not allowed to work in the German economy. With no assets or source of income, a barter system developed, using cigarettes as the main currency. Foods that were received in packages were consumed by survivors whose official rations were insufficient, and other commodities were bartered or sold.

6. Earl G. Harrison was a former U.S. Commissioner of Immigration and United States representative on the Intergovernmental Committee on Refugees, an international body that took no meaningful action on the problem of Jewish refugees from Nazism at the Evian Conference in 1938 and again at the Bermuda Conference in April 1943.

"I Wanted to Get My Own Back"

Maximilian Lerner   U.S. ARMY

Six months after my bar mitzvah and ten weeks after the *Anschluss,* when Austria was absorbed into Hitler's Third Reich, my parents decided to leave our hometown of Vienna, which, undoubtedly, saved our lives.

My father was forty-nine years old, my mother forty-eight. My father was an established businessman, and we lived very well in a nice apartment. We took an overnight train to Paris, and suddenly I found myself in a city I did not know, in a country whose language I did not speak, living out of suitcases in a small hotel room with my parents and younger sister.

I do not know whether my parents expected this to be a permanent move or whether they had hopes that the anti-Semitic excesses would stop. By the time France and Britain had submitted to Hitler for the sake of "peace in our time" by selling out Czechoslovakia in September 1938, my parents realized that there was no place for Jews in Europe. We applied for visas out, but we couldn't get anything. Canada and Australia basically told us that we were of the wrong ethnic origin. The United States accepted our application but informed us that our quota number would not come up for five years.

By the fall of 1938, I spoke enough French to go to high school in Paris, and my father managed to resume some business activities even though our residence permit did not allow this.

When France fell in May 1940, we joined the many thousands of Parisians fleeing the conquering German army. After six weeks of wandering through France by foot, truck, and rail, we wound up in Nice in what then was Vichy France.

The American vice-consul in Nice checked on our quota number, and even though we had only waited for two and a half years, it was now available. I assume that many of the people ahead of us had disappeared.

There were people in New York with whom my father had done business. They obtained the required "affidavit of support" for us from an acquaintance. Considering what we were going through, we were amazed that there were people willing to guarantee with their own funds that unknown newcomers would not become a public burden.

So we got the American visa. In order to get the French exit visa, my father and I had to go to Chatel-Guyon near Vichy. And we weren't allowed to do that, because in order to travel from one town to the other in France, you had to get a safe-conduct from the gendarmerie. So we went illegally, because if we hadn't, we couldn't have gotten the French exit visa. And we got it, came back, and then had to get a transit visa in Marseilles from the Spanish government and a visa from the Portuguese consul in Nice. All of these were bribery visas. And the basis of it was that we had a reservation on the *Yankee Clipper* to leave from Lisbon, because you had to show that you could leave. That was totally fake; we got that from a travel agency for money in Nice.

And so eventually we made our way through Spain to Lisbon. Our American visa had four weeks to expire and there was one ship, the SS *Nyassa,* that was leaving, and it was, of course, fully, fully booked. We ran around for four weeks trying to find a way to get on it. By that time my father had run out of money. There was a Jewish agency in Lisbon that said if we could get the tickets, they would give us money for the tickets but not for bribery. We had enough to bribe somebody if we could only find somebody to bribe. And we were running around looking for the *macher,* for the guy who has the "in." We're sitting in a café on the Placa Rossia, and my sister, who at the time was thirteen, overheard people at another table talking about the *macher.* And that's how we found the guy. Eventually he got us two tickets. My family decided that my mother and sister would leave and my father and I would stay behind and be interned in Portugal in the hope that we would stay in Portugal. At that time everybody anticipated the Germans would take Spain and Portugal and also Gibraltar. There was absolutely no justification for them not to; it would have been the right thing to do. That Franco didn't allow it is miraculous. Anyway, on the day the ship left, we got two more tickets for my father and me.

We were on the *Nyassa,* which was probably the last ship out of Portugal, and we left in the middle of Passover. We had celebrated Passover after a fashion in Lisbon. When we got on the ship, it was incredibly crowded, although when I was on a troop transport afterward that was even more crowded. We ran out of food—we had one meal a day—and ten days later we arrived in the United States. We arrived on April 25, 1941, on Friday. I was up all night waiting to see the Statue of Liberty. It was just . . . we didn't believe it until we saw it, and then when we landed, it took all day to get off the ship. The immigration people came on the ship to check our papers and they were polite to us. You have no idea, they were polite to us! We had been treated miserably by anybody who had a stamp that we needed. And there were the Americans, and they treated us like human beings.

When we got off, my father's friends met us and took us to a hotel on 81st and Columbus. And around the corner there was a deli. And we had, we had the most incredible meal, the best meal. First of all we were starving after a week without food, but then we had Jewish food. And the next morning, Saturday, my father said now we have to go to shul, we are safe. We asked at the hotel where is the nearest synagogue, and they sent us to a synagogue and we walked in and my father and mother said this is a church. We were stunned: This was a Reform synagogue. Someone who saw our astonishment took us around the corner to another one.

On September 4, 1942, when I was eighteen, I volunteered. I didn't want to wait to be drafted. I signed away my right as a foreigner. And I remember standing and getting it notarized. There was a notary public on 103rd Street where the subway station is on Broadway. And the radio was playing "Embrace Me, My Sweet Embraceable You" by Judy Garland. I just remember that moment. I said, "Oh, another change in my life." And I sent it, and then they called me in for examination and I was 1A. Then I waited. And they didn't call me in for induction until I reported for duty the beginning of May 1943. I had anticipated they would get me sooner. Mysterious are the ways of the army.

I was very gung ho, very enthusiastic. This was my war, and I wanted the opportunity to get my own back, which was stupid because I didn't think anything would happen to me. You know, at eighteen you're invulnerable. I wanted to be a good soldier, and I was as eager as can be. I volunteered for everything that there was to volunteer for, some of which was very stupid, worked very hard, and did everything as well as I could from the obstacle course to the courses in aircraft recognition.

I stopped putting on tefillin, but I kept kosher to the extent that I could. It meant occasionally not having the main dish and filling up on potatoes or bread; it wasn't onerous.

I was assigned to the Military Intelligence Training Center at Camp Ritchie, Maryland, because of my language skills. The group that I was in were people like me, a group of bright guys who did the best that we could and that were all feeling like I did. They were all—some were Austrian, some were German—but they were all Jewish refugees. I got to be an American citizen while I was in Camp Ritchie. I had only been in the United States two and half years, but the rule was, and I think it is a correct thing, that you can't go overseas if you're not a citizen. So I became an American citizen at the circuit court of Washington County in Hagerstown, Maryland, on September 23, 1943. There was a whole group of us from Camp Ritchie that were taken there. And we were, of course, in uniform. And it was very nice to be sworn in, to be an American citizen.

We shipped out to Europe in March 1944. We arrived in Belfast, which was my one and only glimpse of Northern Ireland, except for going back and forth. We were put into trucks and were taken to the estate of Lord Londonderry near what was then called Londonderry, which I think is now only called Derry. On this estate we saw the manor house in the distance, but that was off-limits. There was a tent camp, and we stayed in that. It was

Maximilian Lerner,
Piccadilly Square,
London

Maximilian Lerner
posing in Nazi uniform
for special agent
identification

a replacement depot. We had been sent over, as many other soldiers had, to await casualties whom we would replace. But of course this was long before D-Day, so we were hanging around and it was boring and unsatisfying. Some officers from the OSS, the Office of Strategic Services, came around to our group and asked for volunteers to jump behind the lines. And, as I say, I was foolish and young and I volunteered. So that's how I was transferred to the OSS.

I was taken with three others. One was a Quebecois and the other two were French. The four of us were given orders to go to London, which was the first time that we were on our own since being in the army. We were given passes. We took a ferry across to England. We took a train to London, and we reported to a particular address. From there we were taken to another stately home outside of London and spent a number of days there being tested and trained. At the end of it, a group of officers, French officers, came around from De Gaulle's Free French Forces and said to me, "You speak excellent French, but you have an accent." And I said, "Yes, I know." They said, "If you go to France, they're going to recognize your accent. We can't send you to France. You'll have to wait, and we'll send you into Germany when the time comes. In the meantime go back to your replacement depot." So I was sent back to London. But in London I went to ETOUSA, the European theater of operations U.S. Army headquarters, which was on Grosvenor Square where the embassy is now. And I went to the G-2 section, the Intelligence section and asked to see somebody. The colonel came out, and I said to him, "Look, I've been so highly trained in this and this and this and now they're sending me back to a replacement depot. Can't you find a job for me?" He took the information down and sent me back. I went back to Northern Ireland and found that the unit that I had been assigned to had been transferred to a camp near Chester. So I went back to the camp near Chester, England, and within a few days there were orders for me to report back to London. This colonel had done what he had said he would.

I went to London and worked for him in his office and had a lovely time in London. I was there from probably June until the end of July. I missed out on D-Day because I was in London at the time. I did experience the V-bombs that came across, but so did everybody else there. And it was wonderful to be in London. My aunt, who had escaped, lived in the suburbs of London. Her husband, my uncle, had not made it, and we found out later he had been killed in Auschwitz. But I got to see her. And I had a great time, until after D-Day, until Cherbourg was taken.

We flew, my colonel and I, together with a lot of other high-ranking officers—I was the low end—across to Cherbourg, so I had an easy way to get into France. We landed in Cherbourg, hung out there. It was at that time that we had the breakthrough, and the Allies decided to allow the French the privilege of liberating Paris. I was transferred away from my colonel, who had taken me along as an interpreter. By that time suddenly they needed people who spoke French. There were lots of them up in the replacement depot, or "repo depot" we called it, but I was on the spot in Cherbourg.

I was transferred to liaison to General Leclerc's Armored Division that was spearheading into Paris—there were only five Americans with him at the time. So I entered Paris on August 25, 1944, with the first French troops. I was one of five Americans to do that. It was incredibly exciting. There was still fighting going on. I had to fly across in a small plane to meet Leclerc's division. There was still sniper fire going on. And as soon as we got in, we took over the former Rothschild mansion on Avenue Foch, which had been Gestapo headquarters during the occupation. There was a huge courtyard and the FFI, the Forces Françaises de L'Intérieur, the "resistance," kept arresting people and bringing them in. We had a courtyard full of people—men, women—full of people. There was an emergency about sorting them out and seeing which ones were just arrested because their neighbors didn't like them and called them collaborators and which ones were German prisoners, German soldiers who were trying to escape, and which ones really were collaborators.

So I spent several weeks in the Rothschild mansion interviewing these people and deciding whether to let them go or whether to send them forward—there were quite a few Germans who had put on civilian clothes—into prisoner-of-war camps or to hold them for further interrogation by the French. I spent several weeks there. It was an incredible period to be in Paris in an American uniform. You owned the city. If I had only had the time and strength . . . it was just a wonderful experience to be in Paris then.

After a few weeks I was transferred again. This time I was assigned to a special unit, finally, and went on to Verdun, France. And in Verdun again we took over an old jail that had been used by the Germans. We had cells in which we had prisoners that were brought to us, and we had cells that my team members and I lived in. We were working together with a group of French officers. By that time I had been commissioned. We interrogated prisoners and went out on missions from there. I finally was able to put on a German uniform and get involved in some of the missions. I spent several months in Verdun.

We wore a kind of civilian uniform. At that time I was CIC, Counter Intelligence Corps, which was a division of the OSS. And I was called a special agent—this is what my documentation showed—and wore an officer's uniform without insignia of rank. The purpose of that was so I could talk to high-ranking officers as Mr. Lerner from the War Department, Special Agent Lerner in the fulfillment of various missions. If I came in as Lieutenant Lerner, then any captain or major doesn't talk to me but yells at me. But if I come in as Mr. Lerner, then my rank was irrelevant and was confidential. So I was simply Special Agent Lerner. I can't go into too many details, because at the time I swore confidentiality, in spite of the fact that it's so long ago. But there were times when I put on civilian clothes in order to meet with people in France, and there were a couple of times when I put on a German uniform and managed to get across to the German side to meet people.

Let me tell you about the Battle of the Bulge. I was in Luxembourg City at the time, which was three-quarters surrounded, and everybody went out to the front lines to fight. I had gone to Luxembourg for a specific reason, to see some people there. I got caught in Luxembourg City. This was a great surprise to all of us. I had an officer's carbine, and we were lined up in trenches in the snow. When somebody said "Fire," we fired. I never saw anybody on whom we fired, but there were forward observers who said, "Fire," and we fired. We spent three days lying in the snow in these trenches and being scared. And then the famous cloud cover lifted, and our planes came in and the attacks were over. So those were the three days during which I was in actual combat. Any other time I was not in combat. I was in danger of being caught on various missions, but that was the only time that I was actually in combat. It was wet and cold; I wasn't afraid because I wasn't smart enough. I really wasn't.

I'll tell you the one incident which was probably the most important one. When the bridge at Remagen was taken, the Germans sent underwater swimmers to try and blow it up. A couple of them were caught and we interrogated them. They had been trained at an indoor pool in Vienna, which is interesting because I knew it very well, so that helped in the process of interrogation. They told us where their camp was and, of course, that they were going to go after the next bridge. We captured another bridge, the Oppenheim Bridge, shortly afterwards. And at night I went in German

Maximilian Lerner
(center) outside Dachau
concentration camp

Maximilian Lerner
in Munich, standing
on the ruins of the
Brown House, former
headquarters of the
Nazi party

uniform with a group of American MPs who volunteered, and we took a boat across the Rhine, which was still German on the other side except for the bridge. I wore the uniform in the expectation that if we got caught, I would stand up and the Germans would see I'm a German. We managed to get across the Rhine. We went over to the camp, attacked it, machine-gunned everybody that could be machine-gunned, and then found ourselves a hayloft and hid in it for two days until our troops came across and we could come down. There was fighting involved, but I didn't do any shooting—it was my companions who did it.

We did not use torture, but we did make it uncomfortable. One of the things, for instance, was not to allow people to go to the bathroom if they didn't want to talk. It wasn't terribly difficult. One of the best methods was when you had two people and two different interrogators getting information from one and then the other. I did not find Germans to be too eager to keep secrets once they were captured. It's not so different from the cross-examination that you see in the movies. It really wasn't.

It was more difficult with the French who were collaborators and, of course, had to justify everything they did. But if you understood what the circumstances were, you could also see whether they were really collaborators or not. For instance, in Paris there was a man of Russian origin who had a nightclub. He was arrested because his nightclub was frequented by Germans, and I let him go. Well, who else would go there? In 1947 I was in Paris and I was walking around, and he recognized me and stood me drinks. But there were other people, industrialists who had worked for the Germans.

By that time we were in Germany. It was almost an anticlimax. I mean, we knew the war was over. We had won, we were there. We started to advance and cross the river, and we went down to Augsburg and then toward Munich. On the way to Munich we drove past Dachau and stopped in Dachau. It had been liberated two days earlier. There were still bodies lying all over the place, and there was a smell that is just indescribable. I knew about Dachau, oh yes. Dachau was the oldest of the camps. And I knew where Dachau was, outside of Munich. We went to Munich, which was badly destroyed, I'm pleased to say. I specifically looked for the ruins of the Brown House, which had been the headquarters of the Nazi party, and had a picture taken of me standing on the ruins of the Brown House. And that was satisfying. But Dachau was a horrible experience.

I knew about Dachau in Vienna, when I was a kid in Vienna. But Dachau was not an extermination camp. It was the first camp in Germany. I

knew people from Vienna who had been taken to Dachau, and I knew people who had been in Dachau and had gotten released. My first wife's father was arrested in Vienna, taken to Dachau and, on the promise that he would leave the country and leave everything else behind, released. And they left. So Dachau was a known concept. And when I saw the sign, I said we have to stop and go and look. And the first American troops had just been there two days earlier, so there were still a lot of people in there starving, and medical help was just coming in. And the bodies were not buried. They were just starting to get things organized.

After the end of the war, I was in charge of the criminal police in Wiesbaden. This was after V-E Day in the summer of 1945. There was a book the size of a paperback, which had been issued by the Supreme Headquarters Allied Expeditionary Force, which listed all ranks in various Nazi paramilitary organizations and administrative officers who were subject to automatic arrest, all SS but others as well. And you know that to identify the SS, one of the easy ways was to look under their left arm to see the blood-type tattoo or the elimination scar. And a partner of mine, a fellow named Tompkin, and I went to an apartment. We had to interrogate a guy whom we had suspected of being in the SS, and we went into his apartment and interrogated him. I decided that he should come along with us for further interrogation. I didn't like the way he talked. And I said, "You come along with us." He ran into the back room, pulled out a handmade rubber club, and started to swing it at me. I closed my eyes and fumbled for the revolver I had on my belt and fired and by sheer accident broke his elbow with my shot. If I had not, he probably would have hit me. I kept it afterwards, that club. So that was the one time when I probably could have been killed if I hadn't been lucky enough to hit his elbow.

Even though we had won, we didn't of course know the extent of the disaster, the numbers. We did not know. We did not know the methodical slaughter of Auschwitz and the other extermination camps. We didn't know that. But even though, it just confirmed me in my efforts to de-Nazify, which brings me to the story of the fire chief. This was toward the late fall of 1945 and I, as I said, I was in charge of the criminal police of Wiesbaden. Military government called me and said, "We need to appoint a fire chief. We are going to send you the man we think you should appoint. Investigate him, interrogate him, and let us know whether we can." So they sent him to me and I arrested him. He was subject to automatic arrest, because during the Nazi period he had had a rank in the fire department which was subject to automatic arrest. And I said, "Can't do it. He's arrested." So they sent me another man. Well, anybody they would send who had the capacity to be fire chief had had a high enough rank to be subject to automatic arrest. So they sent me a third man and I arrested him too. And I got a telephone call from headquarters in Frankfurt and they said, "You have to pick the most innocuous of those three." And I said, "No. Those are not my orders. My orders are to arrest them." They said, "We've got to have a fire chief." And I said, "I am not going to do it." Within a few days I got my papers to go home.

They had asked me initially to stay on for a little longer, to extend my tour of duty by six months and I was considering it, but after that the question didn't arise anymore. This was fine with me; I was ready to come home.

"An *Eigene Mensch*"

Victor B. Geller U.S. ARMY

I joined the enlisted reserve of the U.S. Army on March 1, 1943. I was called into active reserve duty in September 1943 at Cornell University and then went to basic training December 11, 1943. I started as a private. I ended as a sergeant. I served in a battalion Intelligence section in the 346th Infantry Regiment, 87th Infantry Division. I might tell you that in addition to the duties I had, I was also the acting Jewish chaplain for our regiment. In those days in order for a division to have a chaplain of any given faith, there had to be a minimum of 1,000 men of that faith in that division. Our division had 15,000 men, but there were only 825 Jewish men. They did not have enough chaplains, so when they found out my background, I was made the acting Jewish chaplain for the regiment, which meant that in addition to all the other military duties, I conducted services and buried the dead and reburied them and all of the things that a chaplain would have to do.

We landed in Scotland in the Firth of Clyde, having crossed the Atlantic on the *Queen Elizabeth*. The date, let me see, was sometime in October 1944. We proceeded from there by train to Cheshire, where we were stationed in a little town called Congleton, not far from Macclesfield. This was like an English shtetl, and we spent approximately one month or so there living in a cigar factory. We moved from England to France on November 27. We landed near Le Havre and then bivouacked in the area of a little French town called St. Säens on December 5. We began our forward movement

Victor Geller,
ca. 1944

Administration build-
ing at Buchenwald
concentration camp
after liberation

into the combat area in the vicinity of the city of Metz, where the first units of the division moved into action. Our regiment moved to the line of combat on December 9. And I remember very clearly that December 10 was the night of our first attack. And that was the first night of Hanukkah that year. And we observed Hanukkah in a German pillbox, December 11, 1944, in a little French town of Gros-Rederching. It sounds German, but that was because we were in Alsace-Lorraine at the time. And that's where we began combat.

The only concentration camp that I personally entered was Buchenwald. The exact date that I went into Buchenwald was June 7, 1945, because I have a letter that I wrote home to my family simply telling them, "This afternoon I visited Buchenwald concentration camp at Weimar. What I saw and felt I shall not try to put on paper. But when I get home, please G-d, I shall try to tell you about it." Now, at the time, this was, oh, I would imagine, this must have been more than a month after the liberation of Buchenwald. But what happened was that Eisenhower had given orders that every American soldier who could possibly visit the concentration camps should do so.

I knew what I had read before going overseas as a teenager about, of course, the Jewish persecution by the Nazis. As a matter of fact, that's why I gave up my 4D deferment at *yeshivat rabeinu yitzhak elchanan,* and even though I was exempt, I volunteered and joined the army because I felt that it was a Jewish war. So I was aware of this. I knew enough to know that I had to be careful, for example, as a Jew, if I was taken prisoner. And that's why when I went to the forward area, I did not take my tefillin with me because I was afraid that I would be captured with tefillin. But the details of concentration camps we did not know.

It bore out in painful, horrible details the worst fears that I had. Of course, at the time, I did not realize that among the concentration camps, Buchenwald was a country club compared to the ones in Poland. But what I saw in Buchenwald was enough . . . what Americans in general saw. First of all you saw the barracks where you had the shelves where people lived and they were simply warehouse shelves. The people that you saw at the time were those who had already survived; they were in better shape than the emaciated skin and bone skeletons that subsequently became commonplace. Because those that survived had already been the beneficiaries of medical attention and had gotten food for some period of time. So they were already on the mend. But what I saw, for example, aside from the shelves . . . they showed us where, in the basement crematorium, there were first rows of small . . . of cubbies. These cubbies were about four or five inches square, and in those cubbies were little urns. And in those urns were the ashes of people that had been burned and on the cover was stamped the name of the person, when he was born and when he died. And they showed us postcards which Germans sent to families, how methodical they were, saying that this is to advise you that so and so member of your family died of general illness and was cremated for reasons of health. If you pay a certain number of marks, we will send you the ashes in the urn, all neatly ready for shipment. Of course, many of the urns were already open and the ashes were all over. On the other side there were huge hooks like in a butcher shop. If you ever go into a butcher shop, when you get a whole side of meat, they have to hang it on a heavy long steel hook so that then they take it on a wheel, on a pulley, so the butcher can cut it down to size. And we were told people were hung there whether they were dead or not quite dead, half dead. They were hung there prior to being taken up on the little elevator into the crematorium. The crematorium there, of course, was small. I took a picture, there were about maybe six ovens, so the capacity to burn bodies there was really very limited. When they took the body off that butcher's hook, they put it on a little elevator like a dumbwaiter, and then there was a stretcher on wheels, like an operating table. They just pushed it on there, and it was the same height as the crematorium opening, and they had a pole—like a butcher has one of these big sticks with an end to it—to push the body in until it was burned and only ashes.

Buchenwald Concentration

Inside Crematory showing ovens

Now, how many years later, it is not easy to reconstruct the emotion. You also must understand that this was being shown to soldiers who had been through a war, a combat where there was killing and there was death. And there were bodies and parts of bodies. Death, cruelty, this kind of thing, was not a shocking, abnormal circumstance. We had been living in a climate of abnormal inhuman relations. So it was numbing. It didn't wake the kind of rage that seeing thousands of stacked bodies had for the first people who came in, because they were long since taken away. It was already partially cleaned up . . . it was neater. It was already almost for display purposes—we saw a little sign, THIS AREA WAS FOR CHILDREN AND FRENCH GENERALS. In that sense tidier and less of a terrible jar to the senses of soldiers who had just a short time before stopped killing and stopped getting killed, you see. It was probably more of an education for the *goyishe* soldiers, those who did not know why they hated the Germans. After the fact, they understood why they hated the Germans. Because what the army was doing was they were bringing divisions—thousands of men—constantly. Eisenhower wanted all the American troops to be there, because when he saw it he was horrified. He wanted the Americans to see it and then to remember. The element of *zachor*—remembrance—from the point of view of a non-Jew, existed.

In the concentration camps there were many, we were told, who were Germans, liberal Germans from way back. There were some western Europeans, French and others. Then there were Jews. I don't know if I did know the numbers . . . the sense that I have, and from what I recall, they were the largest members. In other words, the political prisoners were the elite. They were the ones who had the privileges of the canteen. They got certain money, like scrip money. I saw no women. There may have been, but I don't recall seeing any. In the pictures that I have, I don't think there are any women.

There was only one crematorium. There was only one building, and that was a small building, and they had six ovens there. And those ovens were not large. There was no gas chamber there. See, what they did was they used the crematoriums to burn bodies that were dead already. I don't think it was intended as part of systematic extermination the way the gas chambers were at Auschwitz.

At Weimar the people, of course, protested that they knew nothing about it—*"Ich habe nicht gewust."* And what happened was that the American units that got in there collected all the people of the city of Weimar and brought them in, brought them in to look at it and to clean it up. The mayor of Weimar, after that day, committed suicide. They knew because some of them said that the location of Weimar was such that when the wind would blow in a certain direction they would have the odor. The answer was they knew, they knew. The Germans could not not know. But, after that, the Germans, except those that were pressed into service to take care of the people who were ill, they were arrested, and we didn't see much of them anymore. As a matter of fact, people were brought in both for the practical purposes of their needing the manpower and also as an object lesson for the Germans so that they would know what they, in fact, were responsible for. They went into Weimar and they pulled people, so-called nice middle-class citizens, out to deal with, to take care of, the camp and the people who were there at the time. And they were involved in the policing, in the improvement, and in the maintenance of the facility for quite some time afterwards.

In most cases there was fear. There were others who were sullen and angry, not angry at what happened, but angry that they lost. And, of course, every German that I came across later insisted that he was not a Nazi, that he was a very good man, and that he had a cousin in Milwaukee. They were very anxious to tell you all the things that you wanted to hear about— Hitler's *kaputt* and that Hitler was terrible and *nicht gut* and everything else.

The ones that I had contact with were out to persuade us that they were the best. I remember there were two little towns, one by the name of Rodewisch and another one by the name of Aue, which were not too far from the Czechoslovakian border. I was for a while the mayor of both towns because we were the first troops in and, of course, *"Nicht Nazi. Ich bin ein gute Deutsche."*

There was not, again talking about the civilian population, an active venom. You have to realize that the civilian population in those towns at that time, the population was composed of females. There were very, very old men and little children, and the only males between the ages of fifteen and fifty were French, Polish, from many nationalities, Dutch, Belgians. In some cases I let them know that I was a Jew, yes. They were very, very anxious to be accommodating and to persuade you that they were very kind, you know, and that they didn't know any Jews: "We didn't have any in our town, you know, but what they did to them was not nice."

I did not have any experience with triage or anything related to the life and death care of survivors. As I mentioned, having come in substantially after the liberation, those who did survive were already recovering. And those who were not destined to do so had long since passed away. I had nothing to do with this particular area of survivors. I do know that as soon as a camp was found—not only Buchenwald but whatever camp was found . . . because in addition to the big camps they found clusters, groups of people—the medics, the medical unit of the organization that came across it, whether it was a regimental aid station or battalion aid station, immediately sent personnel to deal with the dying. The basic notion that they had was the same that applied to regular casualties: Keep them alive. You do what you can to keep them alive long enough for a higher headquarters where they had better facilities to be able to deal with them. It was done with combat wounded, and in the camps they treated it the same way.

What had happened was this. When Buchenwald was initially overrun, before we even got to it, there were Germans, there were people, you know, running all over. Not only Jews, but there were the refugees, the slave laborers. They were German and they were Polish and they were French; they were from all over. And they ran. And what we tried to do was to collect them, because those who were running had no place really to go and had no access either to food or to medical facilities. As a matter of fact, I recall that at one point—I don't even know where we were, but we were bivouacked for a while—we had collected a number of these people, the slave laborers, and a number of Jews, and they were not in good shape. So, because I was in Intelligence, and I spoke German, and I was a graduate of military Intelligence school, and even though I was only a corporal, I had a lot of clout, and I scouted around and I found a small German hospital. It must have had about twenty or thirty beds. And what I did was, I commandeered the hospital and told the chief doctor that I wanted all the patients out by the next day because I'm moving in people who are seriously ill from the camps. He said, "You can't do it. It's not humanitarian. These people are seriously ill." So I told him, I said, "If you don't have them out, none of them will be sick tomorrow. They'll all be dead. So you have a choice. They're gonna risk recovering elsewhere or you won't have anything to worry about." I scared the hell out of the Germans, so they cleared them out and we filled up all the beds. And then, you know, I made believe—you see we didn't wear ranks so he didn't know what rank I was—I was an *Oberst,* I was a colonel. He didn't know the difference. And we hung around long enough until American military government guards came in. We told them what happened, and they took over. But we tried to collect the people and return them to the camps. As a matter of fact, Buchenwald was a collection point; they had a better chance of getting food there.

I spoke Yiddish and I looked for Jews. I found some and we began to talk and they started to tell me the stories of how the Germans had treated them. I got to know one of them. A group of them remained, sort of as

guards, because they had captured a certain number of guards who had not yet been able to escape. Even though by the time the war reached that stage, most of the guards who were left at Buchenwald were old men, people who were handicapped or wounded, because the more able-bodied were taken off to combat or they ran away more rapidly. So what was left was the garbage of the guarding German units.

We did what other units did, I think, we collected the survivors. We tried to get them off the roads because on the road they would starve. They would be cold. And as I told you, they were diseased and ill. What we tried to do was to collect them and put them into one central place and then let the higher headquarters know that these people were collected in this place and in that place. We brought them there, kept them there, and then once they were identified as a depot of some kind, then a quartermaster started to send food for them, so at least they knew they were getting food.

It was not an official policy of the American army to look for sick and helpless Jews. If it was, I was unaware of it. It was of concern to us. Look, when we went overseas, I think we had about 212 Jewish men out of 3,000, about 7 percent, which is pretty large—about 825 in our division. We were concerned and we were aware. Remember not all of the people on the roads were Jewish. They were French. They were Mongolians. The Mongolian was

American soldiers
at Buchenwald,
marching through the
Appellplatz, where
inmates were forced
to attend a grueling
roll call twice a day

the German prototype of the *Untermensch*. He was an Oriental and looked to them to be subhuman, and they used to use them on farms to pull plows and so on and so forth. We collected these kind of people too, you see. But when you got somebody who was Jewish, you knew he was Jewish because he was a concentration camp person who had run away. He was not somebody who was working on a farm. Those on the farms had been generally fed as much as the civilian population was. The Jewish people you could tell more readily by the physical appearance, and it didn't take long to establish, through Yiddish. If they understood *"a guten rosh hashanah"* as a Jewish New Year greeting, we knew they were Jewish, and they would, they would cling to us, whereas the Mongolian wouldn't because he didn't care.

Later on I was assigned to a small *Arbeitslager,* a work camp, for Hungarian and Polish Jewish girls. It had the survivors there. It was called Renchmulle. This is what they later called a Jewish DP camp. It was close to the Czechoslovakian border. Here I found some 400 Jewish girls. Half of them were Hungarian, half of them Polish. They had been working nearby. This was a work camp. The Hungarian girls spoke only Hungarian while the Polish girls spoke Polish and Yiddish. I was the only one in Intelligence who spoke both Yiddish and Hungarian, so they sent me in there. As a matter of fact, it was probably the most moving experience I had. I got in there on an *erev shabbes* and there were these 350 to 400 girls and about 20 to 25 men, refugees who had run when the camps opened. We had a Sabbath service, davening, *kabbalat shabbes,* and when it came to the kaddish—I will never forget the kaddish—because of the crying and the wailing and the tears and the sobbing of that kind of davening. It was at that point that I decided that I had to start to do something. See this list, it's the information I compiled on the inmates of the camp for Hungarian or Polish Jewish girls at Renchmulle, Germany. I tried to get as much information about their people as I could, and I sent this to my mother in New York, and my mother turned it over to the Yiddish paper to publish. Here is an example, this person was looking for her cousin, Ernest Solomon or Shalomon, forty-five, in Pittsburgh, Pennsylvania. He has an electric factory and has been in the United States twenty years. He has two daughters, five and three. His wife's name is Edith. His mother's maiden name was Edith Rosenfeld of Khust, Hungary. Tell him Charlotte Rosenfeld's daughter is asking for him. And I sent these back and, you know, some of them made contact.

The personal experience that I had was more intense with the young women of Renchmulle because I kept coming back again and again. I

brought the medics, I brought the food. I was the one who spoke Hungarian, and I was Jewish, even though I was an American, so I had a fair amount of authority in telling people what to do. There was an enormous outpouring of regard and affection and identification and gratitude on the part of these young women because, you know, it was an *eigene mensch,* one of our own, who could do something and who apparently was inclined to do so, and that's how I got their cooperation.

There were girls there . . . I had the experience myself and, you know, you can understand it. There were a number of girls who wanted to get very, very close and to identify immediately, and one of them considered herself my girlfriend. You know, for one hundred good reasons, you can understand why. Among the good reasons was the hope that she could come to America very quickly. There was also . . . I'm talking about the case of these girls. I was, look, all of nineteen and a half, and girls would walk around, would walk around without clothes . . . now, for me this was shocking. Of course, if you looked at it from the experience that they had been through, they probably didn't realize, you know . . . but for me it was this kind of familiarity, indifference, if you want, or casualness. It was one of the indexes of the fact that they had been through a great deal, and when GIs were nice to them, brought them a chocolate bar . . . you know, they were emotionally hungry, so they lent themselves to liaisons in friendships. Most of the GIs, as long as the response was positive, they were very democratic. I didn't ask them too many questions. Most American GIs did not make a significant distinction between a German girl—there were plenty of them—as opposed to a survivor. They made no distinction. I was too young to really be that sophisticated. You must realize, you're talking about an abnormal situation. Anyone who would come through that kind of experience with equanimity was capable of incredible denial.

When the war ended, our division was maintaining a front-line sector, not too far from the German city of Plauen, which is in Thuringia, not too far from the Czechoslovakian border. The Russians were about sixty miles on the other side. They had stopped, and we had stopped, and the Russians were giving discharges to all German prisoners who lived in the American sector. They were sending us thousand of people because they did not have enough food. So to anybody who lived in the American-held or the British-held territories, they gave a military discharge. They came to us in the thousands, waving it. They wanted to get across. Our people didn't want it. At one point, we had to put our tanks out to keep these Germans from coming in. Then our regimental commander sent me as part of an Intelligence team to go to the Russians and say, "Hey fellows, stop it!" And we did. We went to see the Russians. We drove sixty miles to the Russian area. And the Russians said, "Nuts to you." There were hundreds of thousands of Germans squeezed between us. The Russians wanted to make sure that they didn't have to feed any more prisoners than they had to. So what they did was they collected all the prisoners and divided them by geography. All those who had their homes in western Germany, they immediately gave discharges to and made up their diplomas—they graduated from the army—and said, "Go home!" and they sent them west. We were getting tens of thousands of Germans, and we had no food for them. There was no infrastructure to feed these people. We had to line up tanks and armored cars to keep them from coming. When it got really serious—there were thousands of Germans, acres and acres of Germans sitting there—somebody had to feed them. Our division commander sent an Intelligence team to talk to the Russians, to tell the Russians, "Hey, stop discharging these guys and stop sending them to us. Keep them." So we went there, and, of course, the Russians couldn't care less. First of all, none of them spoke English. We had to do it in German. They had some people who spoke some German, but they weren't interested. We talked and talked and talked, for about an hour, and then the officer said, "Look forget it. It's a waste of time." And we went back.

I had tried to become detached from my unit and applied to be transferred to American military government. But, they . . . I don't know exactly why . . . they didn't want to let me do it. Part of the reason was, at the time, our division was slated to go to the Orient to fight the Japanese. This was before the atomic bomb. So they wanted to keep the division intact, and therefore, they didn't let me go. I did not have—I was a *Bürgermeister* of a lot of towns and some of the letters reflect on that. I played *macher* in terms of the Germans in cases where we found individual people who were Jewish and others who came back. There we tried to do something for them. But other than that, I didn't have any extended stay because when the division left, I had to go with them.

"I Just Couldn't Face It"

Jack Scharf U.S. ARMY

I went to public school and I used to play hooky and things like that, so as a disciplinary measure, my father sent me to Yeshiva Salanter, which was on Washington Avenue in the Bronx. And I was kind of old and tall. I didn't start from the beginning, so I was even behind in that school, too. The children there were sons of rabbis or they were all Orthodox and I wasn't. I didn't take to Orthodoxy or anything like that.

My teenage years, believe it or not, they were happy years because I now went to a secular school, James Monroe High School, and I wasn't in only with Jewish kids. I was in with all types of people and it was great. They taught me to play the clarinet, so I was in the band. And I was in the orchestra, so I learned classical music. I used to go to football games; I was the class president. And I always went out with the prettiest girls. I was an equal-opportunity person. In fact I went with Irish and Italian girls and all that. And my parents never objected. They were very happy to have them in the house and all. These were kind of religious Catholic girls, and they were very fine people.

I would say I became aware of Hitler in college. I had really no knowledge of any politics whatsoever. I went to City College uptown and it was a hotbed of activity between the Communists and the Stalinists versus the Leninists. And I really didn't know the difference. And they always tried to propagandize you in the lunchroom. But I knew of Hitler. And I think Russia at that time was affiliated with, yeah, that's right, with Germany. And I could not understand it. And that's why I enlisted in the ROTC. That's the Reserve Officers Training Corps. And I worked myself up—I had this citation—to cadet sergeant. I felt I was going to become an officer in the infantry because of Hitler over there. And as I used to walk down in the lunchroom, both sides used to attack me, because I used to wear my army uniform. They called me a fascist. So I was always a minority within a minority.

Well, things came up like smashing windows, Crystal Night, things like that. *Mein Kampf,* I read *Mein Kampf.* I felt that was a blueprint. I guess many Jews I talked to felt, well, it can't happen and it's not going to happen. And I felt it can happen and it will happen. My parents, they sent money all the time to relatives. We'd been getting reports from relatives, but they were very, very sketchy. But we knew that the Jews were in trouble.

I was out on a date. It was Sunday, and I came out of this movie on Jerome Avenue with this girl, and somebody said that Pearl Harbor was attacked. And I said to this girl—her name was Bernice, I still remember her name—and I said to her, "You know what, it looks like I'm going into the army." Well, I was in school. I was in City College. And I was in the ROTC. But I switched down to the Bernard M. Baruch School of Business because I was told by an adviser that I don't have a chance for engineering because there was discrimination against Jews. It was very difficult to get a job. He says, "You have a better chance of getting a job in the government as an accountant," either with the IRS or the Customs Department or whatever department it would be. So I switched over to there. And downtown they did not have an ROTC, so I had to leave the program. And then the army recruiters came, and they said that they were going to let us finish the term if we enlisted. That was great, so I enlisted. So did other fellows. But you know the army. They never listen to their promises. And one day they just said, "Okay, you're on call." So they took myself and several other fellows who were listed from City College, and we got inducted and went to Fort Dix.

They sent us to Camp Gruber, Oklahoma, and they gave us basic training. Then they put us into what they called Task Force Lindon and they shipped us overseas. We landed in Marseilles, France, and then we became part of the 42nd "Rainbow" Infantry Division. And the thing was, we were supposed to show the Germans that many troops were coming over. We were supposed to be the backup, like the tenth line of defense, so to speak. But guess what? The Germans broke through. And that's where I got all my medals. I had the training, thank God.

We had to cross the Rhine in rubber rafts until they could put up bridges. We were in Schweinfurt, where the Germans were making ball bearings, which was very important. Our planes really bombed that place to hell. And that was the first time I came across slave labor, Polish and Jewish, and other slave labor. And that was quite an experience because the Germans ran out of the town, and they were left over there. And they came over to our place to get food, you see. Where do you get food? So they were in our scrap house. What the GIs throw away is unbelievable. And they were in the garbage pails. And naturally, being Jewish, the other guys, what do they know? For me, I went to speak to them and find out what's happening and all. I said, "What a terrible life," you know, slave labor. And they didn't think so. They said, "Are you kidding? We at least had some meals. Not such great meals, but . . . " He says, "My brother, my cousin and all, they're all dead. They were in concentration camps." They told me the story, and I couldn't believe it. It sounded too exaggerated, you know. How could a human being throw somebody else into a furnace or something like that? But apparently they knew and I didn't, and neither did my buddies until we got to Dachau.

There must be something, there must be a built-in radar in us with which we can identify who's Jewish. I found that many times, even when I was in Rome, Italy, and there was a vendor where I stopped to buy some crucifixes for my Catholic friends, and he knew immediately I was Jewish. And he was Jewish. You see that? And he wanted to invite me to his home and all of that. There was something built in. When I went to Paris, wherever I went, there was somebody there, whether I was in Muskogee, Oklahoma—only one Jewish family, they invited us for Passover—or St. Louis, Missouri—the people who make the denims, the Levis, they invited me for Passover. Or I go to the USO . . . wherever it is, it's amazing. I can't understand it, but it's true—you're never alone. Wherever you go—I don't care where in the world—you'll always find the connection and somebody will take you in.

You want to know something? They say there are no atheists in fox-holes. And I lived a lot in a foxhole. We were never even allowed to take rest in a farmhouse, because the Germans used to booby trap them. And since we lost some people like that, we always had to live in the woods or in fox-holes, or whatever. And the foxholes, I showed you, I brought in a siddur, which the Jewish Welfare Board gave to all the Jewish soldiers. And even though I wasn't religious, I did have that little background from yeshiva. A

siddur is a prayer book and you really want to pray, you understand? Because bombs are falling, and mortars and missiles from airplanes and all of that. You're alone. You're really alone. And there's only one thing. You can't call a friend because the guy's in the next foxhole, the foxhole over there, and you're all alone.

So you do crazy things. Like on a Friday night, I dig a foxhole, and then I dig a hole into the side, all the way in. So what I do is . . . My mother, she used to send me wine. Now, it was illegal to send wine. So she went to the doctor and got a medicine bottle for cough medicine. And she'd take the cough medicine, spill it out, put in the wine, and mail it to me, and also mail me a salami. And she made me a candle. She told me to light the Shabbat candle—because she always lit the Sabbath candles. So I kept this in my grenade bag. In other words, let's say you can fit in four grenades. I threw out two and kept the salami, the wine bottle—the medicine bottle—and a candle. And what I did was, on Friday, I would take my canteen, throw it in the snow over there, and I would take out my wine bottle. I just knew the initial blessing. I really didn't know the whole blessing. But I did know the first part of it of it. It's called *borei pri hagofen*. And I'd make that thing, but you're not allowed to light a fire. Because if you light a fire, they can see you, and you can get killed. One of my friends got killed that way. So what I did was, I dug in, took a C ration can, put the candle in there, put it like two feet in, and lit the candle. I took my salami and I had my Shabbat meal on Friday night. And that was Friday in a foxhole.

I was thinking about how you get out of this thing alive, because you're really concentrating on living. I tell you what, I had a responsibility, which was also good. I told you we lost a lot of officers. My friend Ralph Bald Jr. received a battlefield commission, and they wanted to do the same thing for me. I refused the battlefield commission. I was under a lot of pressure, and the reason I refused is because all my officers were killed between the first battle and Hatten—chaplains, doctors, and all like that. We lost everybody practically, over 500 GIs. They were either prisoners or dead. And my group, and a couple of others, we were fortunate to get out. That's a miracle from God also. And I think, I am not going to be . . . I don't want to be responsible for other people. You have to send other people out into combat, and if they didn't come back, that's your responsibility. So I never minded, and I even used to volunteer to go out on patrols. And I went out, and we always came back alive because I was always concerned to take the responsibility. I was always the point man. I was seldom the rear man. I had to see that they had food, that they had first aid, water, and things like that. It was a responsibility.

I wrote letters. I always wrote letters. And they were very good about letters—they used to pick them up in the foxhole, believe it or not. There was a mailman. In fact, one of the mailmen got killed going around picking up these letters. It was unfortunate. Nice guy. Name was Kinney. I still remember him.

This is a very funny thing. I was in a foxhole one day. And it was nighttime, really late at night. And somebody comes in, and I thought it was an enemy. Someone comes in the foxhole and says, "Hey, Scharf. You got to get back to the command headquarters." I said, "I don't have a replacement." So he says, "Look, that's an order. Get out of there." I went out of there, followed him through the lines, and there was a truck waiting for me.

It was a graves registration. And in there were all dead bodies of the soldiers who got killed, you know, in our particular engagement. And he told me get on the truck. I says, "Where am I going?" He didn't know. He says, "We just got orders that we had to take out Scharf and the Jewish soldiers." And they put me in the back, and here I see this guy's boots. I didn't even have leather boots like that. I attempted to take them off and put them on. Because your feet are frozen. In fact, I have trench foot to this day. I can get a pension. I never claimed the pension because I saw friends who lost their legs. I just didn't feel I deserved it.

So I got into the jeep, and the driver didn't know where he was going. He just knew he had to go to Dahn, Germany. And we had to go through very bad territory, the Germans were all around. In fact, this particular jeep had to have—it's a long stick—because the Germans used to put up wire and you'd get decapitated as you went through. And this steel bar would cut through that barrier. It was pretty bad. But he only knew he had to get to Dahn, Germany. When we got to Dahn—and this was the biggest shock of my life—they said it was Passover, and they were going to have the first Passover service in Germany. And there was Chaplain Eli Bohnen, who was a Conservative rabbi from Rhode Island. And here are German women and they're cleaning, and the fish, you know, the gefilte fish, and wine, and they've got matzohs and all of that. It was just incredible. It was like a scene out of Kafka, you know what I mean? Just wild.

And here we were, we're sitting down with the dead bodies and all that for a Passover service. And I have a picture of that in my division magazine of the first services in Dahn, Germany. But that was a great experience. And the reason they took us out—there weren't too many Jewish soldiers—the reason they took us out was because the general wanted to show Americans, the P.R., the public relations, he wanted to show how we celebrated the first Passover. It was a great victory. That shows you that Hitler was now being defeated, if you can take his people and they have to serve you. They have to do the cleaning and the potatoes and the washing. Oh, it was really great. That was one of the greatest services I ever attended.

Our division was the one that was supposed to take Munich. And we consisted of the 222nd, the 232nd, and the 242nd Infantry Regiments. I was in the 242nd. We were going down the autobahn—the autobahn is the highway to go down into Munich. Our job was to take Munich. And the ones from the 222nd, they made a left and they took Dachau. But the thing was, thousands of soldiers—German soldiers—were surrendering. So we

Dachau concentration
camp

American Seventh
Army troops at
Dachau, examining
a train car
containing corpses

didn't have so much difficulty in getting into Munich. It was just cleaning up operations.

So, more or less, the whole city sort of surrendered. And then when the fellows from the 222nd came into Munich, that's when you can sleep and drink and eat and go to the tavern, et cetera, et cetera, confiscate the beer, girls. They came in and they began to tell us stories which were unbelievable. And they told us about Dachau. And naturally, being Jewish, the gentile GIs said, "Scharf, you won't believe what's happened here." And so what happened is the next day—this is about April 30—I remember, because this was unusual—it was snowing lightly, a very, very unusual thing. The next day they had orders to round up prominent German civilians. Because the Germans would say they never knew about Dachau, *"Nicht verstehe,"* and that they couldn't smell the odors or anything else like that. It was ridiculous because maybe it was eight, ten kilometers away from Munich.

So the United States Army had trucks and jeeps to take the personnel over to Dachau to see for themselves what was happening there. I hitched a ride in a jeep, and as we were riding along the driver was describing to me exactly what, what was going on there. There were bodies piled up and all. The thing is, the more he talked to me—and as we rolled into the railroad yards, there were all these cattle cars with bodies—I was getting sicker and sicker and sicker. And I says, "Did you go in?" He says, "Nah, I won't go in

because there may be typhus there." So we got to the entranceway and I was really sick. What I did was, and I can never forgive myself for this the rest of my life, I took the next jeep back. I couldn't face it. I just couldn't face it. And to this day it kills me. It kills me. I'm sorry.

There was a little moat, and there was a barbed wire fence. And some of the prisoners when they were freed, they were so anxious to see the GIs—the fellows from the 222nd were telling me—that they actually got onto the fence before they were able to de-electrify it, and they got killed the last day. Incredible. It just boggles your mind. But what they did was very understandable because you could see they'd killed, I would say, between twenty-five and fifty SS guards over there, and the blood was running into the moat and all that. The Jewish inmates got their guards—they had to get revenge.

Now, I talked to prisoners, but in Munich they were the ones, the inmates who escaped. In other words, because the United States Army said there might be typhus and all types of diseases, they wouldn't let them out. But some of our Jews are pretty resourceful, especially people who are on detail outside. And they got to Munich and I talked to these people. They were very bitter. They were so bitter it was unbelievable. And I said, "Gee, here we came, we sacrificed our lives, gentile guys and all that, and you're bitter?" And they said, "Well, we're always thinking and dreaming that the day that the Americans would come and free us that we would be in Munich

Dachau inmates raising
an American flag after
liberation

and we would be in the warm rooms and we would be in the beds, and we would not be amid the bodies and the stink and the stench and everything like that. And the Germans who were there, we would take them over there instead of loading up trucks and showing these Germans and then bringing them back so they can stay in their warm beds." Then he says, "And you keep us in prison yet?" And I tell you, I was at a loss. In fact, I was always at a loss with my Jewish brethren. Because you say, maybe they don't have any gratitude or appreciation. But when I look back, they were justified.

Those people who we were defending in Munich—and I tell you I was really defending them—because my own men, and they were pretty good men there, they were so outraged by the atrocities that they were starting . . . they wanted to rape the women, and in fact some of them were holding up civilians, taking away their watches, taking away whatever valuables they had, smashing up furniture and windows. And myself and several other GIs had to stop this. And here's a Jewish guy, I'm stopping this? It wasn't right. The army should have taken these people in these jeeps and the armored trucks, whatever, just bring them over here. And yet they were still behind bars.

They were behind the electrified wire because the army was right. There was typhus, there were all types of sicknesses. There was dysentery. There was everything. They didn't want it to spread. You go into the civilian population, Lord knows, you can have a plague. But you can't explain that to people who have lost everything.

I was still attached to the 42nd Infantry Division. But let me tell you what I did. On my free time, and I had a lot of free time, I found out—naturally I spoke to the young ladies and all—there were shortages of everything. So I wrote a letter to my mother. And I wrote this letter to my mother saying, if you can send me anything—lipstick, food, stockings—anything would be greatly appreciated by the displaced persons. I didn't know, but my mother takes this thing, puts it into the Jewish paper, the *Forward*, and packages start coming from all over the country. They had to go to a local synagogue, and they actually set up a special post office for us. I have an article on it with my picture, which was sent into the paper, the Jewish press. Well, it wasn't only me. It was other Jewish people too. Whoever we can gather together, we worked as a team, including the chaplain. We had our own organization. So, you see, even over there we tried to help our own DPs.

All the time, I had contact with Germans because, first of all, after the war we were assigned in Bruck, Austria, and we had to take the civilians to do clean up, to do the KP, to do all the types of menial tasks which our GIs used to do. So I had them come in every morning and chop the wood, put the fires on, make the baths, the water. That's what we did. So I had contact with them. Fortunately in Bruck I also took a course in German to learn to speak a better German. You know, all the Germans, they all loved the Jews. It was their neighbor, not them. They helped them, you know. They're best friends. "I went to school with them," and such and such.

I told you I really wasn't religious. I enlisted, and when you enlist you have to, you know, you can't observe the Sabbath and things like that. But I would tell you the first great influence was this rabbi, Eli Bohnen, from Rhode Island, the chaplain. Because he first made me realize I'm Jewish because he always called upon me, whenever there was a problem, you know, of services and anything else like that. So even if I didn't want to, I was forced into it, you see, because I couldn't let him down. Many organizations have asked me to speak in front of them, and I just couldn't do it. You saw how I broke down. I couldn't face it. I can't even to this day. I'd have other people read this thing from Dachau. I just can't do it. I'm afraid I would crack. I have guilt. I left a lot of good guys behind. These are the real heroes. I'm not a hero. That's a lot of . . . I'm a survivor. You know, we're the liberators, so to speak. But we're not the heroes. It's guys like Sgt Merle Todd, who could have gone home. And he wouldn't leave us, because we were raw recruits, and he says, "You're going to get killed." And he told us, "Put your head down," do this, do that. He got killed. He never came back to see his wife and his children. These are the real heroes. Carl Zahm, the Jewish fellow from Carleton College. Great brain. Got killed in a foxhole. These were the heroes.

I suffer nightmares every night of my life. The only thing to do is to remember that camaraderie I found in the army. The Hebrew expression is, the greatest tranquilizer in the world is to do mitzvahs, which means— mitzvahs are not good deeds—it's just common decency to your fellow human being. It is very important.

"*Sholom Aleichem Yidn, Ihr Zeit Frei!*"

Rabbi Herschel Schacter   U.S. ARMY

In the summer of '42, after Pearl Harbor, with my clergy exemption from military service, I debated with myself whether or not I should volunteer. I knew that Hitler was persecuting Jews. I knew that, once the United States entered the war, this would be—at least I felt so in my heart of hearts—a "Jewish war." I also knew that in anti-Semitic circles in America, and many other places, the term "Jewish war" was one of derision. I heard people saying "Why should we Americans be fighting and risking our lives for a Jewish war?" I volunteered to serve as a chaplain in the American army, because I felt this was the right thing to do. I don't mean to wave a flag or demonstrate my patriotism, I simply felt that this was the natural and proper thing for a young Orthodox rabbi to do.

When I left chaplain's school at Harvard in December 1942, my orders were to report to the port of embarkation in New Orleans, where I was stationed until approximately the fall of 1943. My orders arrived for duty in San Juan, Puerto Rico, where I served as Jewish chaplain for the entire Antilles Department in the Caribbean for almost another year. I then received temporary orders to conduct High Holiday services in Greenland and other remote outposts way up to the far north, an assignment that I truly enjoyed.

When I returned to New York in October '44, I found orders to go to Texas. After pressuring the Office of the Chief of Chaplains in Washington, I succeeded in having them cancel that order and found myself on my way to Europe. Reporting first to army headquarters in Paris, I waited at the

replacement depot outside Paris. Orders arrived from headquarters of the
Ninth Army somewhere in Holland. I walked into the office of the senior
chaplain of the Ninth Army and gave him a snappy military salute.
"Chaplain Schacter reporting for duty, sir!" Maybe I shouldn't say this, but
this senior chaplain, a full colonel, looked up at me and said, "Who needs a
Jewish chaplain now? How did you ever get here?" To which I replied,
"Sorry, sir, I did not ask to be sent here, these are my orders." I simply had
no choice but to wait around. This was really absurd because there was a
war going on! There was such an acute shortage of chaplains on the front
battle lines. And I was sitting around and waiting. Finally, I received orders
to report to VIII Corps headquarters, where I was courteously received by
the senior corps chaplain.

The VIII Corps included divisions with front-line combat troops and
was in need of a Jewish chaplain. I came at a critical time, immediately after
the Battle of the Bulge. I was not in Bastogne, but I was in that area and the
fighting there was fierce. This was a shattering experience. There were so
many boys who were killed, and I was the only Jewish chaplain. I had to
officiate at the burials of many young Jewish soldiers, nineteen and twenty
years old. It was a very trying experience to write condolence letters to their
families. How do you answer, how do you explain to a family when a young
son, or a daughter, or husband, or brother is killed?

At the height of the war, the front kept moving. Our tanks, trucks, and
vast numbers of troops were pushing eastward across the Rhine onto the
huge superhighway that Hitler built, called the autobahn. Little did he
realize that he was building the road to his own destruction. We kept
moving eastward until we were just outside the city of Weimar, where we
stopped. A friendly colonel, a nice fellow, approached and said to me, "You
know, this may be of interest to you. We just got word that our troops pene-
trated a place called Buchenwald. It is some kind of, I think, concentration
camp. We don't know what went on there or what is going on there."

I started to shake. I had never heard the word *Buchenwald,* but I had
heard the words *concentration camp.* I heard this was a place where Jews
were being tortured. I never dreamed of seeing what I ultimately saw. I said
to this high-ranking officer, "Do you think I could pull out and try to find
that place?" He replied, "Well, I wouldn't advise it, wait a little while." I
couldn't wait, and I pulled out with my jeep and driver. Buchenwald, I soon
learned, was right outside of Weimar. In Weimar I found American military
personnel, who directed us to Buchenwald.

We drove until we saw a big gate that was open—the gates of hell. I had finally reached Buchenwald. We drove through and we found a huge open area. I learned later that it was called the *Appellplatz*, where inmates were dragged out early every morning and late into the evening for roll call. They were forced to stand for hours in the broiling sun of summer and the freezing cold of winter. This vast huge area was now empty, but as we looked around I caught a glimpse of a tall chimney with billowing smoke still curling upward. I went forward to look at it, and of course, it was the crematorium. As I approached, I scarcely could believe what I was seeing. There I stood, face-to-face with piles of dead bodies strewn around, waiting to be shoveled into the furnace that was still hot. It was just an incredibly harrowing sight. I stood there for a while, in utter confusion and disbelief. I turned away in a daze; I just couldn't bear to look at such a gruesome scene.

Walking back to my jeep and driver, I met a young lieutenant, who, recognizing the insignia on my uniform, said, "I am a Jewish boy." I replied, "Oh, my God, do you know what's happening here? Are there any Jews still alive here? He led me to an area that was called *das kleine Lager*, a horrible place which was utilized primarily, as I understood it, for the torture of Jews. I could not believe my eyes. There I saw many dilapidated and filthy barracks. Hesitantly, I walked into one of them. A foul, smelly odor hit me. What I saw there I shall never forget as long as I live. I saw a series of shelves, hard cold planks of wood from floor to ceiling. There were hundreds of men, a few boys—there were no women in Buchenwald—lying on these stinking straw sacks, looking out at me from dazed bewildered eyes, skin and bones, more dead than alive.

I stood there overwhelmed and terrified. I did not know what to say or do. Impulsively, instinctively, I shouted out in Yiddish, "*Sholom aleichem yidn, ihr zeit frei!*" continuing in Yiddish with, "The war is over, I am an American rabbi, you are free!" There was dead silence. A few who could approach me, touched my uniform. Many of them spoke Yiddish and, thank God, I spoke Yiddish well. "Is it true? Is the war really over? What happens now? Where do we go from here?" A few started to follow me, and I went through this agonizing experience in barrack after barrack—I don't remember how many—until, just exhausted, I stopped going into barracks that day.

That was it! That's when a whole new chapter started in my life. Under the impact of those moments, of those hours, I decided that as long as I possibly can, I am staying in Buchenwald. I ran back to Weimar, which now became the headquarters of VIII Corps. I settled in and ran back to Buchenwald. For the next eight weeks, Buchenwald was my place.

I soon found myself coming early every morning from my quarters in VIII Corps Headquarters as I began to roam around the camp. Buchenwald had a huge public address system that reached the entire camp. On the very first Friday, I found the location of the microphone and spoke to the GIs in charge. "Look, I want to make an announcement of a religious service for Jewish survivors." The sergeant in charge said, "OK, go ahead Chappie." So I spoke into the microphone in Yiddish, "Here is the American rabbi talking to you. I want you to know that tonight at seven o'clock there will be an *oneg shabbes* evening service in the *Kinohalle*." I found this large open space that was a "movie hall." You can imagine the kind of movies they saw there. But everybody knew where that was because they had been herded into that room for, oh, a million beastly reasons.

From the earliest days I found myself building acquaintanceships with a number of army medical officers who were helpful in saving the lives of many survivors. I cannot praise them enough for their remarkable devotion. One of these officers guided me to the dispensary, a minihospital of sorts where I managed to find this little clean room. I put a little cot in there. That was my headquarters for *shabbes,* because I wasn't going to drive back and forth. I walked into the *Kinohalle* on Friday evening, and there were at least 1,000 people packed to the rafters. I got up on a small platform. I had a little GI prayer shawl and started with *"sholom aleichem"* and slowly but steadily we were singing and praying.

I had no prayer books to distribute. I had nothing other than my voice. Yes, I did have one very interesting item, which I carried with me throughout my military career. I had a little *hupah.* Sometimes the chaplain was called upon to officiate at a marriage ceremony. So I brought this little canopy, embroidered with *mazel tov* in Hebrew lettering, put it on my little table serving as my "lectern." I led an abbreviated Hebrew service with a traditional *nigun* for *lecha dodi* with many singing the familiar melody with me. In a paper cup I poured some grape juice and recited kiddush. After it was over, many people gathered around me. I will never forget those moments! Everyone spoke Yiddish—the lingua franca was Yiddish. "Do you know where is . . . I have an uncle who lives in Chicago . . . I have a niece somewhere in . . . " On and on it went. It is impossible to describe their excitement or their pride. This was the first moment that they could openly express their Jewish identity since the war began. They remained with me until late in the evening. These Friday night services continued, with lesser attendance, for several weeks.

Electric fence surrounding
Buchenwald concentration camp

Rabbi Herschel Schacter
leading *Shavu'ot* services at
Buchenwald for liberated
inmates and GIs

In the little room in the dispensary which now became my headquarters, there were almost always people lined up to talk with me. I collected many lists of names, ages, and last address of these survivors. Before long, I had hundreds of names on these lists, and I forwarded them to the senior Jewish chaplain in Paris, Rabbi Judah Nadich. I enclosed my own military return address. He then forwarded these lists to the Jewish Telegraphic Agency. Before long, I was deluged with letters from people seeking their relatives.

When I received a shipment of GI prayer books from the Jewish Welfare Board, I hurriedly distributed them at another *oneg shabbes* gathering. Young and old quickly snatched these booklets as though they were diamonds! A young Communist leader rose and shouted, "To whom are you praying? To the God who threw your parents in to the crematorium?" It is interesting to note that this outburst made very little impact on that crowd.

One day, a group of young men whom I knew from Friday evening services approached me. "We have nothing to do, we're just hanging around," they said. They told me that before the war they were members of a *hachsharah* group preparing for aliyah to Palestine. Some of them were religious and all were people of conscience, people with heart and soul. "Maybe we can reconstitute some kind of a camp here that would be similar to the camp that we used to have where we worked the farm and we were preparing physically for life in a kibbutz in Israel." This impressed me.

I knew a friendly, sympathetic colonel who was in charge of G-5 civilian affairs, which included the instructions governing the return of refugees to their countries of origin. I asked, "What about the Jewish survivors?" He quickly answered that they also had to return to the countries of their origin. I told him, "There are Jews who have sworn never to return. How can these Jews return to Poland? It's a giant cemetery drenched in Jewish blood." He was sympathetic and answered, "Unfortunately, my orders don't give any specific instructions for Jews."

I described to him the nature of the group that had come to see me and their sincere desire to prepare for a meaningful life and work on a farm in Palestine. He was impressed by what I said and told me he would give the matter some thought. Within several days, the colonel found a large farm estate in Eggendorf which had been in Nazi hands during the war. The group settled there and adopted the name Kibbutz "Buchenwald." The group was under the leadership of an inspiring survivor named Chaskel Tydor. What a tzaddik! He survived Auschwitz, Birkenau, and Buchenwald for over six years and he helped save many people after the war. The group

was composed of people with varying views, but because of Chaskel Tydor's inspiration, they all agreed to observe the basic Jewish traditions.

Before long, women began showing up at Buchenwald. These were women who had been working in slave labor camps in the area of Buchenwald. Word reached them that Buchenwald was free and, somehow, they heard there was a rabbi there. Many of them found their way to my headquarters in that dispensary, where I tried to help them. Some decided that they wanted to go to *hachsharah* and joined the men.

Another rabbi, Chaplain Robert Marcus, also assisted many Buchenwald survivors. He was instrumental in helping the *chalutzim* of Kibbutz "Buchenwald" to obtain seventy certificates for aliyah. He accompanied them on an ageing British ship, the SS *Mataroa,* to Palestine to fulfill their dream.

Another historic moment was when I was called into the office of the VIII Corps commanding general who told me that word had come down from SHAEF, Supreme Headquarters Allied Expeditionary Forces, in Paris, where Dwight Eisenhower was in command, informing the VIII Corps that orders had come from the Swiss Government inviting several hundred children who survived Buchenwald to come to Switzerland. There they would be enabled to regain some measure of health after a few months, then eventually go on to wherever they wished. This was a moment of rare largesse on the part of the

Swiss government. I was asked to be in charge of this transport by the military authorities in Weimar, an assignment I happily accepted.

The Swiss government sent a woman, a nurse, to interview and accept only youngsters under the age of sixteen. She was not a kind, sympathetic person. She insisted she must see everyone under sixteen, young enough and able to go. Tragically, Hitler did not leave so many young Jewish children alive in Buchenwald. But we sent loads of people to her. The ones she accepted received a rubber stamped card as a train pass. She rejected all those she thought were over sixteen. With Tydor's help, I made liberal use of U.S. Army rubber stamps, and we were able to forge train passes and distribute them to the people she rejected.

The following day, the train, loaded with all the card bearers, rolled out. Once on its way, the nurse began to pass through the cars. She was stunned by the sight of so many people and, in a fit of rage, she cried out, "Where do all these people come from?" The number far exceeded the number of cards she distributed. She ran around like crazy, but there was nothing she could do. The freedom train was on its way.

When we approached the Basel station, the train stopped. A Swiss officer asked for the person in charge. I walked up to him, saluted and said, "I am Chaplain Schacter, I am in charge! What is happening?" He spoke in a very heavily German-accented English, "I am sorry to tell you but my orders are that this transport has to go back to where it came from." "What are you talking about, 'It has to go back'?" I said. To which he responded, "Well, the arrangement was, I am told, our government invited only children under the age of sixteen. I understand there are many, many people on this train who are far beyond the age of sixteen. This is a violation of my government's invitation, and it is cancelled."

Oh God, what do I do? Where do I go? I had no idea, I was really at a loss. I wasn't a military general; I was a young, little *rebele* who was trying to do a good deed. I stood around awhile shifting from foot to foot. Then I went back to this Swiss officer and said, "Look, I want to tell you one thing. I am an officer of the United States Army. I am here on a mission that I was ordered to fulfill. Did you ever hear of General Eisenhower? General Eisenhower gave me an order to bring these people into Switzerland on the basis of an invitation from your government. I just want to tell you that if this train does not move within the next hour, there will be an international press conference. I will bring to this station hundreds of journalists from newspapers all over the world. Not only can I do it, but General Eisenhower will do it and the world

will know how generous and kind and humane the Swiss government is to turn these people back to hell. The entire world will know, I promise you!" He said "Oh, just a minute," and sure enough, he contacted some people and in less than an hour, the train was rolling into Basel.

When everyone got off the train, the arrangements were fine. The Swiss had a number of local Jewish leaders to welcome us. Our people were escorted to various facilities. I had to leave from there; otherwise I would be AWOL. Traveling alone, I found my way back to Weimar. When I finally arrived back in the very beginning of July, the Russians had already taken over. A huge sign across the Buchenwald gate, with a big portrait of Stalin, declared in German and Russian: "Long live Stalin, the liberator of Europe."

I drove through Weimar and found the location of the VIII Corps Headquarters, where I served until we were returned to the United States in July 1945. After a brief furlough, the VIII Corps Headquarters had orders to move on to the Far East until, thank God, President Truman authorized the dropping of the bomb in Japan while we were still in New York. The war was over.

U.S.PRESIDENT
GENCY ACT

JAN 8 1944

UNITED WE WIN

Race, Ethnicity, and Religion in World War II

William L. O'Neill

Before the war most Americans associated largely with their own kind. Urban residential areas consisted of separate neighborhoods, each one peopled by a given ethnic group. Many spent their entire lives in the neighborhood where they had been raised, leaving it only to work, take vacations, or visit family and friends. Outside the South, small towns and rural areas tended to be homogenous, inhabited largely by native-born white Protestants. Catholics were typically in the minority. They were a minority in the South as well but were outnumbered by the nation's only significant racial minority, African Americans, then called Negroes. In 1940, of the slightly more than 132 million Americans, about 10 percent, some 13.5 million, were identified as Negroes, the majority of whom still lived in the South. Owing to restrictive immigration laws, very few Asians and Hispanics lived in this country. Together with American Indians, the U.S. Census Bureau designated them as "other races." All told they probably numbered about 1.5 million persons. In one of the most flagrant violations of civil rights during the war years, anti-Asian bias would lead to the relocation and internment of Japanese nationals and American citizens of Japanese descent on the West Coast.

Most Americans self-segregated, choosing to live with people like themselves. Negroes constituted the major exception, being segregated by law in the South and by custom everywhere else. In the suburbs, home buyers often had to sign restrictive "covenants," promising not to sell their homes to Negroes, Jews, and sometimes Catholics. Bigotry ran rampant. Racism led the list, but anti-Semitism clearly came second and manifested itself even in small towns and rural areas where few, if any, Jews lived. Anti-Catholicism persisted also, as did the tendency of Protestants to look down upon ethnic groups that had immigrated from southern and eastern Europe, nearly all of whom were Roman or Orthodox Catholics or Jewish. These recent arrivals were often called "new immigrants," to distinguish them from the earlier wave of immigrants from northern Europe, chiefly Irish, Germans, and Scandinavians. Far from being the proverbial "melting pot," America consisted of a great many racial, ethnic, and religious groups who retained their distinct identities and usually their traditional prejudices against other nationalities and religions.

Two things, one of them already at work, would change the way white Americans treated each other. The huge influx of new immigrants had come to an end in 1914 when the First World War broke out. In the period just before then, nearly a million immigrants a year had been pouring into a country inhabited by fewer than 100 million people. Although in the long run

United We Win, 1943

Poster distributed by
Office of War Information

these newcomers would enrich the nation, in the short term they strained its facilities and its tolerance. Antiforeign prejudices lay behind the Immigration Act of 1924 that all but closed America to aliens, but, ironically, the act had positive consequences.

The end of mass immigration meant that gradually, and for the second and third generation of immigrants in particular, white ethnic groups became more alike. The children and grandchildren of immigrants spoke English as their first language, attended English-speaking public schools, went to the same movies, listened to the same radio shows, and danced to the same music. All bathed themselves in the popular culture, which was much more of a piece than it is today now that cable TV and other new mediums have created so many niche markets. Bob Hope was everyone's favorite comedian, Bing Crosby the most popular singer. By 1941, despite widespread prejudices, the Americanization of new white ethnic groups had progressed much farther than most people realized. The Second World War would make this clear and, at the same time, accelerate the process.

The armed forces were the real melting pot for white Americans. Sixteen million men wore uniforms during World War II. Young men from all parts of the country, all walks of life, all ethnic groups and religions served on average three years in the military. They lived in close quarters in barracks, tents, foxholes, and ships. They had to work together, and sometimes fight together, regardless of differences. And, thanks to the unifying effects of public schools and popular culture, they discovered how much they had in common. In Great Britain, through which millions of GIs passed, American soldiers seemed much like one another. They were all "Yanks," not Jewish Yanks or Polish American Yanks, just Yanks, gum-chewing, jitterbugging, generous, loud, overpaid, young Americans. Negroes were the obvious exception, not on account of their color so much as because of segregation. The army even attempted to impose racial segregation upon British communities near their camps.

American war movies trafficked in more specific stereotypes. Every bomber crew, or army squad, or whatever had to be ethnically balanced and have a Jew, an Italian American, a Texan, someone from Brooklyn, and

so on. But stereotypes are based on reality, however much they simplify it. And the reality is that war brought young Americans together, bonded them with common experiences, and revealed the unifying effects of schooling and culture. It did not abolish ethnic prejudice or anti-Semitism. Indeed, many Jewish veterans interviewed for the Museum of Jewish Heritage's oral history project seem to have experienced anti-Semitism to a greater or lesser degree in the armed services. But living, working, and fighting alongside Jews humanized the Jews to Christians and reduced anti-Semitism among veterans as a whole. Further, this new understanding carried over into peacetime. Polls showed a marked decline in anti-Semitism during, and long after, the postwar era. Partly this was because Hitler's death camps revealed to all but the most benighted where anti-Semitism could take you. For another, American Jews outdid all other groups in supporting the war effort, putting paid to slurs about Jews being slackers or in some way less than American.

The GI Bill of Rights enabled millions of white veterans and their families to move into inexpensive new suburbs, such as Levittown on Long Island. And they did so as Americans, not as ethnic Americans or hyphenated Americans. Veterans did not self-segregate by ethnicity and religion in these communities but as men who belonged to the same generation and had shared a powerful experience that produced common values. Their wives shared their values as well. They had gone through the war without men, living together on male-free campuses or sharing apartments as war workers and the like. Millions of them took factory jobs formerly held only by men. Norman Rockwell's famous poster *Rosie the Riveter* honored these women, who worked as riveters, welders, and took just about every hard and dirty job industry had to offer. Over 300,000 served in the Women's Army Corps and the other uniformed auxiliaries. And more would have done so except for scurrilous rumors that all WACs were sluts and/or lesbians, false charges on the whole that impaired the war effort. Eager to make up for lost time, veterans went to college, got married, and had children all at once, instead of in sequence as previous generations had done. In cramped and overcrowded family housing on college campuses, men and women worked together to create new lives for themselves and their growing families.

Older Americans found the war generation hard to understand. Social critics feared that it was excessively conformist. One, William H. Whyte, wrote an extremely popular book called *The Organization Man* (1956) embracing this thesis. But unlike many critics, Whyte visited the new housing developments and observed the war generation on its native ground. Although he failed to identify the source of its values, the war generation impressed him with its tolerance and its belief in service and cooperation. He called this the "social ethic," and it worried him as being incompatible with rugged individualism and entrepreneurship—although at the same time he saw how much it benefited children and the community. Whyte missed the point. Entrepreneurship did not decline in the 1950s and 1960s. Census reports show that business starts, far from declining, rose along with the population, falling only during recession years.

A veteran himself, Whyte should have drawn the correct conclusion. Veterans and their wives had gone through a unique generational experience, one that was forged in separation and war and sealed in their shared postwar experiences raising children on campus and in housing developments such as Levittown. Their social ethic was the logical result of what they had gone through. Much more than previous generations, they discounted ethnic and religious differences and judged people by who they were rather than going by group labels. Subsequent generations had different experiences, producing different values, but what the war, and the war generation, did to promote tolerance has proved to be lasting.

Negroes did not benefit from the war to the same degree as whites. Most served in segregated noncombat units, racism dominating the services as it did civilian life. But Negroes, a majority of whom served in Europe, which had no minority races and therefore no segregation, discovered what equality looked like in practice. Broadened by their overseas experience and profiting from the GI bill, Negro veterans would play important roles in the postwar Civil Rights movement; and, segregation notwithstanding, they also went on to have higher incomes and more education than their civilian counterparts.

Anti-Semitism still exists, expressing itself in private mostly. Once in a while a synagogue is defaced with swastikas. But housing covenants are a thing of the past, as is religious discrimination in just about every walk of life. Jews have been mainstreamed along with other descendants of the new immigration. Jews still maintain their own schools, social organizations, and country clubs, as do Christians. However, outright bans are rare and membership is usually based on choice and tradition. By and large white ethnic and religious groups have made their peace with each other. Group identifications persist—the Irish march on St. Patrick's Day, Italian Americans turn out for Columbus Day and invariably complain about movies and TV shows that identify them with the Mafia. But in all the areas that matter—education, business, politics, government, and marriage—integration has prevailed over bias and ethnic and religious defensiveness. World War II is not the only reason for this great improvement, as we have seen. Yet America would not be what it is today without having gone through that experience.

"The Lord Would Provide"

Marty Silverman   U.S. ARMY

My given name was Morris, but for generations I've been known as Marty, Marty Silverman. What happened was, there were three Morrises in my class at public school, and one teacher decided it was too much for her to handle. "So you we'll call Marty." My mother's name was Fanny. My father's name was Simon. I have two older sisters, since deceased; they were born in approximately 1902, 1905, somewhere in there.

My dad was a tailor. It was a very simple story—they arrived at Ellis Island and somebody from Troy, a cousin, went down to meet them, brought them back to Troy, and that's where they lived. They came to Troy as immigrants. They had nothing. But the community took them in, and since he was a tailor they finally got him a little store, got him a sewing machine, got him an iron, and put him in business. It was just that simple. The Jewish community, for the most part, they knew how he was. They knew he was trying to make a living. They were trying to help him. So I would say 90 percent of his clientele were the Jewish people in the community.

Troy was a Catholic town. They used to teach the kids in Sunday school that the Jews killed Jesus Christ. Every Monday morning we had to either fight or run. It was very difficult, and we finally had to establish ourselves. But on the other hand, looking back at it, it probably created a lot of character. I think more than anything else the Catholics made a Jew out of me. If they'd have left me alone, I don't know if I'd be so sensitive about being Jewish.

Marty Silverman, 1945

There was one word that describes Troy to me and that word was *simpatico*. No one had very much, but everyone would help you if they could. There were the usual shuls. There was the shul that my grandmother went to, which was extremely Orthodox. We went to another shul, a little less Orthodox, and then there was the German shul. In the German shul were those people who had come from Germany with an education. They were really the industrialists of Troy. They were so far above us—they had the money, they had the education, and they always looked down on the rest of the community. We were not welcome in their shul, and they didn't come to our shul. The other people were either merchants, or like my dad, a tailor. It was a very tight community. Everything revolved, at least when I was a kid, around the shul. And the shul saw to it that the Jewish community stuck together and helped each other. It was very close, very tight.

Our house was a simple house. It was a wood frame house, three bedrooms. The usual house. You have a dining room and a living room—we used to call them parlors. It had a porch; it fit in with the community. The houses weren't row houses, but there were similar houses on the block. It was my mother, my dad, my two sisters, and myself. The interesting thing about the house was, as I grew up, it was converted from gaslight to electricity. With that one step, many things happened. As a child it was my job to empty the pan under the icebox. So there came a time when we had no more icebox—I didn't have to empty the pan—we had a refrigerator. A very important part of my life.

Sunday was a very important day in my house because it was the only day my dad stayed home. He worked very hard, and as a result, no one in my house moved until my dad woke up on Sunday morning, and then we all had breakfast together as a family. The rest of the time my mom ran the house. She took the coal in. She took the ashes out. She got the kids to school. She did all the things that Jewish mothers did in those days. She saw that I went to school, that I behaved, and that my sisters behaved. Everything revolved around her, except for one thing—a tremendous respect for my father.

We spoke English for the most part, but when the adults didn't want the kids to know what they were saying, they would speak Yiddish. But for the most part we spoke English at our house. We did the *Shabbos* candle deal on Friday night. We were not religious people. We went to shul on Rosh Hashanah, Yom Kippur. It was very important for us, and it was very important for the community to be shown as together. Passover was a big holiday. We went through the whole thing of getting rid of the *chometz*. We changed the dishes. We changed everything—it was a big holiday and a happy holiday.

In Troy there was only one rabbi who could teach you to be a bar mitzvah boy. As we looked at it as kids, he was a tyrant. If he kicked you out of class and you had to go home to your mother, she would plead with you to please try to behave yourself because if Rabbi So-and-So didn't make you a bar mitzvah, you couldn't be bar mitzvahed. It was very difficult. And needless to say, they taught us by rote. We had no idea what we were saying. Whatever they told us, we read the book, we read it back to the book. When we finally were bar mitzvahed it was a great occasion for the community. And it was nothing like we have bar mitzvahs today. They had an *oneg shabbat* in the shul; then you went home and the relatives came back to the house for dinner. But it was a very important occasion. After bar mitzvah I retired from Jewish schooling.

In the capital district—the capital district was known as Albany, Troy, Schenectady—there was a Jewish high school fraternity called Alpha Beta Gamma. The fact is we were such a minority when we started to grow up, and so after we were bar mitzvahed, we couldn't wait to join Alpha Beta Gamma, which brought all the Jewish kids together. It was a social thing—they would have a convention and they'd have meetings, and we would attend. The meetings were always in a shul somewhere. It was a gathering place.

In my opinion I was an average student. I wasn't outstanding. I went to a public school. I went to a high school, but I went to a very unique high school for a particular reason. There came a time when my two sisters got married, moved to New York and had children. My mother decided that she would like to be near her daughters and her grandchildren, and they convinced my dad he could do the same tailoring in New York City as he could in Troy. And so for a period of time we moved to New York City. He opened up a little tailor store, and I went to high school in New York but at a very unusual high school and at a very unusual time. In an effort to keep the kids in school at this particular period, there was a high school in New York City called Harren Cooperative High School. And what did Harren Cooperative High School do that no other high school did? They got you a job, and they teamed up another student with you so one week you would go to school and he would take care of the job and the next week he would go to school and you would go to the job—and you'd get eighteen dollars a week. It was a tremendous education, far and beyond an ordinary high school education.

They kept the kids in school, which they might not have done if they didn't have this program.

And so the most exciting thing of it all was the week when you went back to school after having worked for a week, you met all of the other kids who had worked. We had a big lunchroom in that school and the chatter was unbelievable, everyone exchanging their experiences. Wanamaker's down on 9th Street, that's where we—the other boy and I—worked. We were stock clerks and that's where we went, that's where you got paid.

On Saturdays and Sundays I would get a job as a soda jerker in the local drugstore out in Washington Heights. It was beautiful—we got paid, and I could do all the things that I wanted to do and I could help my parents. Ten dollars. I could get five bucks on Saturday and five bucks on Sunday. It would mean I could keep five bucks and bring five bucks home to my parents.

We were teenagers and at that point in time girls really weren't that interesting to us. We all had a friend somewhere to go to a dance with, but we were not social, the times were not social, and we didn't have the availability of funds to be social. We pretty much did what we had to do to make a living. Everybody I knew was in the same position. We never considered ourselves poor. We never considered ourselves broke because no one around us had any more than we did. It was very simple.

I graduated high school and went down to NYU at Washington Square—business course. NYU was no problem. Remember, I came from a town where there were three thousand Jews out of seventy-five thousand people. NYU was no problem for me. All my friends were Jews. We congregated. We didn't know there was anybody else. We didn't know there was any other kind. At NYU we were all Jewish. There was a quota in place but not at the college level. The quotas came in at the university level. At college level, at least as far as NYU was concerned, there were no quotas. And they were a city college and, you know, it was a good community.

I must explain that everything I have done in my lifetime was just getting into the stream and letting the stream carry me. I made no big decisions. I did whatever was necessary. So at this particular point, when I was finished with college, my dad was finding it very difficult making a living here in New York City. So we go back to our security blanket in Troy where we knew people, we had friends, we had relatives, and they would help out. Once again my dad opened up a little tailor store in Troy. And since I'd made a good bar mitzvah speech, my mother had decided I would make a good lawyer. They really needed my help and I did work with them, but in the meantime my mother had this notion that she wanted her son to become a lawyer. If that would please my mother, that would be fine with me. I had no real intention and I had no desire. I wasn't going to be a great litigator, but my mother wanted me to go to law school, so I went to law school. It was that simple.

The problem was that there was only one law school in Albany—Albany Law School—which is five miles from Troy, and they had a quota. As a result of working in New York, my grades were average grades, Bs and Cs, and this particular law school was extremely difficult to get into even if you had good grades. They were extremely selective, so I had two strikes against me. First of all, I didn't have great grades, and second, they in fact did have a quota and generally didn't permit more than 10 percent of their student body to be Jewish. Everybody I knew—and they all meant well—my friends, my relatives, all assured me that I would never get into Albany Law School. And since they already warned me that I wouldn't get in, I had nothing to lose. Instead of sending an application to the registrar with my grades, I decided that I would call the dean of the law school and ask for an appointment—if anybody was going to turn me down, I'd like it to be the dean. So I call his secretary and I set up an appointment. You must understand Albany Law School was a small school. It had two hundred students. So I called the dean's secretary and tell her I'd like an appointment with the dean, and she asks me why and I tell her why. And she in fact arranges an appointment for me. On the appointed day I meet the dean, he looks at my transcript, and he tosses it aside and asked me why I want to go to law school. I suggested to him my mother wants me to. I really think that shocked him because he expected a big answer. All I wanted to do was satisfy my mother. He reminded me that when I was in New York and going to NYU, I could work my way through college. Where would I get the funds to pay to go to Albany Law School? I said I did not know the answer to that question, but the Lord would provide me with that answer. And that seemed to impress him. After looking at me for about a minute and a half, he said to me, "Let's give it a try." So to everybody's amazement, I'm now going into Albany Law School.

The issue was tuition. The city of Albany is based on the state payroll. Nobody in the city of Albany works nights or Saturday or Sunday. That's just not one of the things they do. So as a result it would be very difficult to get a job nights or Saturday or Sunday. So after leaving the law school, I'm driving home back to Troy, and I drive across a brand new bridge called the Menands Bridge and on the right hand side of the bridge as I'm driving over there's a little farmhouse and a farm. As I drive by this location, I keep hearing this voice say, "Build a gas station here." So I go over the bridge and I come back again and I go over the bridge and every time I pass that spot I get the feeling that somebody ought to build a gas station on that site. The very next morning I call Standard Oil Company, who had an office in Albany, and suggested that I had an excellent location for a gas station. They agreed to send two people up to review the location, and if they were interested they would help us in some way.

Sure enough, they did send two people up. They agreed that this particular site had possibilities and suggested to me that they would build a gas station on that site, make me the manager, and let it go at that. And I said, "No, no, no, you don't understand. I want to go to law school, and I can only work nights and Saturday and Sunday. I'll build the gas station. You loan me the money. I will build the gas station, and I will hire somebody to work days when I cannot work." They supplied you with the tanks and the pumps so that was no big deal, but I needed $6,500 with which to buy the land and

Marty Silverman's
gas station during
flooding of the
Menands Bridge

build a little building and a grease pit. They agreed that they would loan me the $6,500, and I would build a gas station and I would run the gas station.

The gas station was an instant success because everybody in the Jewish community between Albany, Troy, and Schenectady knew I was using that gas station to help pay my tuition at Albany Law School. We did 75 percent of our business on Saturday and Sunday. People would drive from as far away as Schenectady, which at that time was twelve miles, and the kids in the back seat would ask their fathers, "Why do we have to drive so far to buy gasoline?" And they would just sit straight up and explain to the kids, "Because we're helping this young man go to college." That's the way it was.

After three years I passed the bar exam, and it's customary when you pass the bar exam to have your name published in the paper together with the other names of people who passed the bar exam. The Sunday that my name appeared as having passed the bar exam my business fell off 75 percent. Everyone felt they had done their thing. It was so bad that the Standard Oil Company refused to believe anybody could lose 75 percent of their business in one week. They came up and we had a big discussion and we finally decided they would forgive the balance of the debt I owed them. They would give me twenty-five hundred bucks and they would take over the gas station. Frankly, now that I'm a lawyer, I really don't need the gas station any more. To my mind all of these things prove the way the tide carried you: I needed the gas station to a certain point. When I didn't need it any more, it went away. And that's just been happening to me most of my life.

I got out of law school in '36. It was very interesting but nonprofitable. In those days they paid a law clerk ten bucks a week. They had just started up the Legal Aid Society in Albany, so my first job was with the Legal Aid. I was making ten bucks a week as a lawyer. I wanted to get married. My sister had married a man whose name was Mel Rosen. I'd gone to the wedding and met his sister. The country's in a depression. Her mother was a widow, and she was working to help support her family. I was working and helping to support my family. We'd wanted to get married; we just couldn't commit ourselves because of our financial obligations. At the end of seven years, we finally decided, hey, we'll never get any better than this in today's world, we'll get married. I got married in 1937. My wife had moved up to Albany. She was making eighteen dollars a week as a secretary. We lived with my parents, and as far as I was concerned, we were still in the depression.

I got a very low number and I was drafted. To make a long story short, I went down to their personnel office and suggested that, as a lawyer, I

should be in the Judge Advocate branch of the armed forces. The young man at the desk—I was then about thirty, he was about twenty-two—suggested to me that now they need riflemen, later they'll need lawyers, so now we were going to put you in a rifle company and send you to Harrisburg, Pennsylvania, for basic training.

I was probably the oldest man in the company—almost the oldest—the sergeants may have been a little older. I was a Jew. There were 180 men in the rifle company. It was not easy. There was one other guy who was a Jew, his name was Bernard Rosenberg, who's still a good friend and lives nearby. We caught every lousy detail and all the abuse one could take. But on the other hand, it kind of strengthened us, kept us together—number one and number two—we knew we had to survive this. There was no other way. So we suffered the indignities, we suffered being called a kike, Jew bastard, and all the other good things these guys who came up from the South, these redneck, never-saw-a-Jew-before guys called us. What they expected I do not know, but it was extremely difficult, especially for one who was senior—most of these kids were in their twenties.

All day long you drilled, you kept plowing bayonets into straw baskets, you wallowed in the mud, you followed every command, you suffered all the indignities. The only time you could be alone was when they dismissed you in the evening to have your meal. That was the only time you could be alone. The rest of the time you are completely surrounded by men, you're completely given orders. To an entrepreneur—remember up until this point I had been an entrepreneur—I didn't work for anybody really, so it was very difficult for me. Bernie Rosenberg was eighteen years old. For him it was a little easier. They took him out of the ASTP program. For me it was most difficult. About the only place you could really be alone was the latrine. If you know what the army latrines look like, a series of bowls, but down at the far end of this latrine there was a wall and at least you could be alone on one side. You didn't have to have a guy sitting on both sides of you. On this particular wall somebody had scribbled or inscribed, "The only man in this fucking army who knows what he's doing is sitting right here." I read that sign for twelve weeks, and I was convinced that I was the only guy in the army who knew what the hell was going on.

When we finished training, we went through a couple of maneuvers, but in the final analysis they shipped us overseas. First they took us up to Boston to a camp called Miles Standish, then we shipped out of Boston for England. We got to England and remained there for a period of a few weeks until they were ready for the invasion at Normandy.

We arrived at Normandy on D-Day plus seven. We didn't get there on D-Day. As a matter of fact, when we got there we walked up the hill. We didn't have to climb up the hill—we walked up the hill. Our first engagement was at Saint-Lô; we started with the hedgerows at Saint-Lô.

Two things happened. All the anti-Semitism was left in England. By the time we got into Normandy and were beginning to have casualties and the noises got louder, there was no anti-Semitism. It was the last thing we heard about. All we wanted to know is you're wearing the same color suit, you're firing in the same direction, and you're in a foxhole next to me. We left all that behind. Fair is fair. We proceeded up the hedgerows, which were very treacherous because every time you thought you were finished and could move to the next hedgerow you discovered there were mines in these other hedgerows and there were Germans there too. So as we started up the hedgerows, we continually lost men. Every day we lost men. They were hurt. They were killed. They stepped on mines. By the time we finally got to Metz—that was some time about November—things changed. We

had isolated resistance all through the hedgerows, but when you got into the cities you got real resistance.

In spite of the training, you're never prepared for the experience. I mean, first of all you must understand what happened. You're up there, you've been there now let's say ninety days, we won't talk about long-term— and by this time your ranks have been decimated. Half the guys, at least half the guys, are all replacements. You don't know who they are, what they are, or where they came from. You're paying for the stupid mistakes they make because they have no experience. So you have that problem. To give you some idea, we started with 180 men. There were probably eight of the 180 men still surviving when hostilities ceased in May of '45.

I was wounded twice. I was wounded at Metz, and I was wounded at the Battle of the Bulge. The one at Metz was a very simple thing. We were in the process of taking a pillbox, and as a result, two things happened. We lost half of our unit—the lieutenant was killed—and we took the pillbox. The artillery fire was quite heavy. We finally succeeded in taking Metz, which was considered a city that had never fallen before. It was a bastion city. And as a result of taking Metz, the 95th Division henceforth was known as the Iron Men of Metz. We got our reputation at Metz.

I got hit by a piece of shrapnel in the throat. I had a muffler on—my old muffler. That muffler probably saved my life because it slowed the schrapnel down. It made quite a hole in that muffler, but they patched me

American troops come
ashore in Normandy,
France, shortly after
D-Day

up and that was the end of that one. When I got hit at Metz, I got a battle-field commission and became a second lieutenant because I was one of the few remaining guys. The officer was killed. I was a sergeant. Patton came up in his big jeep, and he wanted to know who was in charge. I was in charge. He said, "What happened to the lieutenant?" "He got killed." I was very critical of the lieutenant. They'd send up what we called "ninety-day wonders." They'd get a nice young guy, they'd put him through officer candidate school for ninety days, and they'd send them up to us as officers with no experience. It was difficult and treacherous, but after a while we didn't pay much attention to those who didn't have the necessary experience. This particular poor guy was killed. So Patton said, "Could you have done it any better?" And I said, "I sure as hell couldn't do any worse." I had an attitude: If they didn't like the way I ran the army, they can send me home. They didn't do that, of course. "Well," he says, and takes a pair of bars out of his pocket, "All right, Lieutenant, let's see how good you are." So, at that point in my army career, I became a second lieutenant.

At the Battle of the Bulge, I got hit by a sniper's bullet. You wore a steel helmet and underneath the steel helmet you wore a plastic helmet. When I got hit by the sniper's bullet, the bullet actually pierced the steel—tore the hell out of the steel—ran down between the steel and the plastic right down my back and stopped at my butt. I was removed to a station hospital. They were tremendously short of people. They patched you up and sent you back. I could make a big shtick out of it, but these were flesh wounds—they healed up. Put a patch on it and send you back.

There was a time when we had what is commonly called a "mopping-up" operation. We were terribly shorthanded—I'm still a sergeant at this time—and we're taking over a compound in the Saarland, I think it was. Suddenly we put guys upstairs to see if there were snipers up on top. I take the basement, and when I got down there, I hear a lot of noises, guttural noises. So I kick the door open and lo and behold there's a whole room full of Germans sitting there at a table, and I capture twenty-two Germans single-handed. Then I have a problem—I'm all alone and I'm speaking in Yiddish, but when you have a weapon in your hand, Yiddish and German sound very much the same. You can get along with that. Finally we get them upstairs. I've got twenty-two guys strung out against the wall. I'm a sick guy; I haven't got the heart to mow them all down. They've already surrendered. They've laid down their weapons. They're all hollering, "*Nicht schiessen, nicht schiessen.*" They've got their hands on top of their heads, and half of them are

on their knees praying. By this time they made so much noise, the rest of the outfit began to gather around, and we finally got these guys together and sent them back. But it was a tremendous experience . . . a tremendous experience. Remember, up until now I had seen a lot, and I knew about the German concentration camps. I just couldn't do it. To have twenty-two Germans . . . the one target that everybody would die for, I had it.

Our company did not liberate Dachau. We were part of a unit that liberated Dachau. It's a very difficult . . . really . . . it's a very difficult sight to describe. The prisoners were in their striped suits; they were pathetic figures to look at. The guys who had been in combat for a long period of time couldn't handle it . . . guys openly cried. It was an extremely painful sight to see the skeletons of figures and the joy and the tears. It was a very difficult sight. We saw the place liberated, but interestingly enough Patton was in charge and he wouldn't let these guys out at that time. He let them out eventually, but at that moment when they were liberated, he did not let them out. And that kind of bothered me personally.

So, you know, you do what you have to do. We moved on. Other people took over at Dachau. Eventually we came back. After hostilities ceased, we took Dachau back as a center for war crimes, for rounding up the minor war criminals. At that time I was still a rifleman in a rifle company and had nothing to do with war crimes. There came a time, probably I would say six, seven weeks later when hostilities ceased, about May 25, when they suddenly decided they needed combat-experienced lawyers to determine what is a lawful order. You know, if a guy tells you to shoot and you shoot, does he give you a lawful order? Should you have done it? You know, you're getting into a lot of technicalities, which nobody paid much attention to, but if you read the books, they tell you what's a lawful order and what's not a lawful order. So they suddenly begin to look around to see where they have lawyers, and of course they pull up a name and they say, "Your outfit is going to go to Japan. You've got a choice. You can either go to Japan as a rifleman with your company or you could stay here and go to war crimes." "I'll stay here and I'll go to war crimes." So I was then assigned to a war crimes unit at Nuremberg.

My first assignment was to go out and pick up a particular group of Germans who, after an infantry outfit had surrendered, had mowed them down. Now that's not a lawful order. My first assignment was to go pick these guys up and bring them back to Dachau. Like most things the army does, it turned out to be a fiasco. We spent days picking these guys up, schlepping them back. The civilian group was very eager to point out the guy who did it . . . this guy did it or that guy did it. So we have probably one hundred men in Dachau, and Patton in his wisdom comes in and says, "Forget it. These guys were only following orders." And they turned them all loose, which really took the heart out of us.

After we got through with these guys at Dachau, I went back to Nuremberg to work in what would be called a law office, reviewing the cases that they brought in. When they brought us the cases, we determined in our mind which were war crimes and which were not. So now I was with the war crimes team of six men. We were working our asses off, and we loved what we were doing. The people in the army and in the States said, "You know what? Let's get the guys who've been over there now for a couple of years, let's get them home and let's send over replacements." Suddenly the six men grew to twelve and the twelve grew to eighteen because they were sending guys over—JAG officers who hadn't seen any combat. When they got over there it was a party for them. They were whoring around, they were drinking. And so what we used to produce as six men, eighteen men were not producing. And pretty soon, you know, you say to yourself, hey, we've got to be a bunch of schlemiels here. These guys are having a ball and we're breaking our asses. We had enough points to come home, so I came home, probably about May of '46.

You have to understand when the hostilities ceased, war was over. All we wanted to do for the most part is go home to our families. And now we had communications—we could write, we could receive, we could get a telegram with Western Union. While I was away I had a baby boy. And my mom and pop, they were still alive, thank God. We were all glad to get home. It was over. I mean, what . . . what was there to say? It was over. Now the question is, how do you make a living? The big deal for everybody was, when I get home what do I do? Could I practice law again? I don't think so. Since I left the law school in '36, a lot of exciting things had happened, and I could never go back and practice law.

I wish I could tell you that I thought of great things and that I was going to do great things. All I ever did was live from day to day and try to make a living and try to make every day count. Everything that ever happened to me happened because, once again, it was just in the stream. The Lord provided.

"If You're Waiting For Me to Get Married, Don't Do It "

Evelyn Schecter Perlman   U.S. MARINE CORPS WOMEN'S RESERVE

I was born Evelyn Schecter in 1922 in Brooklyn, New York, in a house that my grandparents owned, like a tenement. They owned two of them, and we lived in one until I was a year old when we moved to Englewood, New Jersey. In those years Englewood was like the country. It *was* the country-side. And our relatives would come out and dabble in the brook—we had a brook across the street. I grew up in Englewood and lived there with my parents until my dad got sick. We lived very well. We had a good life. I had a sister thirteen months after I was born—she was born in Englewood. And I have a darling brother who's a rabbi now. A graduate of Yeshiva College and the Jewish Theological Seminary.

There were very few Jewish girls in town. It was a town then; now it's a pretty big city. We felt discrimination. I felt it. Because in high school we weren't invited to join these upper-class clubs, but you know, we grouped together. We grouped together and we stood our ground and we got the best marks in the school. And among ourselves we were very happy. We laughed all the time.

My father was for a time president of the synagogue—it was an Orthodox synagogue. I went to Hebrew school maybe twice or maybe even three times a week, and I learned Hebrew up to a point.

Evelyn Schecter
[Perlman], 1943

For all the holidays we would travel to Brooklyn. There wasn't the George Washington Bridge then. We used to go over on the ferry, the Weehawken. And we would keep asking, "Are we there yet, are we there yet?" Then my sister and I used to say, "We're in Brooklyn, we're in Brooklyn, we're in Brooklyn!"

When we did get there on the holidays—I have some pictures in my album of seders there—we used to sleep in drawers. There wasn't enough sleeping space. My brother wasn't born yet, but my grandmother used to take out the drawers, and she and my mother they used to put pillows in the drawers and that's where we slept.

Oh, I remember my grandfather wore—they call it a *kitel*—a white robe. And a high white hat. He was very stern. He wanted silence. We always took turns saying the four *kashes* and reading and singing. We did a lot of laughing. I remember I laughed through my whole young years.

My mother kept a kosher home. We had a kosher butcher in Englewood, and that's where my mother went. My mother didn't know any other way but to keep kosher. Her parents were Orthodox. But my mother was very American—she'd been in this country since she was two. She drove a car in those early years, and she played bridge. She had a circle of women friends. My mother was very American. She went to something called normal school—she had a good education.

In back of our house we had a garage, and there was a big tree over the garage. We found ways to climb up into the tree—we used to have so much fun up in that tree. In the back we also had a wall, a cement or brick wall, and we used to play ball against the wall. And I remember we used to go swimming in Rockland Lake. That's in Rockland County. My father also used to take us to West Point. He was a soldier. Actually, I think that's one of the reasons he let me go into the Marine Corps. He thought it would make me more disciplined.

I was working in those years before the war. When I graduated from high school, my father became ill with tuberculosis, which, really, that's what killed him at such an early age. He used to go to Saranac Lake for treatment. It was very difficult for us because we had to move. He didn't work and make money because he was hospitalized. So we went back to Brooklyn to stay with my grandparents in one of their apartments. And I worked. I worked from the time I was sixteen years old.

I was a legal secretary. I worked for famous lawyers. And I always fell in love with these lawyers. They were so different from what I knew. They

Pinchas Schacter,
Evelyn Schecter's
maternal grandfather

Leon (Louis)
Schecter, Evelyn
Schecter's father,
age twenty, in his
World War I uniform

were wonderful, wonderful experiences. One of my jobs was for a law firm that represented Rogers and Hammerstein. I did the contracts for *South Pacific*. But it was during the war and there were no men. All the men were in the war, and it was just at that time that I started to date—or I wanted to—and my parents couldn't wait until I got married. I was the older sister. I have a letter to my sister that says, "If you're waiting for me to get married, don't do it."

So that's when I had feelings of maybe I wanted to leave home, because we only lived in a four-room apartment and my dad had TB. He had to have a room all to himself, so the rest of us, three children and our mother, were crowded into one bedroom and there were no closets. And I was growing up. I had such glamorous experiences on my jobs and then would come home on the subway to Brooklyn to this apartment and this kind of life. I wanted to get away. I felt that joining the service would be an adventure, and I'd have an excuse to get away, and I'd feel important and maybe I'd make a contribution, which it turned out that I did.

My mother was devastated. That's why I had to write all those letters and pretend that I'm really looking for a nice Jewish boy. And if a gentile spoke to me, I was very reluctant to speak to him. Every other letter tries to excuse the fact that I left them.

I picked the Marine Corps because it was the most exclusive, elite. I did a lot of research. And it sounded so exciting to me. But I was very realistic about it. I had these skills, and I had a letter that outlined what was needed. Some went to technical school, others were clerk typists. But I was a legal secretary, so I really had some skills. I was placed right away. They could use me and I really did so well, that is, I did better than the other girls. Because of my legal secretarial background and the shorthand that I had, I started with summary court-martials. And then I moved up to general court-martials. I took all the testimony even as a kid. I was only twenty-one.

As soon as I signed up, I was sent to Parris Island, South Carolina. Well, it was the boondocks. It was. I never thought it was anything else. After boot camp we used to go to Charleston and Atlanta. I was in the aviation section—I'm not sure how it was called. Cherry Point was an air station, and we went there after boot camp to be assigned. That was in North Carolina.

In boot camp we used to get up at 5:45 in the morning, and we had to mop our floors and dust. We only had a double bunk and a locker. That was all we had. And then we had to take showers, well, we didn't have to, but we took showers and we had to muster at breakfast. It was still dark outside.

Evelyn Schecter
in grade school,
Englewood, New
Jersey, 1932

Evelyn Schecter
after mess duty
at boot camp,
Parris Island,
South Carolina

We used to be in our uniforms and we used to sing. The stars were out and they would ask us to sing. They tried to instill a spirit of camaraderie. And they succeeded.

The women in the aviation barracks stuck together. The Jewish women became friends. There were maybe seven or eight. But I had other non-Jewish friends. Years and years later I went to visit one of them. She lived in one of the Twin Cities. And I once traveled out to see her. I became very attached to the girls, even a few non-Jewish girls. I adored them.

In boot camp we didn't do very much. What we did, we had to be up at a quarter to six. So by ten o'clock at night lights were out. And before that you wrote letters—letter-writing was a big thing. We used to go to the post office. The military had an envelope where you didn't use a stamp. You just wrote *Free* on the envelope. I wrote home—you know, it depended how busy I was in the office—but I wrote home at least three times a week. Very lengthy letters on the typewriter. Such detail.

I heard often from my parents. I had an allotment out of my salary, which was so minimal. My dad was not working and he was ill and in the hospital so much, so I felt a responsibility to send some money home. The allotment, I think, was taken out automatically. But I always needed extra. My mother wrote at length. I never kept her letters. So I have very little of what she actually said. I sent them every little detail . . . I got up this morning . . . I mopped my room . . . it's a lovely sunshiny day . . . and after work I'm going swimming and then after swimming we're going to the movies. I made a big thing about the movies—everybody went to the movies at night. They were free.

Everything was contained in that area. We used to have chow, no, we went swimming, and then I think we went back to eat. And then we went to the movies at night. The movies were educational. I learned a lot from the movies. They were wonderful movies in those years. They knocked them-selves out trying to see that we were occupied and entertained.

The men were also going to the movies. We would have a date to go to the movies, but we never ate together. Oh, my goodness, no. The men couldn't even come near our barracks unless it was by special permission or there was a special event. And when we went to Cherry Point, we were the only girls there, and they weren't prepared. It was the first time. They had to whitewash the windows halfway up so the marines couldn't look in.

In my heart I knew it was fine. But I felt when I wrote to my parents I had to say that, well, number one, I couldn't say that I talked to anybody

ENGLEWOOD

who was married. I mean, then I'd have my head cut off. But I also mentioned marines who were lonesome and away from home. And also that men and women met at the Jewish Welfare Board in Savannah for the holidays so we were invited together to somebody's home. Jewish families tried to entertain us over Jewish holidays. I remember sending a Mother's Day card to my mother . . . I wrote, "Parris Island is a motherless place."

The uniform was a skirt, but for mess duty and for other things on the base we wore dungarees. We had to stick pretty much to regulation on the post. But after swimming, we went to the PX in our slacks. That was really a no-no, but we did it anyway. Our excuse was that we just came from the pool.

I would always send home messages like, "There's a flannel pair of pajamas in my drawer at home. And it gets pretty cold up here." I would write that to my sister. One good story is we had to wear regulation lipstick. The red had to match the trim in our hat. So we had to wear regulation red lipstick. But I would ask my sister to get me a Revlon red lipstick next time she sends me something.

Basically, the men were protective toward the women. Well, the chaplains, that was their job. The men weren't, except for the men that I worked for. One man was Jewish, a lawyer from Jersey City. He was thirty-four at the time and I was twenty-one. He was very protective. Number one, we couldn't talk to officers. But at the chaplain's—it was called a chaplain's circle—he would sometimes sit us all in a circle after services and ask who's married here and who's single. So he would try to fix us up. We did go to services. You know what, it really was someplace to go. And it was so familiar to me. And I felt I belonged and I loved going.

I have a letter that talks about Yom Kippur and how everybody had to go to work anyway, because the war was on and some of us had jobs that needed to be done. So I made a point of saying that it had to be done. But it was difficult to work on Yom Kippur. I always felt guilty. I had that Jewish guilt instilled in me. So I felt guilty. But on Rosh Hashanah, we would go to Savannah. I had a lady, Mrs. Polefsky, who kind of took me in and had me go to synagogue with her and sit next to her. And she would also make a meal. I will say that the Jewish civilian families really went out of their way to host us, make us feel comfortable on the holidays.

These ladies were Southern ladies. They were Jewish but they were Southern—it was different. I came from New York and the yeshiva, and at the synagogue we used to go to in New York the women sat upstairs and the

Dear Folks :—

It is Monday afternoon,
Rosh Hashana, and I'm at the
JWB in ~~Savannah~~. I went to
Schul this morning and sat
upstairs with Mrs. Palefsky,
who saw me and called
me over to sit with her.
The atmosphere I could see Jackie in every boy and people his age were so much ~~like home~~ ↑,
that I really felt awfully
lonely, and even cried a
little. Mrs. Palefsky invited
me to eat dinner at her
home, but I met a very
sweet WAC downstairs,
who was also alone and
in the same boat I ~~was~~, so

men didn't wash because it was Yom Kippur. It smelled and I hated it, but I had to go.

The food, by the way, was the same. Maybe I'm not giving them enough credit. Like Mrs. Polefsky, she was much older than I was, of course. She wasn't a Southern belle. She was a Jewish lady who happened to live there.

I wasn't aware of discrimination in the South. We were always on the base. When we went off the base, we went to the JWB, which as I said was a precursor to the Federation. We even slept there. They put us up. We used to sleep on the couches if we didn't have a home, a private home to sleep in. I think Mrs. Polefsky charged one dollar a night. Sometimes we stayed at a hotel. A couple of us in one room.

Money was always an issue for most of us. We literally had no money. So if we wanted to buy something at the PX, or I needed a new pair of shoes. . . . One story is that my bunkmate, Connie, and I—Connie was much slimmer than me—our coats were regulation and I had a larger coat. Somebody took my coat by mistake and I was stuck with a tiny coat. I couldn't button it. But Connie was slimmer than I, and she liked fitted things. So she said she'd switch with me. She'd take the tight coat and give me hers. That was a big problem that was settled.

We did go to a lot of dances. Everything was a dance. I can't imagine myself dancing in my uniform with that shirt and tie. I mean, how do you dance? But we apparently did that.

Before I got good enough to do the court-martials, I had to sit in and I had to train myself. As a matter of fact, the job that I took for general court-martial, I relieved a man to go overseas. I don't think he was too happy about it, but I worked myself up so that I was able to do it well enough. I couldn't do it as good as he did.

I had another job too. I was what we called a port-and-starboard liberty clerk. They posted us out in the sentry box, way out—I tell you it was the boondocks—and we had a whistle and a billy club. Or at least I did. I requisitioned a stove, because it was cold one winter. The men who had liberty had to check in at the sentry box. I used to check them in and out, see them going out and then check them back in. It seemed a bit ridiculous, as I look back, to see myself sitting in a sentry box all by myself.

I remember once there was a scare on the base. This was in the aviation section so there weren't thousands of men coming in—just the aviation. One time there was a story about a prisoner of war or somebody who was on the loose, and we were supposed to be on the lookout. There was no phone. There was no connection. But they wouldn't have put girls there if it wasn't safe. There were just a few of us. We were always safe—too much.

We knew very little about the war actually. And I don't know if it was because of who I was. I don't think newspapers were really available. Certainly not television or instant replay. We were never informed, as I look back. But I should have known. I have some letters that talk about the men who came back shell-shocked after two years fighting in the Pacific. And they caused . . . oh, they just tore the place apart when they came back. It was mostly over girls. They felt that the men who were on the base were sissies and had access to the girls. There was enormous fighting and resentment and a lot of our court-martials were a result of the way they acted. I don't think they were able to access rehabilitation the way they do now. They would come and then they would go. And then another. This was mostly in 1944. There was Iwo Jima and Guadalcanal and Guam. And the fighting in Iwo Jima . . .

I also had another job. We had entertainment, various shows that came in from the outside. So they asked me to preview the show to see that there was no objectionable material in it.

Anything to write notes. To this day, I write notes and keep track and take minutes. That's what I spent my life doing.

 I helped sell war bonds. A lot of the marines were buying war bonds. And then I got a letter from my sister enclosing a voting card so I could vote away from home. And with all kinds of instructions. It really got my ire up. I wrote back to her, "Harriet, do you think we don't know what's going on here? Captain Lake—that was my boss at the time—is giving out voting cards to everybody. We gave out 400 cards with all kinds of instructions on how to vote. And you're telling me from New York? I know you're socially conscious, but please." There were always things to do—if it wasn't a court-martial, it was something else.

We were moved—apparently they built another barracks. Boot camp was one thing. And when we graduated from boot camp, we got not just lockers. We had dressers. And we had a rec hall. And we had a library. And across the street there were rowboats. We could go rowing. Everything was in a proscribed area.

There were maybe a few hundred women where we were. But people got shipped, you know. There was a bulletin board that gave you assignments. And people went to Quantico. And they went to California. And they went to technical schools. They were teletype operators among other things.

Of course we had mess duty. I didn't mention that. I have in my letter, it says you're not a good marine until you do mess duty. Not a real marine. First of all, we wore the dungarees. And we had to dish out the food. And we had to clean up. They didn't have dish-washing machines, so I think it was called slop duty. We had to be there to clean and we had to dish out the food. The food was wonderful. Oh, they had such desserts. And the girls gained weight. Except we swam every day . . . swimming was a big thing. We had fun on mess duty. We used to sing and poke fun at what we were doing. And again there was this camaraderie that built up.

There was a lot of excitement in the early years, in '43, and even at the end of '43 and in '44, there was still excitement about being in the marines. At the end of '44, toward '45, when the war was almost over, I said, you know, I'm restless and I'm bored. And there's so much routine here. And it was so inefficient. In the beginning, we didn't know the difference. But later the repetition and the inefficiency was apparent. You had to stay until the war was over, yes, unless you got pregnant or something.

In November of 1945—I think I got out when I was twenty-three—I went back to the office, to the very same office I had left. They held my job for me. They were being patriotic. And it was a glamorous big law office. Except for standing in line to register for college, I don't remember those years well. I was twenty-three, and I wanted to get married so bad.

My parents were on top of me. I just had to get out. So what happened was, I went to California. See, going into the Marine Corps gave me a lot of courage to get away and be on my own. So when things weren't going so well, I moved to California just like that—didn't know a soul there. And I got a job at Paramount Pictures. Paramount interviewed forty people to be a legal secretary, and I got the job. I suffered through a weekend while they made their decision. I worked in the musical copyright department at Paramount.

The service certainly opened my eyes to being independent and away from home. It propelled me toward a life that was a little askew—adventurous and on the edge. I've always—and Connie, too—we've always lived on the edge. But I've got to tell you, when I got out of the service, I didn't talk about it much. Because people immediately assumed that you slept with every man on the base and that you were no good. This was early women's lib before there was any such thing as women's lib. To be on your own and to go away and to be one girl among 200 girls with thousands of men. It just gave us such a bad reputation that I never spoke about it really.

When I finally heard what had happened in Europe and in the Pacific, I was really angry. I realized that our government censored what was in the newspapers. They had to, because it wasn't just me who didn't know. There was a whole population that didn't know the severity and the nature of the death camps. They didn't know. If they had known, they couldn't have . . . they wouldn't have let it go on the way it did. It was really a horror . . . the men who went and fought and died. It was terrible. But war is hell. I mean, that's what it is.

"Abnormally Normal"

Milton Mollen U.S. ARMY AIR CORPS

When I arrived in England, the situation was pretty much what I antici-pated. I mean, we got to the base and we finished up some more training there, and then we started flying missions—to different points in Germany, sometimes occupied France. The target of the mission on which I was shot down was to bomb Munich, which at that time was a very long flight. It was one of the longest missions in the Eighth Air Force. We were hit pretty hard over the target, but we managed to get away and we were flying back. Then we got hit by fighters again—we had a tough trip on that mission.

We found, as we went along, that our fuel tank had been hit too because we started to lose gas. Our pilot did an excellent job in trying to get the plane back. What we were trying to do was nurse it along. We didn't have the protection of the formation. See, the major protection when you flew missions was the formation because each one protected the other. They would cover each other with the guns, you know, the machine guns in the plane. Because we couldn't keep up with the others, they had to go and leave us so we had a pretty tough time. Our pilot was trying to get back to the North Sea, because if we could ditch in the North Sea, the English had these small patrol boats on the English side of the Channel, on the North Sea, and they would send out these boats to pick up those aviators, those air crews that had to ditch in the sea.

Milton Mollen, 1943

We did what was called precision bombing. We always flew daytime. The English would fly at night—they didn't do precision bombing. They did area bombing. That's how we kept bombing twenty-four hours a day. Munitions plants and certain railroad terminals, things like that that were, they felt, strategically important. At that time I remember things were getting a little rough. We were having a fairly heavy percentage of losses. Initially the Germans didn't, but they perfected their antiaircraft fire, and they also concentrated their fighters to combat our bombers. On the short flights we would usually have American fighters to protect us, but if there was a long flight, the fighter planes didn't have the range to accompany us to the target. They couldn't protect us all the way. So we would have sometimes a difficult time, particularly over the target. The Germans would always have a lot of antiaircraft fire concentrated over the target, you know. Once we'd reached what we called the initial point, IP, we never deviated. We wouldn't do evasive action to avoid the antiaircraft or the German fighter planes—we went straight for the target. I remember, interestingly enough, when I was shot down later and was talking to some of the German soldiers, they used to tell me—so apparently what our Intelligence officers told us was the truth—that the Germans used to watch. They couldn't understand that when we went for a target we'd go through antiaircraft fire, we would never deviate. We'd just keep going. Either you kept going or you got hit and exploded. But this had a very destructive impact on the morale of the German people. It made them feel that ultimately defeat was inevitable because the bombing, it just seemed to them endless. They'd be bombed at night by the RAF, they'd be bombed by daytime by the American air force, but what it reflected to them was a total determination to hit the targets. We would do so, but you took losses because of that; you'd get hit.

I still remember one time we were being briefed. We'd had some heavy losses. Some general who'd come down from London for morale purposes was telling us what a great job we were doing, what an impact we were having on the German morale. So one of our squad, a typical American sergeant in the back of the room, yelled out, "Yeah, what about our morale?" because we were taking heavy losses. So the general tried to ease it a little bit and he said something to the effect, "Well, you're still keeping the losses no more than 5 percent," something like that. And the sergeant—they never stop—the sergeant said, "That's fine if you're not one of the 5 percent," meaning if you weren't knocked down the statistics were pretty good but if you were one of the ones knocked down the statistics weren't

B-24 Liberator in
flight for an air raid

More B-24s were built
than any other American
airplane during the war.
By 1944 over 180,000
people were engaged
in B-24 production.

very good. So it's always move and countermove. As we would perfect our bombing, they would perfect their protection, the antiaircraft, the fighters that they would send up to try to knock us out.

You were always prepared to have alternate routes planned if you got hit and you couldn't get back to England. I, as a navigator or radar navigator, had to know to tell the pilot what course to take, say, to go to Switzerland or to Spain if we thought that the plane couldn't get back to England. We always were planning to get to the target and back, but in addition to that we had to be prepared to do whatever was called for, whatever emergency would arise. You would just do it, whatever you had to do.

I was very conscientious. I'm not very mechanically inclined and therefore I took extra pains to make certain that nothing ever went wrong with the equipment. I was a little bit proud of the fact that our plane was never what they called "aborted." A plane would be "aborted" and not be sent on a mission if the equipment wasn't working perfectly. When I got into the plane, first of all, the first thing I would do would be to pin up a number of photographs of my wife. She'd always send me pictures from home to remind me she was there and alive and well, and there were some nice photographs. So when I'd get into the plane, automatically the first thing I would do was put up the photographs of my wife. And in fact it was kind of, well, crazy, but I never regretted it because I was glad I had them with me. When the time came to bail out, the first thing I did was take all my photographs, put them in my pocket, and then I did something that I guess was kind of foolish. You don't think. Normally I never wear a hat—I don't like to wear hats. I don't like things on my head. When you were on the ground, you know, you're supposed to wear your full uniform. I'd carry my hat in my hand because I just don't feel comfortable with something on my head. But here I was, I was about to bail out, I took my hat and put it on my head and my wife's photographs, which I put in my pocket, and the moment I stepped out of the plane and opened the parachute, the first thing that happened was my hat went flying off and that was the last I saw of my hat, but at least I had my wife's photographs.

I was always very fatalistic; I felt there's nothing I could do about it if we got hit and destroyed and I got killed. So I try not to worry about things I can't do anything about. When I'm confronted with situations where I can do something about it, then I try in every way I can. And if I have to fight, I will fight to do what I think can be done. But if it's something I can't do anything about, I try not to worry about it. So when we were flying in these

missions, I accepted the premise: We're up there to do a job. We had to do our job. And therefore I tried not to worry about it and just concentrate on doing my job. I was lucky and survived it.

We were over occupied France. This is July 11, 1944. And we bailed out, I think starboard, like at about nineteen thousand feet, something like that. We had come down from higher altitude. The pilot was fighting to keep the plane under control. I found out later—I didn't know at the time— ultimately of the twelve of us, eight were killed; four of us survived. I bailed out. We'd bail out one after the other; you've got to do it pretty quickly. The ones who got killed were in the back of the plane during the attack. Those of us in the front—command pilot, pilot, the navigator, and myself—we landed near one another. It was late in the afternoon, over French farmland, and three of us landed close to one another in this field. The fourth landed not too far away from us. And we were kind of hidden. We decided we'd stay in the field until night and then try to escape. There were some French farmers in the field who gave us some bread and cheese and we remained hidden. We saw the German squad cars. They knew—they'd seen the plane going down—they knew we were somewhere there, and they were on the roads looking for us. And we just stayed hidden until nighttime.

My leg wasn't badly hurt in the plane. There was some bleeding, but I didn't feel like I was in any real danger of something terrible happening to me. But when I landed the parachute, because I was trying to favor my leg—it was bleeding on the way down—I think I didn't land straight as I should have and I fractured my ankle. We just lay there. There were two of us and then the third fellow came over. He landed not far away from us. I didn't see the fourth fellow. He joined the others later. Anyway, we discussed it among ourselves. We had maps and things like that. We were always prepared to think in terms of how we can get back. So we planned to move by night, try to contact the underground until we got back to either Spain or Switzerland.

So we lay there until it got dark. When it got dark, the three of us who were together we started to plan to move out, to try to go in the direction that we thought would get us to Spain. That's where we were aiming for. But finally when we said, "Okay, let's go," and I stood up, I couldn't stand on my foot. It was excruciatingly painful. I didn't realize my ankle was that bad. I didn't know it was fractured. I knew it was hurt, but when I stood up on it, then it was excruciating. The pilot cut my boot off. We were wearing flying boots. He cut the boot and then he saw it was a real problem and it was bad. They were very nice, the two of them. They didn't want to leave me. They wanted to stay. But I insisted they leave because I couldn't walk. They weren't serving any useful purpose to me by being there other than the comfort of their presence. But beyond that, they couldn't do anything for me so I told them to take off. I said, "My only chance to get back is to either get a doctor to fix it up so I can get out on my own or get into the hands of the underground and with their help get back to England or to Spain."

I finally convinced them to leave and they left. And I started to crawl, because I couldn't stand on my leg, to try to find some French farmhouse where I could get some help. That was probably the single most excruciating experience of my life, because I couldn't stand and I was dragging myself for quite some distance at night until I got to a farmhouse, some strange farmhouse. I knocked on the window and a Frenchman, a farmer I guess, came to the door and then he put me into his barn for the night, and I rested the rest of that night there. In the morning he came around and told me I had to leave. He brought me some food, but he told me I had to leave. I said, "I can't leave. I can't walk. Either get me a doctor to fix my leg up and then I'll leave, or contact the underground and let them know that I'm here." I assumed they would do whatever they had to do to protect me and to help me get back to England.

He insisted I had to leave. In fairness to him, you have to understand the circumstances at that time. The Germans were very, very upset—angry—about the fact that when American or RAF crew members would bail out for one reason or another, they'd be helped by the French. So they had issued orders that if they found any Frenchman helping an Allied aviator, they were going to execute him immediately. It was obvious he was very terrified of them. I didn't have a gun because the Eighth Air Force had issued orders that we were not to carry guns because of what was happening. What they found was happening was that some of the air crew members who bailed out and landed were, in a number of instances, being killed by the Germans. If they landed in Germany, the Germans would kill them. I think it was a mistake, but the theory was—the excuse was—that the air members had guns or were threatening to shoot them. My view of that was, I think, a little bit more practical. If they wanted to kill you, they didn't need any excuse. If they were so angry at us, they'd kill us anyway whether we had a gun or not. At least if we had a gun, we could to some extent protect ourselves.

I didn't have any gun so I couldn't even threaten the farmer. I tried to reason with him. I spoke some French. I still remember—I'll digress for a moment—when the farmers came over to us in the field and we were conversing, one of them was pointing at my leg and he kept saying *blessé* and I couldn't think, what is *blessé*? I thought he was giving me a blessing. I just didn't know what the verb meant—then later on I remembered that it's *wounded*. Are you wounded? Because he saw my leg—I had the blood seeping through my uniform.

Anyway, coming back to the Frenchman whose barn I was in, I tried to get him to get me a doctor or to find out where the underground was. Finally he said he was going to speak to the village priest. Now, whether he ever did or not I don't know, but he left. About an hour later a German jeep came into the barn—four German soldiers with machine guns—and they captured me. Then they took me to the local army base. They had an army base nearby and they drove me to the base.

That particular unit treated me decently. I was brought before a German lieutenant who spoke perfect English. He was trying to interrogate me, and all I would do was just give him my name, rank, and serial number. Under the Geneva Convention that's all you're required to do—give name, rank, and serial number. He kept trying to find out from me what group I was with, what kind of planes we were in, and all of that. They found the plane. They knew. They had found a crashed plane. See, they knew that the air force was using radar equipment. They were particularly interested in that. But I wouldn't answer any questions.

His manner was decent, you know, considering we were enemies. But then he said something, because I wouldn't answer anything else, so he said, "You know, I have a choice." He says, "I can turn you over to the Luftwaffe." See, they had a system in Germany. If you were in the air force and they captured you, they would turn you over to the Luftwaffe, the German air force. Each service kept its own prisoners. So he said, "I can turn you over to the Luftwaffe, and you'll be treated according to the Geneva Convention, or I can turn you over to the Gestapo, and the fact that you're Jewish will not be very good for you." He saw my dog tag so he knew I was Jewish because, as you must know, they had either *H* for Hebrew or *P* for Protestant or *C* for Catholic. In prior wars the religion didn't matter very much. But of course with Nazi Germany it was different, and being Jewish might result in being treated very differently than other prisoners were. And when he said that, I said to him, "Look, Lieutenant, if you were captured, I'm certain as a German officer you would just give your name, rank, and serial number and nothing else. That's all I intend to do, and I think you must understand that."

What went through his head I don't know, and I wasn't sure, frankly, whether he was bluffing or serious. I found out later that he could have been serious. But he turned me over to the Luftwaffe. First they sent me to a jail—I guess the nearest big French town was Lille—that was one of the most unpleasant experiences I had. It was like a dungeon. I kept asking for a doctor because my leg was really excruciating. I couldn't stand on it—it was difficult even to crawl—and I'd lost some blood and it was bloody and everything. He told me if I kept asking for a doctor, they were going to take me out and shoot me. Then they sent me to Frankfurt by train. They loaded us up, not only me but others, and sent us. That was the central place where

you would go first for interrogation and then to various prisoner-of-war camps. And there I did the same thing: name, rank, and serial number. They finally, I guess, gave up on me and sent me to a hospital. Finally from Frankfurt they sent me to the local hospital.

At the hospital they treated me, I guess, as they did anybody else. They washed away the blood and whatever else they had to do to my leg, and they set my fractured ankle. And then they sent me for a couple of weeks to a convalescent home. Small place, they had one doctor. I remember him with some fondness. He was an Austrian and he hated the Nazis. He used to taunt the guards. When a German plane would fly overhead, you could tell it was a

German plane because the engine would sputter. They didn't have high-octane gas. They didn't have enough gas so they would use low octane, and you would hear it sputtering up in the air. And every time he'd hear a sputter, he used to tell the German guards, "There goes the last of the Luftwaffe." Oh, he used to drive them crazy—why they didn't kill him I don't know. I guess they just didn't. I developed a kind of semifriendship with him.

As a matter of fact, a young American was brought in while I was there who had been a radar operator. That's one of the reasons I was interested in him, but he was one of the enlisted men operators. I was in the first class of officers to get radar training. He'd been one of the radio operators they had trained to use the radar equipment. And he had been turned over to the Gestapo when he landed and they did terrible, terrible things to him. He told me some of the things they did to him, which were pretty bad. When we were at this convalescent place, he couldn't walk without holding onto the wall. He would hold onto the wall one hand at a time and, you know, walk that way, kind of push himself off the wall. The doctor told me, this Austrian doctor, that physically—medically—there was nothing wrong, there was no reason why he couldn't walk, but psychologically, I mean, they had pretty much broken him as a person. And he just was afraid to walk. He would just hold onto the wall. So when I heard that story, I realized I was pretty lucky that the lieutenant who had first captured me didn't turn me over to the Gestapo, because this fellow, this other American, had been.

From there they sent me to a rather infamous or well-known prisoner-of-war camp, Stalagluft III, which was the camp from which they had the mass escape at one time of seventy-two men and they executed fifty of them. I was sent to that particular prisoner-of-war camp. I was on the escape committee. Because of my knowledge of Yiddish, and I knew Yiddish quite well, I was able to converse with the Germans to a great extent. I never studied German. I studied French and Spanish, but I was able to converse with the officers, either those who spoke English and those who didn't. I'd make myself understood and I understood them. So I became a contact person and we would trade with certain guards. For example, periodically the *Abwehr*, which is this German secret service, would come through the camp and do a sweep. We always had a hidden radio going, which we built ourselves to get broadcasts from London, the BBC broadcasts. So invariably they'd put us out in the open and they'd go through everything and they would find it, destroy it, punish us, and then we would build a new one. We would trade with the German guards for cigarettes, whatever, and we'd get the material together.

The camp was mostly RAF, not American. There were some Americans besides myself, but it was mostly RAF and some of them had been shot down in the early days of the war. I'm talking about from 1939 and this is 1944. There was one fellow, he was only twenty-four then, he'd been a prisoner for five years. He had been captured when he was nineteen. He was one of the first. He was shot down like three days after the war started, September of 1939. So they were very ingenious. We had Englishmen, we had Australians, New Zealanders, Canadians, and some volunteers. One of my roommates was a Danish fellow who had volunteered, had joined the Royal Canadian Air Force, and then he was shot down while he was flying with the RAF. They had learned to survive. They knew how to survive. They knew how to build radios. They knew how to do a lot of things. So we would, we'd always rebuild the radio and continue to get our broadcasts, secret broadcasts from London from the BBC.

This was an officers' camp, anything from second lieutenant up to colonels. I don't think we had any generals there, but we had colonels. And because under the Geneva Convention officers could not be compelled to work, we didn't work. We probably would have been better off if we had something to do like work, but we survived. We built a little basketball court and played basketball. They put on theatricals. I was fortunate when I came in there. I moved into a room; there were eight of us, seven had been there quite some time, and they had adjusted to prisoner-of-war life. The Americans had come in more recently. With my own approach of fatalism, being fatalistic that is, I adjusted temporarily. Well, other than the times when I was trying to think of how to escape, I adjusted to it.

In fact, interestingly, when I played basketball one of the fellows I played with, an American, had one arm. His name was George Kelly. He was a fighter pilot, and he crashed and lost his arm. He was ultimately repatriated before I was. Years later when I went to law school, I was walking through the library and he saw me and called out, "Hey, Milt." He was at law school at the same time that I was. He was quite a person and we became good friends.

We made some kind of a way of life in prisoner-of-war camp. To survive, to keep from going crazy, we did certain things. The English were very good at growing gardens to get some additional food. They would get seeds, I guess from England, and develop gardens. Some of them were very bright. We had discussions. And every week—I guess it was Friday night—they put on a show, and they were great shows. They were very ingenious. The Australians and New Zealanders were great fun people to be with. They were kind of wild. If you had to be stuck in that kind of circumstance, they were good people to have as your comrades. They made life bearable under very unbearable conditions because we lived off mostly sawdust, which they made into ersatz bread and some soups or something that they'd throw whatever they threw into it. The food was not very much and conditions were not very great, but somehow you'd try to keep your spirits up.

We didn't identify as such, but I'm sure there must have been other Jews there. In my room there were no other Jews. I was the only Jew. There was one who was a Mormon from Canada. In my room they were all Canadians except me. There was this Danish fellow who had flown with the Royal Canadian Air Force. He had volunteered. I remember his name—Sorensen. He was a Danish fellow, very nice fellow. I had a high-ranking Royal Canadian Air Force fellow by the name of Jack Beggs. We had an Irish fellow, actually an American, who'd gone to Canada to volunteer before the United States entered the war, and he made life somewhat interesting. He was a tough Irishman. He'd get up in the morning—he was very surly and very unhappy in the morning—but as the day would wear on he'd come around. The Mormon, from Alberta, he always tried to be upbeat and happy. So he'd wake up in the morning and he would try to be cheerful. "Good morning, everyone!" And this Irish fellow from Boston wanted to kill him because he was in no mood to be happy. We used to practically hold the Irishman down to keep him from killing this fellow, this Mormon. We'd tell him, the Mormon, "Be quiet. When you get up in the morning, you feel good with life, just be quiet. Enjoy it yourself." Sullivan was the Irish fellow. I'd say, "Sully"—we used to call him Sully—"Sully is in no mood to have somebody be cheerful in the morning in this terrible place, so just leave him alone. Don't be cheerful. Be cheerful by yourself." And he wouldn't, he couldn't learn. He was just being natural. He'd get up and say something like, "Isn't it a wonderful day?" and Sullivan would go crazy, you know. But we kept him in check. It was an interesting combination of people.

They didn't give me a synagogue there to go to on holidays. What the RAF people would do because they'd been there a long time is they would sometimes brew their own kind of homemade beer out of something, but they weren't celebrating Jewish holidays. They were celebrating Christmas, things like that. We didn't really recognize holidays. You're just waiting for each day to pass in the hope that the war would end. See, we were getting two kinds of propaganda. The BBC, you'd listen to them and they would tell you what great victories we were winning and how the war was almost over,

and the German newspapers which we'd get in camp would tell you how they're winning the war and it's almost over because they're winning it. So we used to take the two, put them together and split them in the middle and figure out just about where the war was because they both were exaggerating, they were both propaganda, whether it was the British or the Germans, and we didn't believe either one of them. Until the Russian front started moving. When the Russian front started moving westward, the Germans, what the Germans were doing is they were letting the Russians recapture their prisoner-of-war camps, most of them, except for air force officers because they felt apparently that if we were liberated that the next day we would be flying and dropping bombs on them again. So, the Russian front started moving and the Germans did not want us to be liberated. In the middle of the winter—and I'll never forget that experience—it was either late December or early January, they started us on a forced march to vacate the camp. We were in Eastern Silesia. We were not too far from the Russian front. So they made us march for like twenty-four hours in freezing weather until we got to a certain barn on the next night. My leg was still bothering me. I had difficulty walking on it, but I tried to help the others to keep moving so you didn't freeze and to keep everybody's spirits up. When we got to the barn, I'll never forget, I laid down on the ground and my body was so cold that I started shivering so hard that I was actually bouncing off the ground and I couldn't stop. Sorensen—because our group we tried to stay together—took his shirt off, opened up my shirt and lay on top of me with his body to give my body warmth and finally I stopped shivering. The next morning they put us on trains that took us westward. We finally ended up in another prisoner-of-war camp outside a little town near the Danish border called Tarmstedt. I don't even know what the camp was called, but it was a POW camp. And even though we were getting, I won't say orders, but we were getting requests from London to not try to escape—they were telling us the war's going to end soon, don't try to escape, you'll get killed. We had these secret BBC broadcasts, and they knew that prisoners of war were listening to it so they would tell us to not try to escape—but a Canadian and myself decided we didn't want to stay there any longer, and we were able to get out one night.

Well, we had an arrangement with a guard and he was kind of friendly to us. We used to trade with him for things we could build—radios and things like that. And we told him we were going to give him a good conduct message, that he was helpful. We took a chance finally that he would not shoot us or something, and when he walked away—he was on a certain post—when he walked away, the two of us got out. Things were getting pretty chaotic because the Germans knew by that time that they were losing the war, and they were getting worried about how they were going to be treated by the Americans or the English when the war was over. So we managed to get out and we traveled by night. We stayed hidden by day, traveled by night. This was northern Germany, near the Danish border, and we were heading for the Elbe because we had heard on the radio that the British were getting ready to cross the Elbe. When we got near the Elbe, we met the first British troops coming across the river. Finally, we spotted someone who looked like an officer, and we came out of the woods. They were very nice to us. In fact, this officer put us in a jeep, and he stopped the troops from coming across into Germany so that we could cross over into Belgium. A fellow drove us to Brussels, and then from Brussels we flew back to London. Then in England they put us into a hospital. That was automatic. If you were an escaped or released prisoner, you'd first go to a hospital for observation for two weeks, medical and psychological.

I remember there I had a Jewish doctor, a major, who was a psychiatrist. He was the one that did the mental, you know, psychological testing. He said something I thought was kind of cute. He'd asked me questions: "If you go back into active duty, would you be willing to go back into bombers again, bomb Germany?" And I said, "If that's where I'm assigned, yes." You know my fatalism came into play. So then he said, "Well, if we win the war here, how would you feel about going to the Pacific and flying there against Japan?" And I said, "Well, if that's where my assignment is, I'll go there." Whatever he said, I'd give the same kind of answer: "Whatever I'm assigned, I will do my job." And this went on for about two weeks while they checked me medically. I was okay. They gave me food so I put back a few pounds that I had lost. Finally he had to do a report. So the last time I saw him, he said, "Would you like to see my conclusion about you?" So I said, "Sure, if you don't mind. I'd like to see it." He said, "Considering what he's gone through, this man is abnormally normal." After I came back to the United States, when people sometimes would try to get me excited or upset about things, I always tell them, "Look, don't waste your time. I'm abnormally normal. I have a certification from a psychiatrist that says that."

"V-E Day: We Picked Up Our Gear and Went Overseas to Fight the War"

Mitchell B. Schulich   U.S. ARMY AIR CORPS

After we got our operational training, we were assigned to a bomb group and we flew to our destination. And the story was this: On May 8, 1945, which was V-E Day, we got up very early in the morning because we were leaving Herington, Kansas, with a brand-new B-29, and we were taking that B-29 over to Guam. We didn't know that was where we were going at the time, but that's where we ended up. We walked into this little coffee shop—it was very early in the morning—to get something to eat before we took off. Of course, the time frame was such that in Europe it was much later, six hours later or eight hours probably. The girls in there were shouting, and we asked, "What's wrong, what's the matter?" They said, "The war's over, the war's over." And we just finished our breakfast, we picked up our gear and went overseas to fight the war.

From Herington, Kansas, we flew to Mather Field in Sacramento. We spent about two days at Mather and then from there flew on to Hawaii, Oahu, and spent about three days there. Then we flew on to Guam, but we had to stop at Kwajalein Island and spend overnight at Kwajalein, which was just a coral rock with big land crabs crawling all over it—in our tents and everywhere else. From there we went over to Guam, and fortunately we were not shot down by the U.S. Navy antiaircraft gunners, because we did violate some of their air space. It's happened, by the way.

Cutaway of B-29 Superfortress

Technically more advanced than all other heavy bomber types in World War II, the Superfortress was pressurized for high altitudes and featured remotely controlled gun turrets. The B-29's 3,700-mile range allowed it to carry large bomb loads across the Pacific Ocean.

The popular name of the B-29 was the Superfortress. It was the prototype of the modern aircraft in that it was a pressurized plane, and you didn't have to wear your oxygen mask when you flew above 10,000 feet, which was very comfortable, very good. Of course, we always had them dangling from our chest in case we needed them. It was quite an aircraft. We were shot at, and we took holes in the aircraft from antiaircraft fire—decompression did exist, but it wasn't explosive; it was gradual.

You had the aircraft commander, who was essentially what most people call the pilot, and then there was the pilot, who was what most people call the copilot. So you have those two guys flying the plane. The flight engineer sat right behind the pilot, the bombardier in the front, down below where the bombsight was, and the navigator behind the aircraft commander but a little bit removed. There was a big turret next to the navigator, and around the other side of the turret was the radio operator and a little place that had no window. That was my space. In the mid-section, you had three gunners. The top turret gunner they called central fire control. This was a system whereby you controlled the guns remotely. You didn't fire the guns by holding the actual gun. They were electronically controlled. There were electronic computations so that the angle of sight, the target, and the gun itself formed a triangle, and you focused on that. You could also switch

Mitchell Schulich with his father and
mother, Reuben and Lillian Schulich, at
the training base in Herington, Kansas

Radioman Mitchell Schulich (bottom row,
right) with B-29 crew, Guam, 1945

control over the guns from one gun to another. The central fire control gunner was in charge of this whole operation. If an aircraft came at you and it went from the left side of the plane to the right side, the port to the starboard, then he would switch the control of the guns to the gunner on that side. You had a tail gunner as well, who sat isolated in the tail section, and you had a radar operator, who was just in back of the gunners in the midsection. I was the first aid man on the crew, and the only training I ever got was how to put a bandage on and how to inject into the vein. It was very haphazard training.

The officers and the enlisted men were separated. That's clear. You were a different species of life if you were an enlisted man compared to an officer. They lived together in their own area and we lived in our area, and they had certain privileges that we didn't have. I don't know whether they ate better than we did, but there were fewer of them so maybe they did. We lived in a Quonset hut. I became very friendly with one guy in particular who was close to my age, about six months apart, named Caris McLeod who came from Ponce de Leon, Florida, a really rural guy, you know, but a good person and we were friendly with the other guys, even though we needled each other. We'd play pinochle to pass the time of day when we weren't flying missions. We'd go down to a place called Hoover Bay Park, and we'd go swimming in this beautiful coral sea and beautiful water. I had a favorite hat that I would wear when I was flying missions, and it became something you sort of depend upon. It was something like an amulet, like a rabbit's foot, or something like that. It brings you luck, it protects you. You had to lean on something. Well, one time on the way back a wind came along and that hat was blown off my head. It landed in the bush and they wouldn't stop . . . and now that hat was gone and we were flying a mission that night, so I was a little nervous. But it was a very easy mission, what we called a milk run. So there it goes. I didn't really need the hat. Some Christian guys wore a St. Christopher medal, that sort of thing, you know. I had my hat.

I don't recall whether they had actual services or whether it was an ecumenical type of service where they involve many groups, many, many religions. But at Sioux Falls, South Dakota, some people in the Jewish community made a seder, and Jewish guys went to the seder, which was very nice. They did have services, though I never really went to them.

I had some good experiences. I remember a fellow by the name of Al Brancatti, Italian. After the day was over, we retired—there were two guys to a pup tent—and of course we were talking a lot, and he was a beautiful, beau-

tiful guy. I really appreciated his receptive outlook toward life and equality and his idealism in what was good and true and just, you know, that it's the individual that you should focus on, not his background. The individual is what really counts, because there are good and bad people in all walks of life from all cultures. And that is one of the good experiences that I had.

I had a few bad experiences also. I can tell you about one when I was overseas. I was flying missions at that time and there was another radio operator, and I had talked to him occasionally and we got into a conversation. He mentioned this Captain Goldberg who was a pilot, aircraft commander they called him, of one of the B-29s, and he commented, "You know, you know how they are." I said, "What do you mean, you know how they are?" He says, "Well, he's a Jew." I said, "Well, how are they?" "Well, you know, they're loudmouthed." And here he is talking to a Jew, right? And I said, "I don't agree with you. I happen to be Jewish." And I walked away from him.

I'll tell you one thing, I was with all kinds of people, but I felt a little bit more comfortable when I was with Jews.

This other guy, he came from Pennsylvania, and he made a comment. He was the left gunner on my crew. We were talking about bus drivers in Philadelphia or wherever it was, Pittsburgh maybe, and he said, "The blacks are doing that—it's too good a job for a black." I said, "What the hell are you talking about?" I challenged him on that, and he said, "You're only saying that because you're a Jew." I even asked him to step outside. I was ready to fight him and he would have creamed me. He was bigger and stronger, but he wouldn't do it. A couple of other incidents took place, but I felt comfortable with these guys for the most part.

There were basically two kinds of missions. When we got over there, the strategy was pinpoint, daylight bombing to hit industrial targets and oil refineries, and things like that. And we did that. We flew in formation, which consisted of fifteen B-29s to a squadron. That was for protection, because when fighter opposition comes across and they try to attack you, if you're together and you have so many, you have great fire power. And there's a story of one Zero coming in a pursuit curve at our squadron trying to shoot down a B-29, and the six 50-caliber machine guns on the top of each B-29 all swiveled around in his direction. He broke his pursuit curve and ran away. He figured he wasn't going to die. He would have been blown out of the sky. So there was that sort of protection.

And of course, the other side of the coin was the nighttime raids. Those were basically incendiary raids, the firebombing of Japan, which was a significant factor in bringing the Japanese to surrender, although it was a cruel thing because millions of people died in those raids. At night we flew at various levels, usually at lower levels, and we dropped magnesium incendiaries, which would explode about fifty feet above the ground and spread little cylinders of burning magnesium into various areas. Of course the construction of Japanese houses was paper and wood, and so it just was a conflagration. We saw this whenever we flew night missions, because what we did was to look out as we hit landfall, and we could see fires burning all over Japan, as far as you could see. And each of those fires pinpointed a bomb group's raid. Different groups were assigned to different locations.

We had a kamikaze on our tail once, and he was gaining on us. Our pilot was excellent, the aircraft commander, Walter Ormond, he was really an excellent pilot. He knew everything about that plane. We were going at a rate of 250, 275 miles per hour and that's unusual for that plane—it was vibrating. And this kamikaze was gaining on us and it just blew up in the air. Another time we were caught in the searchlights—that's sudden death if they've got you in the searchlights, because they see you, they shoot at you, and they knock you down. He put that B-29 on its wing and he went down with it, and then he pulled it out and we were out of the searchlights. So you've got somebody like that who knows how to handle a plane.

There's another experience I had which was very interesting and very frightening to all of us who realized what was happening. We had to land at Iwo Jima six times for various reasons. We'd been shot up, we had engines out, and what have you. The time I'm talking about we had experienced a hit in the gas tank and we didn't know it. We were leaking gas. We just about had enough gas in the tank to get back to Guam, but the pilot smartly did not want to take a chance. So he said, we're going down here, and we attempted to land, but we had no wounded on board and there were aircraft coming in with men who were wounded and aircraft missing one or two engines. They kept on waving us off the approach pattern. The sixth time they waved us off, we veered away, but because of raising and lowering the flaps and the gear so many times, the fuses became overheated and a fuse blew. That meant that the gear and the flaps stayed down, and we were off the approach and were settling fast. There were men working, repairing other aircraft on the ground, standing on these pipe racks ten feet off the ground, and they saw us settling like that. Well, they jumped off those pipe racks at ten feet and they ran. I was standing between the pilot and the copilot to the rear of them. The radar man was in front of me, down below sort of on his knees in a squat position. He realized what was happening and he went into the fuse box, which was located there, and replaced the fuse. The gear and flaps started to come up, and with that we gained more air speed and that took us off. So we didn't barrel into the earth, we probably were cleared by about twenty or thirty feet, which was just amazing. I was standing there and you know, they say your whole life goes before you before you die, well, not so. I said . . . I couldn't believe it . . . I said, you know, "I'm going to die." I looked at the ground coming up, and I said, "This is the end, I'm going to die." That was all that was in my mind.

It was cruel and people died, and the people who died were not the people who were fighting us, they were civilians basically. It was not a nice thing, and in the back of my mind—and I'm sure other GIs felt this—there was very little choice that we had. Not only because the orders were there, but we wanted to get the war over with and this was a technique by which to do it. You have to look at this, I think, as a way of life, as a whole episode. You can't pick it apart. Here you had a country, and in Germany also, where the civilian population was strongly in support of the military population and the military decisions on what to do. And there was a war. They said that if you are shot down, you don't want to be captured by civilians because they'll slaughter you. You're better off being captured by the police or the army. You had a better chance to live at that particular point. And I can understand why they would want to slaughter me. But you try not to think about that. You drop the bombs. War is hell. And there was a lot of bestiality that took place on the enemy side as well, but it didn't make it right. I was a Pfc at that time, private first class. Then promoted to corporal, then to sergeant, and then to staff sergeant, which was the highest rank you could go as a radioman. Twenty-one missions and one mercy flight to Okinawa to ferry in rations after a hurricane hit that island. But the operation was fraught with danger—you could go down like that. I think we had more operational failures than we did combat losses.

While we were flying missions, the radioman didn't do very much because there was radio silence, and so there was—I don't think it was an anti-Semitic framework—but there was a constant joke: If we ever have to jettison any material, we can throw the radioman out. He doesn't do anything anyway. Well, I got the better of them, though. I used to get the weather reports that came over Guam when we were going back and what have you. But on one occasion I intercepted a call from a B-29 that was ditching off

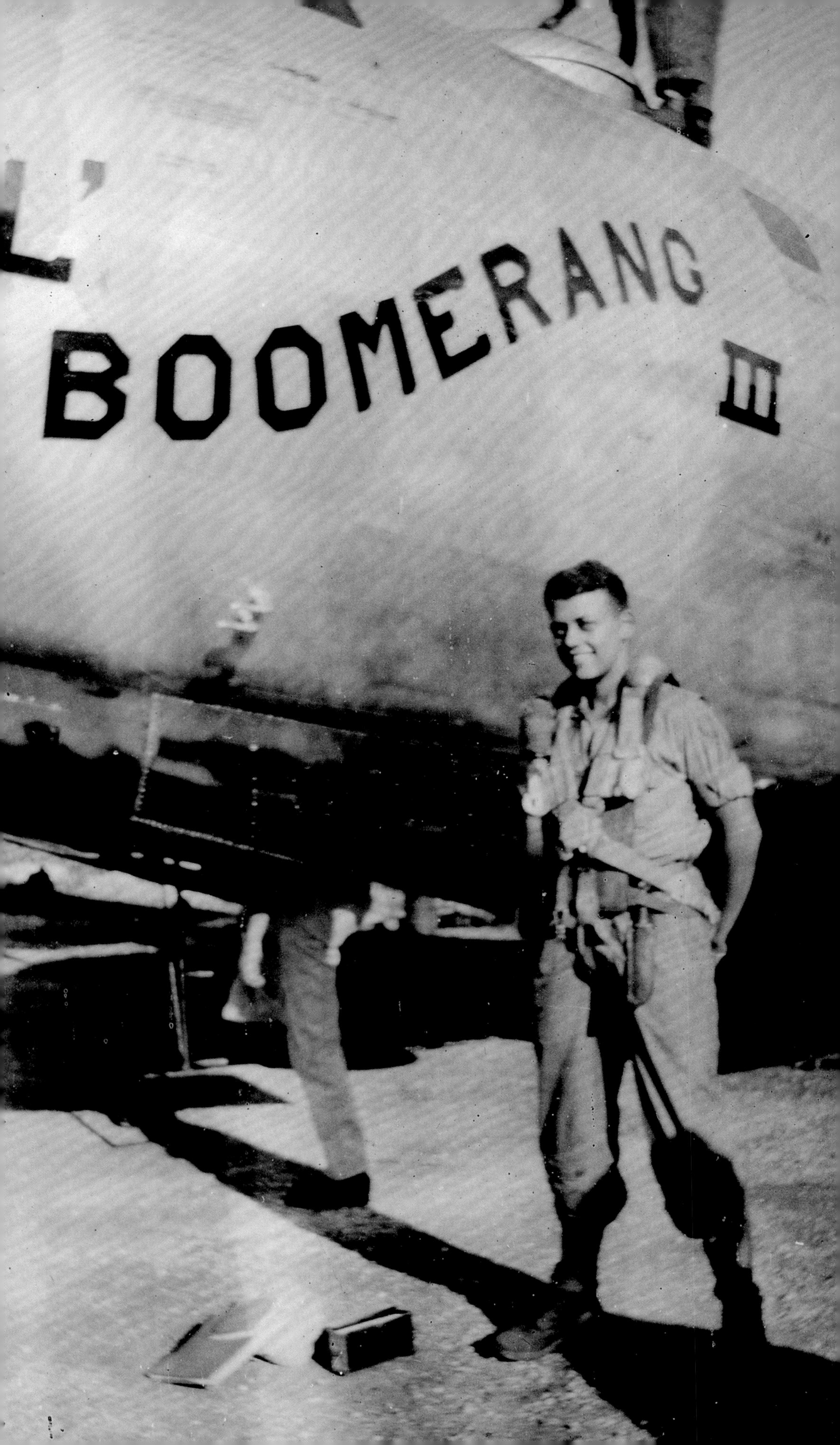
L'
BOOMERANG
III

Japan, and I relayed that message to air-sea rescue giving them the position of the B-29. They acknowledged receiving the message and that was the end of it. I never heard anything about it after that until 1995. In 1995 I went back to Guam with the copilot of the plane. And we went with a group through a travel agency which was run by a fellow by the name of John Misterly. And John Misterly told a story of their ditching a B-29, and I described my experience to him. And he said, "Gee whiz, you may have saved our lives." Could be. I broke radio silence against orders, and I'm glad I did. Nobody knew because this was continuous wave, you know, with a key and a dot dot dash rather than voice, so nobody knew it was going on. But I knew and I was proud of it.

The last mission was after the atomic bomb was dropped, and it was of very little consequence. On September 2, I think it was, 1945, we flew a display-of-force mission over the *Missouri* when the peace treaty was being signed by MacArthur and the Japanese dignitaries. And we flew so low, we were about 200, 250 feet above the *Missouri,* and they were ticked that we dared to do this, mind you. So they zeroed in on us, and they gave us extra duty, extra assignments, you know, flying here, flying there, what have you.

After the first bomb was released—it was spread around that they had dropped an atomic bomb, and I knew all about atomics because I studied chemistry and physics in high school. An atom is very small, how much damage could it do? We didn't understand it, the chain reaction and all that sort of stuff. But we heard of this brand-new weapon—we didn't get too much information about it—a bomb that was 100,000 times more powerful than TNT.

I felt a sense of relief. This would mean I'd be going home. This would mean I would be taken out of harm's way, as it affected me personally. But as far as the effect of the bomb, which was a brutal thing—our missions destroyed more life than those two bombs, the burning out of those cities, much more—the atomic bomb was welcome because it meant the end of the war.

I was a needed member of the crew, and those aircraft had to go back. So, as a radioman, I was aboard the aircraft, while the gunners were left behind. The flight engineer, I think he traveled also by ship. It took them a month or something to get back. I was back in two days. I had the opportunity to fly with the air transport command at that time. I was just about twenty years old at that time. And I had been away for a couple of years, and I was eager to get back home, get on with my life. I knew I wanted to go to college, I wanted to do something. But I'll tell you as I look back, I think I made a mistake. I think I should have stayed there and then have gone to college when I came back because it would have been a great experience. I knew about the shipload of Jews that was turned away in Florida and sent back, our country refusing to take them. There was talk around . . . I knew what Hitler was doing. I knew of his victories, and I knew of the persecution of the Jews and the others. It had an impact upon me. It reinforced a feeling that I had even before this happened, which was that growing up in a mixed society as a very, very shy kid, I felt inferior. I felt because I was a Jew I was inferior.

You'd see this attitude all around at that time, and you'd hear Father Coughlin on the radio. You recognize that this is essentially a Christian country, and the delineations between acceptance and rejections were clear in those days. There was a lot of rejection. The circles people traveled in were mostly homogeneous, ethnically homogenous. And, of course, I looked at these tall good-looking Christian guys and these beautiful Christian girls, you know, the Nordic type. And I'd ask myself, "How come they're so good looking and Jews are not that good looking?" That was my perspective then. I wasn't secure in my own feelings about myself, which made me, I believe, prone to feeling less than equal.

One thing that I thought was really good that came out of the war, the experience, was the intermixing of people from all walks of life and from all areas of the country. That was good because we learned that we were really human beings with very human qualities. That was good. Now, as far as other things, I think that I came of age. I think it made me a more reflective type of person, my war experience. I think it gave me a kind of self-confidence, which I didn't have before the war, that I'd done something really important and did it pretty well. And I was proud of my experience, proud that I came and defended the country, and proud of the fact that I stood up and took the high road. I know a lot of people who didn't. A lot of people worked to avoid being in combat, worked to avoid being in service. I don't respect that.

In a way it brought me closer to my religion, because I did have some occasions when I celebrated the joys of the holidays with fellow Jews, and that was important. And I knew people in the service who were Jewish, and we sort of had similar experiences, which reinforced my identity because of the fact that other Jews like me were serving the country and the nation, that we were doing our part, and I was proud that I was Jewish in doing it. The war was always a good war, a war for the right and the just, a war to counter totalitarianism and brutality—I actually felt that all the way through from the very beginning.

Afterword

Tom Brokaw

I was born in the Great Plains of South Dakota in 1940. My father worked on an army base, so my first memories of life really were of World War II. It was a small base in southwestern South Dakota, and all around me were khaki greens, people going to or coming home from the war, ammunition being tested and then shipped off to distant battlefields.

Given the fact that these were my first memories, I always believed that World War II would go on forever. When it ended, we rushed on with our new lives in peace and working-class prosperity in the Middle West, like so many working-class families from that part of the world. For the first time my parents were able to dream of sending their firstborn to college and having enough money at the end of the year to maybe buy their first new car.

Life went on, and I found myself working through the stages of NBC to the point that I was the anchorman of the NBC *Nightly News*. Then in 1984, in the early spring, I went to the fortieth anniversary of D-Day to do a documentary for NBC news on that historic event. I was tantalized by the journalistic opportunity, but I also looked forward to the sybaritic experience of spending a week or ten days in northern France, sampling the cuisine, drinking a little Calvados, and having a good time.

We took with us a group of veterans, some who had been in the Army Rangers, the boys of Pointe du Hoc.

We had some from the 101st Airborne, and we had working-class guys from the Big Red One who landed on Omaha Beach. And I took two of them with me, Harry Garton, a man who lost both legs in the war, and Gino Merli, who went on to earn the Medal of Honor. The first day that we filmed on the beach with our camera crews in place, we went over those first dunes and onto the beach, with these two men, who looked so much like my high school coaches or the fathers of my friends, and their wives, who looked like the mothers of my pals, my mother's friends, as I was growing up. They were in windbreakers, modest people, very few words.

As we stepped over the dunes onto the beach, they began to talk in muted tones about what they had gone through forty years before. By the end of that walk, my life had been transformed, because I realized how much we owed not just to these two gentlemen but to the entire generation that they represented.

That experience reverberated in me in an emotional, intellectual, and journalistic way, so for the next ten years I began to read and think more about World War II in all of its aspects. By the fiftieth anniversary of D-Day, when I went back to France, it was a much larger event. I was on the air with Tim Russert of *Meet the Press* and he said to me, "Tom, what do you think as you sit there at Colleville-sur-Mer, the large American cemetery overlooking Omaha Beach?" I said, "When I think of this generation, who survived the Great Depression and then was asked to go off and save the world and did so and came home and gave us the lives that we have today, and never whined and never whimpered, I think it is the greatest generation any society ever produced."

There were unintended consequences of my first book, *The Greatest Generation;* letters began to pour in. Obviously, memories had been triggered. Children had been energized and motivated to go talk to their parents about their experiences, grandchildren were asking their grandparents about what they had gone through. And there was an unleashing in this country of the appropriate kind of memories, the kind of memories that are preserved in the Museum of Jewish Heritage's exhibition *Ours to Fight For: American Jews in the Second World War,* for in those memories are the lessons not just of the past but the future for all of us as well.

This was a time when the world truly was at stake, east and west. John Keegan, the British military historian, has said that World War II was the largest single event in the history of mankind. It was fought on six of the seven continents. It was fought on all the seas and in the air over all of those continents. And when it was over, more than 50 million people had been killed, cultures had been realigned, and nations had been destroyed and needed to be rebuilt.

In every aspect of that experience, we learned something about our strengths and also about our weaknesses. I have called those who participated in this collective experience the "greatest generation." I have been challenged on that from time to time. I say it was the greatest generation, but it wasn't perfect. It wasn't perfect because of the terrible, humiliating racial discrimination that existed at that time—the segregation of African Americans, the internment of Japanese Americans, or the anti-Semitism that men and women describe in this book and the corresponding exhibition.

But World War II was also a time during which the fundamental values of life, in this land especially, were on the minds of everyone, including everyday Americans like Maury Robb, whom I learned about from his son. Writing in response to my second book, *The Greatest Generation Speaks,* Robb's son tells of his dad becoming a B-17 pilot and successfully completing

thirty missions over Germany. Maury Robb was preparing to train as a fighter pilot when the war ended. Instead, he returned to the University of Pennsylvania, completed a degree in engineering under the GI Bill of Rights, as so many did, and eventually founded a small plastics company in Philadelphia.

Maury Robb's mother had written to him during the war because he had volunteered to become a pilot on combat missions, and she was hoping that he would ask for reassignment because it was so dangerous. She was, as a good Jewish mother, worrying about his personal welfare. Robb's powerful reply, evoking the steadfast ethics that later guided his career, is a testament to the time that shaped the lives of these people. Maury Robb wrote the following letter to his mother:

I enlisted to serve in the Air Corps and I doubt if I will ever change. Remember, Mother, some *have* to fly so that peace can be won. But it is not this desire to be among the "Elite" that makes me anxious to graduate and be able to wear a pair of silver wings. It is more than that, it is because of the way Dad brought me up, it is because of the love and respect I hold for Dad that I will never voluntarily ask for a transfer.

You remember how Dad turned down a badly needed line, because he didn't want to take it away from another man—who also needed to make a living? Do you remember how Dad paid rent for five or six months . . . while all around people didn't—and got away with it? It is these things—and a lifetime full of other incidents—perhaps nothing which in itself would be noteworthy—but together they point to one thing—Honor. Honor in more than the everyday way people think of it—Honor the way the bible means. To Dad Honor meant more than simply financial integrity—it meant respect for his fellow men, and fair play for everyone.

Today Honor means Duty. And my duty is to serve in the highest position I can fill. So, my dears, looking at it this way, I really think that you will not want to urge me to switch. Remember the phrase, "I could not love you half as much, if I loved not Honor more." Well, today Honor and Duty and Country are all tied up together. Thus, I feel I am doing right and that I am doing what Dad would think right.

This is an extraordinary document when we view it in the context of contemporary life, but it really did represent the sensibilities not just of this young man but of millions more just like him across the country. They felt the call of duty and honor and loyalty. And because of them, we have the nation that we have today, because they came home and they extended that honor and duty and loyalty to the domestic needs of this country as well.

These men and women could have given up on America, but they did not. They are like the generation of African Americans who didn't give up on the idea that the day would come when they would have real rights under the law, even as many paid the ultimate price. Or Jewish Americans, who returned to a society that was still harboring so much anti-Semitism, yet they didn't give up on the idea of America. We were constantly in pursuit—during the Great Depression, World War II, and in the postwar years—of the common higher ground. That I believe is the great enduring legacy of this generation. It is that legacy that deserves

to be burnished today, celebrated, examined, and passed on to the coming generations.

We cannot prevail, despite all of our industrial strength, despite the rule of law, despite the great peace that we have enjoyed in this country, if we allow this nation to be divided up into a collection of victims, each competing with the others, if we allow ourselves to be less than the sum of our parts.

In some small way I hoped that my work in sharing the stories of the greatest generation and all that they went through, the values they held in their hearts and minds, would help perpetuate these lessons for generations to come. So, I commend you and congratulate you on this magnificent museum and on this insightful exhibition and book. They are steadfast reminders to us to constantly remember that terrible time so that these lessons will continue for generations to come. You are the trustees of a great legacy. And Americans, young and old, will now hear these stories and be enriched by them.

This afterword was drawn from remarks made by Tom Brokaw at the Museum of Jewish Heritage – A Living Memorial to the Holocaust on May 30, 2001, in discussing the significance of his books *The Greatest Generation, The Greatest Generation Speaks,* and *An Album of Memories: Personal Histories from the Greatest Generation.*

Veterans' Biographies

Dr. Bernard Branson

After discharge Bernard Branson completed a Bachelor of Arts degree at New York University in 1949. He returned to active duty in the Korean War as an officer from 1951 to 1953. He completed his doctorate in psychology at Syracuse University in 1957. He continued to serve in the air force reserves and the Medical Service Corps Reserves until 1972, retiring with the rank of captain. He taught at Queens College from 1957 to 1982 while maintaining a private practice in psychoanalysis and psychotherapy. After retiring Dr. Branson became a training and supervising analyst for the Alfred Adler Institute. He is now Dean of Academic Interrelations at the Adler Institute.

Jeanne Zamaloff Dworkin

After returning from military service in 1945, Jeanne Zamaloff Dworkin completed a bachelor of arts in history and economics at Barnard College and Columbia University under the GI Bill of Rights. In addition to raising two children, from 1950 to 1963 she was a community activist working in children's arts and cultural programming and the peace and Civil Rights movements. From 1963 to 1968 Ms. Dworkin was an executive administrator at Albert Einstein College of Medicine. She completed a masters degree in psychology at Queens College in 1974, took a teaching credential, then taught secondary school and special populations for two years. From 1976 to 1986 she worked at the City University of New York, running grant-funded community programs and literacy and vocational programs for the deaf. Throughout her life she was active in community affairs, and her commitment continues now in her retirement.

Victor B. Geller

Victor B. Geller returned to Yeshiva University after the war. He completed a masters degree in communal administration and spent most of his career working in the Orthodox community and at Yeshiva University. He was director of rabbinical placement and dean of communal services at Yeshiva. He is now retired.

Maximilian Lerner

After returning home from Europe, Maximilian Lerner earned a bachelors degree at City College and a masters of education at Columbia University. He worked in the import and export field, eventually establishing his own firm importing peat moss. Since his retirement, he has authored a World War II spy novel based in part on his wartime experiences.

Franklin Mellion

Franklin Mellion returned from the service in 1946. After completing high school, he studied retail management in the food business in a course sponsored by the New York State Food Merchants Association at City College of New York. In 1950 Mr. Mellion took over his family's butcher shop and delicatessen, which he ran until 1990. He is now retired.

Hon. Milton Mollen

After receiving his law degree from St. John's University in 1950, Milton Mollen embarked on a distinguished career in public service as a lawyer and a judge for New York City, including thirteen years as presiding justice of the appellate division. From 1990 to 1992 Judge Mollen was deputy mayor for public safety in the David

N. Dinkins administration. From 1992 to 1994 he chaired the Special Commission on Police Corruption better known as the Mollen Commission. He is of counsel to the law firm Herrick Feinstein, LLP.

HON. BURTON ROBERTS

After discharge Burton Roberts earned a law degree from Cornell University in 1949. From 1949 to 1966 he was an assistant district attorney in the New York County district attorney's office and also served as a military Intelligence officer in the U.S. Army Reserves until 1953. In 1966 he became chief assistant district attorney for Bronx County. In 1968 he was elected district attorney for Bronx County serving until 1973. From 1973 to 1998 he was justice of the New York State Supreme Court. He served as administrative judge, criminal branch, of the Bronx Supreme Court from 1984 to 1998, and from 1988 also administrative judge, civil branch. He is of counsel to the law firm of Fischbein, Badillo, Wagner, Harding.

EVELYN SCHECTER PERLMAN

After returning home in 1945, Evelyn Schecter Perlman resumed work as a legal secretary while attending New York University at night under the GI Bill of Rights. Her work in the legal field brought her to some of New York's most important law firms. In 1958 she left legal work to raise her two children. A decade later, she began a second career in the fashion industry, working with such top design houses as Valentino, Ellen Tracy, and Christian Dior. A longtime volunteer for the Women's League for Conservative Judaism, she is now retired.

RABBI HERSCHEL SCHACTER

In 1946, after returning from service, Rabbi Herschel Schacter was invited to become the rabbi of the Mosholu Jewish Center of the Bronx, a position he held for fifty-two years. He was national president of the Religious Zionists of America/Mizrachi from 1965 to 1970. From 1968 to 1970 Rabbi Schacter was the chairman of the National Conference of Presidents of Major American Jewish Organizations. An early activist in the struggle for Soviet Jewry, Rabbi Schacter was national chairman of the American Conference on Soviet Jewry from 1970 to 1972. He served as chairman of the Jewish Welfare Board Committee on Jewish Military Chaplaincy from 1980 to 1983. He is now retired.

JACK SCHARF

Returning from service in 1946, Jack Scharf went on to complete his bachelor of business administration at Bernard M. Baruch School of Business under the GI Bill of Rights. He became a practicing certified public accountant in 1947 and began his own accounting firm, where he continues to work. One of the founders of the Hebrew Institute of Riverdale, he is active in several charitable foundations.

MITCHELL B. SCHULICH

After the war Mitchell B. Schulich studied at the Brooklyn College of Pharmacy on the GI Bill of Rights. He worked as a pharmacist from 1949 to 1957. In 1957 Mr. Schulich began teaching at Seward Park High School, completing a masters of science education in 1959. From 1967 to 1979 Mr. Schulich was assistant principal-administration at Seward Park. He was principal of Curtis High School on Staten Island from 1979 to 1991. For many years a member of the education committee of the Anti-Defamation League, Mr. Schulich has remained active in environmental causes since his retirement.

MARTY SILVERMAN

Marty Silverman returned to business after the war. He went on to found National Equipment Rental, Ltd., which he ran from 1950 to 1984. During his tenure as head of National Equipment Rental, Mr. Silverman had the honor of appearing before the Supreme Court of the United States, winning the landmark case *National Equipment Rental v. Szukhent* in 1964. He is now the president and chief executive officer of the Marty and Dorothy Silverman Foundation.

PHOTOGRAPH CREDITS

Cover: Gift of Rabbi Samson Goldstein, Yaffa Eliach Collection donated by the Center for Holocaust Studies; p. 2: American Jewish Historical Society, Waltham, Massachusetts and New York, New York; pp. 4–5: Collection of the Lawrence Luskin Family, photography by Peter Goldberg; p. 6: Collection of Arthur Coren in memory of Rose Coren; p. 12: Collection of Meyer Birnbaum; p. 16: Collection of Bernard Branson; p. 19: © Horace Bristol/CORBIS; pp. 20–21: Collection of Bernard Branson; p. 23: Collection of Bernard Branson, photography by Peter Goldberg; p. 29: Collection of Bernard Branson; p. 32: Collection of Jeanne Zamaloff Dworkin; p. 35: © Bettmann/CORBIS; p. 37 (top): Collection of Jeanne Zamaloff Dworkin; p. 37 (bottom): Collection of Jeanne Zamaloff Dworkin; p. 39: © Bettmann/CORBIS; p. 42: Collection of Franklin Mellion; p. 43: © CORBIS; p. 45: © CORBIS; p. 47: © Bettmann/CORBIS; p. 50: Collection of Burton Roberts; p. 53: Collection of Burton Roberts; p. 55 (left): Collection of Burton Roberts, photography by Peter Goldberg; p. 55 (right): Gift of Solomon Feldstein, Yaffa Eliach Collection donated by the Center for Holocaust Studies, photography by Peter Goldberg; p. 57: © CORBIS; p. 60 (left): Collection of Burton Roberts; p. 60 (right): Collection of the National Museum of American Jewish Military History, photography by Peter Goldberg; p. 62: Gift of Joseph Wright, Yaffa Eliach Collection donated by the Center for Holocaust Studies; p. 66: Collection of Maximilian Lerner; p. 69: Collection of Maximilian Lerner; p. 71 (left): Collection of Maximilian Lerner; p. 71 (right) Collection of Maximilian Lerner; p. 75 (left): Collection of Maximilian Lerner; p. 75 (right): Collection of Maximilian Lerner; p. 78: Gift of Victor B. Geller, Yaffa Eliach Collection donated by the Center for Holocaust Studies; p. 79: Gift of Victor B. Geller, Yaffa Eliach Collection donated by the Center for Holocaust Studies; p. 81: Gift of Rabbi Herschel Schacter, Yaffa Eliach Collection donated by the Center for Holocaust Studies; p. 83: Gift of Victor B. Geller, Yaffa Eliach Collection donated by the Center for Holocaust Studies; p. 85: Gift of Victor B. Geller, Yaffa Eliach Collection donated by the Center for Holocaust Studies; p. 87: Gift of Victor B. Geller, Yaffa Eliach Collection donated by the Center for Holocaust Studies; p. 90: Collection of Jack Scharf; p. 93: Collection of Katz's Delicatessen, photography by Peter Goldberg p. 96: Gift of Elias Linhart; p. 97: Gift of Harold Conn in memory of Werner Conn, Yaffa Eliach Collection donated by the Center for Holocaust Studies; pp. 98–99: Gift of Harold Conn in memory of Werner Conn, Yaffa Eliach Collection donated by the Center for Holocaust Studies; p. 102: Collection of Rabbi Herschel Schacter; p. 106 (left): Gift of Rabbi Herschel Schacter, Yaffa Eliach Collection donated by the Center for Holocaust Studies; pp. 106–107: Gift of Rabbi Judah Nadich, Yaffa Eliach Collection donated by the Center for Holocaust Studies; p. 109: Gift of Rabbi Herschel Schacter, Yaffa Eliach Collection donated by the Center for Holocaust Studies; p. 111: Gift of Rabbi Herschel Schacter, Yaffa Eliach Collection donated by the Center for Holocaust Studies; p. 112: Collection of Northwestern University Library; p. 116: Collection of Marty Silverman; p. 119: © Underwood &Underwood/CORBIS; p. 123: Collection of Marty Silverman p. 125: Collection of Marty Silverman, photography by Peter Goldberg; pp. 126–127: © Hulton-Deutsch Collection/CORBIS; p. 129: © Bettmann/CORBIS; p. 132: Collection of Evelyn Schecter Perlman; p. 135 (left): Collection of Evelyn Schecter Perlman; p. 135 (right): Collection of Evelyn Schecter Perlman; p. 137 (top): Collection of Evelyn Schecter Perlman; p. 137 (bottom): Collection of Evelyn Schecter Perlman; p. 139: Collection of Evelyn Schecter Perlman, photography by Peter Goldberg; p.144: Collection of Milton Mollen; p. 147: © Bettmann/CORBIS; p. 151: © CORBIS p. 155: © Hulton-Deutsch Collection/CORBIS; p. 158: Collection of Mitchell B. Schulich; p. 159: © Bettmann/CORBIS; p. 160 (left): Collection of Mitchell B. Schulich pp. 160–161: Collection of Mitchell B. Schulich; p. 163: Collection of Mitchell B. Schulich; p. 165: © CORBIS; p. 167: Collection of Mitchell B. Schulich; Back cover: American Jewish Historical Society, Waltham, Massachusetts and New York, New York

RSVP

**The very best
of invitation and
promotion design**

RSVP
**The very best
of invitation and
promotion design**

Sara Manuelli

RotoVision

A RotoVision Book
Published and distributed by
RotoVision SA
Route Suisse 9
CH-1295 Mies
Switzerland

RotoVision SA
Sales & Production Office
Sheridan House
112/116A Western Road
Hove
East Sussex BN3 1DD
UK

Tel: +44 (0)1273 72 72 68
Fax: +44 (0)1273 72 72 69
E-mail:
sales@rotovision.com
www.rotovision.com

Book design by Browns/London
www.brownsdesign.com

Photography by Xavier Young

Production and separations in Singapore
by ProVision Pte.Ltd.

Tel: +656 334 7720
Fax: +656 334 7721

10 9 8 7 6 5 4 3 2 1

ISBN 2-88046-704-7

Contents

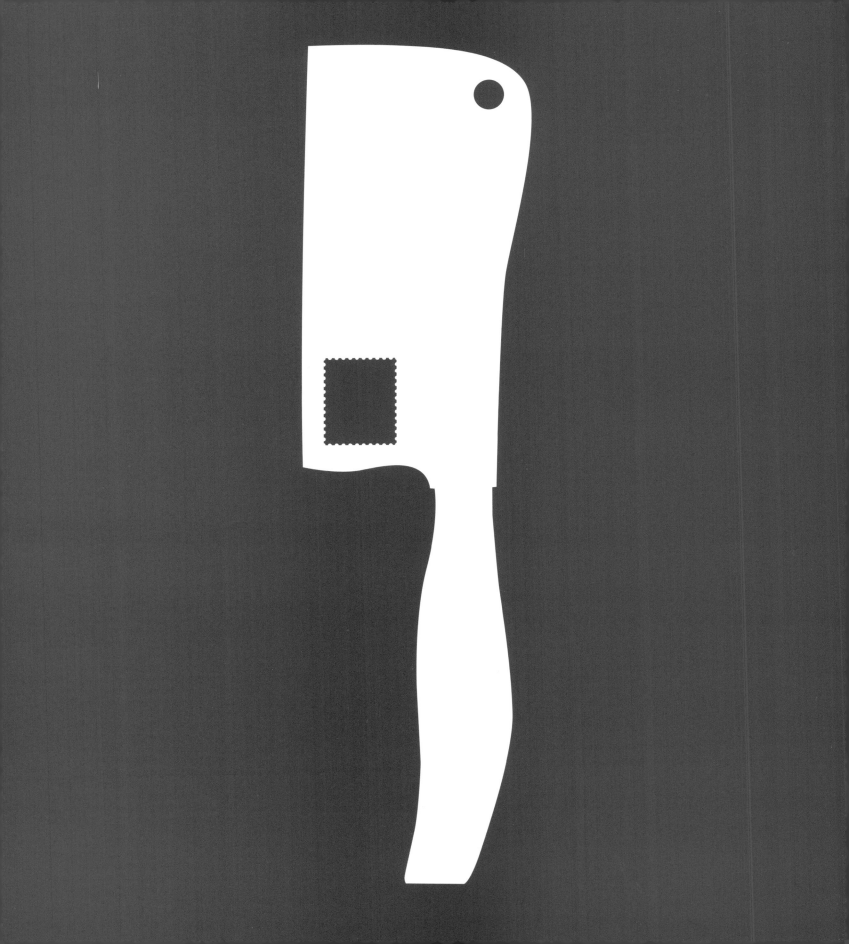

As human beings, our lives are defined by social events. Whether the event is as personal as a friend's wedding or as banal as an annual conference, to be invited to an event is a call to action to behave in a collective, socially accepted way. The relationship between the invitee and the invited is formalised by the invitation. Conventionally, it is a printed card that requests your attendance and denotes the nature and the purpose of the event. It communicates when, where and why you need to attend.

The invitation also represents a complex social relationship between sender and recipient. The event may be exclusive or be open to all. It may be a sobering occasion such as a funeral, or as casual as a warehouse party. It may be something you want to attend, or something you dare not miss. A mantelpiece lined with invitations to exclusive events acts almost as physical proof of acceptance by a social order.

An invitation is both a piece of communication and a complex purveyor of social values wrapped up in a small, postable object. Further, as an ambassador to an event, it has to explain and recall the essence of the forthcoming occasion, through its language, its format or by creating a mental image.

Invitations need to have convincing qualities. They need to establish that the event is worth attending and replying to. To capture the recipient's attention, they need to charm, intrigue and sometimes amuse. Their graphic design needs to employ the tools of persuasion.

The design of invitations can vary from the simple to the wildly elaborate. They can take the form of a card, a website or a three-dimensional object. They can be mass-produced or exquisitely crafted in limited editions. Their size can range from a poster to that of a flyer.

Anything that demands a response and attendance can be defined as an invitation. Call for entries in a competition, a request for a donation to a charity, the giving of an award, the conferring of a lecture, the commemoration of a deceased person; all these are events which are defined by an invitation. Although a telephone call could easily fulfil the same functions, the physical invitation symbolises something ingrained in Western mentality, where the cultural norm is to endow a strong value upon objects – whatever their format – and to turn them into symbols for our social lives.

In the UK before 1800, invitation cards were produced by copper plate engravers. The letterpress printer, armed only with text faces and no embellishments, could not compete with the engraver's decorative and delicate handiwork. For them, invitations for funerals, dinners and functions were an attractive economic sideline to the production of book title pages. Many funeral cards were generic; the name of the deceased and the details of time and place were filled in by hand. The iconography would be one of 'puritanical severity' (see Printed Ephemera, by John Lewis, 1962, published by W.S. Cowell).

At the turn of the 19th century, the creation of display typefaces like Fat Face and Egyptian allowed the jobbing printer and compositor to make more visually powerful work. Heavily decorative elements like frames, borders and more frivolous fonts provided the printer with an easy way to compete with the engraver's handiwork. Letterpress took over the production of printed ephemera such as invitations, and for the next 75 years it was the jobbing printer who influenced the look of the invitation, taking an otherwise artless and functional arrangement of display texts to new levels of craft.

Concepts of modern design, born at the turn of the 20th century, found their way into the printer's studio via the letterpress manifestos of the Vorticists and the reproduction of Futurist poetry. By the 1920s, modernists Theo van Doesburg and László Moholy-Nagy were using letterpress to redefine print communication. Jobbing print work became a format for the modern graphic designer. Typographers like Jan Tschichold and Herbert Bayer created some of their most unselfconscious work in the design of invitations for intimate events or for friends.

Today, art, advertising and popular culture have become visual influences on the designer's way of promoting an event. In addition, the advent of digital communication means that invitations can be sent online. Receipt and response mechanisms continue to change, as online registration takes over from reply slips. In recent years, physical invitations have acquired an additional status, transforming themselves from short-lived conveyors of data to collectible items. As it becomes increasingly challenging for invitations to stand out in the face of low attention spans and constant competition, so designs become ever more unusual. In the fashion world, for example, the imagination of designers has run wild, conjuring up precious or quirky objects-turned-invitations to lure even the most jaded fashion editor. From John Galliano's crimson ballet slipper, enclosed in a box alongside a love letter, to Alexander McQueen's mirror, razor blade, white powder and rolled-up note, there is no limit to the game of seduction and shock tactics. In these cases, the designer has had to expand his skills beyond the constraints of the print medium. Rather than type, photography and paper stock, the attention has shifted onto three-dimensional objects, textures and shapes. This means that a piece of design created with

information purposes acquires an artistic value, defying its original throwaway value. Far from becoming obsolete after the occasion has passed, such invitations are kept as an enduring reminder of the event, and are even collected by those unable to attend the event itself, perhaps in the hope that some of the cachet and glamour may rub off on them.

The message of an invitation varies according to its audience and the type of event. Wit is predominantly used for a recipient with a strong visual vocabulary and knowledge. Invitations for designers' parties, catwalk shows and the media in general need to employ any means necessary to capture attention. A designer may need to use all the methods of intrigue to provoke even the mildest curiosity from veterans of the social scene. Formality may be used by institutions or government bodies to stress not just their understanding of social conventions, but their seriousness of purpose.

Who the invitations are aimed at will also influence their conception. A limited edition poster campaign created by UK advertising agency St Luke's splashed the slogan 'Have you been invited to the Stefan Sagmeister lecture?' on prebooked sites around London. The brief required a poster to be noticed by most of those in the creative community who would have naturally been interested in a lecture by the Austrian designer. The 1,000 posters were then followed a week later by flyers and a postal invitation stating, 'You have been invited to the Stefan Sagmeister lecture.' Thousands would have passed the posters without recognising the name. But for those who did, receiving the invitation was confirmation of membership of a circle whose exclusivity had been publicly advertised.

The following chapters look at the main issues surrounding the design of invitations and how designers from around the world have tackled them, whether as an interpretation of a client brief or for their own, self-promotional intentions. 'Medium' looks at the various formats invitations may take, while 'Message' considers the ways in which verbal and visual languages are employed to communicate. 'Target' focuses on how designers have made invitations appropriate for specific audiences, and 'Response' discusses the various ways in which designers have endeavoured to secure a reply. 'Lifecycle' features invitations to events such as memorials, birthdays and marriages. Each example shows how an aesthetically pleasing object can interact with the recipient and convey the necessary information. Finally, a rundown of practical tips and a selection of work-in-progress case studies reveal the stages of designing an invitation. They show possible routes and indicate some useful hints. Most of the examples shown within the specific chapters could easily have been included in any other chapter of the book. So not only is the medium interchangeable with the message in invitation design, but often the message becomes the target itself, which in turn can determine response mechanisms.

The design of an invitation may suffer certain constraints, like cost and formatting limitations due to the need to go through the mail, and the invitation may have just one essential job, to attract recipients to an event, but as the examples in this book show, there are many tantalising ways of doing it.

Medium

Invitations come in multiple guises. The medium is open to interpretation as designers take it upon themselves to play with formats, textures and materials. Although cards with a sans serif typeface set on a white background are still commonplace, there is an increasing use of illustration, photography, collage, die-cut and foil-blocking techniques. The renewal of interest in letterpress print reveals that hand-crafted invitations are ever more desirable in this predominantly digital age.

There has also been a reappraisal of the textural possibilities in invitation design. Examples included here underline the importance of the tactile experience: cloth, wood, vinyl, stainless steel, special papers, PVC and suede. Expanding the range of materials becomes a novelty, a trusted technique to stimulate the senses of the recipient.

The trend towards glamour has been the main instigator for transforming the fashion world's catwalk show invitations into objects appreciated in their own right. The fashion invitations included in this chapter are not just advertising a season's collection; they have been endowed with a value that survives long after the event is finished. They become ornamental or acquire collectible status. Formats and sizes can also be experimented with. Leaflets, direct mailers, business cards, posters and even catalogues can all be transformed into invitations.

Because the client often regards the design of an invitation as a less important commission than other projects, designers work within constraints of time and budget. However tight the brief, there is always space for creativity. Stefan Sagmeister's controversial body invitation to the 1999 American Institute of Graphic Arts lecture (page 25), has become a legend of its own making. The words of the invitation, mesmerisingly scratched into his skin, announce an intent and a message more powerful than any graphic design lecture.

Event: Habitat press launches Spring/Summer 1996, Autumn/Winter 1996, Christmas 1996 and Spring/Summer 1997
Designer: Graphic Thought Facility, UK. Photography by Andrew Penketh. Spring/Summer 1997 illustrations by Nick Higgins
Medium: Posters

London-based design group Graphic Thought Facility (GTF) started working with retailer Habitat in 1996. The brief for their first press invitation was to convey the change in the retailer's direction with an emphasis on 'back to basics'; something that would express the essence of the season's collection through shape and materials rather than embellishments. A poster-sized invitation was created to coincide with a press release, sent out with the invitation. The idea was to create a consistency of format and narrative, a story started on the invitation and completed in the message of the press release. In tactile terms, the poster allows for a lavishness that a typical A5 format would otherwise restrain.

habitat preview
spring/summer 1996 collection

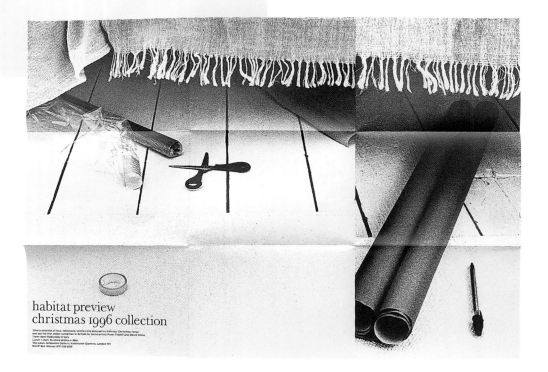

habitat preview
christmas 1996 collection

The first invitation is for Spring/Summer 1996, a series of outlined abstract shapes inspired by that season's materials. The Autumn/Winter 1996 invitation shows a modular seat unit made of packaging, promoting simplicity and the basic idea of using one thing as another. The Christmas 1996 preview invitation visualises the idea of hiding presents and wrapping paper under the bed, while the Spring/Summer 1997 invitation features an over-printed image of stacked chairs.

GTF found that designing for the press inevitably conditions the design, as journalists are often overexposed to and jaded by design-savvy invitations. The invitation has to work that extra bit harder and be slightly more special. A poster format allows for collectibility and longer life span. Because it is assumed that the press will be able to spot upcoming trends, the language of the invitations can afford to be suggestive rather than obviously direct. The design of these press invitations allows for the provision of basic information and a suggestion of the season's collection. The bulk of the story is then unveiled by the complimentary press pack.

Event: Artomatic and Royal Mail call-for-entries and invitation to 'Open Up' exhibition, 2001
Designer: B+B, UK
Printer: Artomatic, UK
Medium: N-Flute corrugated board

The Royal Mail sponsored specialist printer and retailer Artomatic to convey the potential of direct mail to the creative industry as a medium, highlighting its strengths and the benefits of using unusual materials and production processes. Artomatic commissioned UK design group B+B to create an invitation that called for designers worldwide to submit innovative examples of direct mail, which would then be featured in an exhibition. Artomatic and Royal Mail co-hosted the submissions process, selection and exhibition.

B+B decided to employ basic forms of postage and packaging to inform the design of all promotional material, such as packing boxes, labels, stickers and wire mesh pigeon holes. The first item sent out was a call-for-entries pack – a vacuum-flat-packed N-Flute box with descriptive text running on the inside and outside. Inside was a cellophane bag containing a voucher, a spare address label and an entry form printed on the same material that Royal Mail uses for Recorded or Special Delivery labels. The recipients could construct the box, insert their entries and mail the box back.

The invitations for the 'Open Up' exhibition itself were mini versions of the call-for-entries pack but this time sent out as a fully constructed box. To read the information regarding the event, the box had to be deconstructed. White invitations were sent out for a series of special viewing evenings, while blue ones were for the private view.

Finally, for the exhibition B+B continued the theme by creating a 2m-high version of the box for the window display. Wire pigeon holes were used to house the exhibits, and the entry forms were stuck onto Manilla labels to describe the work on show.

Artomatic, in association with Royal Mail host OPEN UP their first exhibition showcasing the best in concept, design and production in Direct Mail from across the globe →

ARTOMATIC   Royal Mail®

You are invited
to attend one
of three special
evenings at
Artomatic

Wednesday 25 April
to Friday 27 April
Open until 9.00pm

The show will continue
until Thursday 3 May
10.00 – 5.00pm

OPEN HERE

OPEN HERE

In association
with Royal Mail,
Artomatic hosts
OPEN UP their
first exhibition
of Direct Mail
celebrating the
best in concepts,
design and
production from
across the globe

DESIGNED BY B+B

Admits one

OPEN UP
Tuesday
24 April 2001
6.30 – 10.00pm
at Artomatic

Artomatic
13/14 Great
Sutton Street
London, EC1

RSVP
Artomatic
T 020 7566 0171
E OpenUp@artomatic.co.uk

OPEN HERE

OPEN HERE

In association
with Royal Mail,
Artomatic hosts
OPEN UP their
first exhibition
of Direct Mail
celebrating the
best in concepts,
design and
production from
across the globe

DESIGNED BY B+B

Event: Jeremy Scott fashion shows Spring/Summer 1998, Spring/Summer 1999 and Autumn/Winter 2000
Designer: M/M, France
Medium: One-colour print posters

M/M is a Paris-based design group which works with many fashion clients such as Martine Sitbon, Jeremy Scott and Yohji Yamamoto. M/M has recently designed the new book Pictures, for Icelandic songstress Björk. The three invitations designed for Jeremy Scott display a constant theme in approach and format. Each season, M/M designs the invitation as a 'pamphlet' in poster size. The invitation carries a 'slogan' and is printed with one colour only to emphasise the bold messaging. The slogan provides the mood for the show and is reflected in that season's collections.

Spring/Summer 1998 carries the slogan 'Viva Avant Garde', the Spring/Summer 1999 is 'Duty Free Glamour', while Autumn/Winter 2000 is 'A Tale of 3 cities'.

Medium

Event: HKF yearly golf tournament, 1997
Designer: Factor Design, Germany.
Illustrations by Uwe Melichar.
Copywritten by Hannah S. Pricke
Medium: Mixed materials

HKF is a German advertising agency which annually sponsors a golf tournament for its clients and friends. Every year, Factor Design is asked to create the invitations as well as related packaging and certificates. The client's brief was to provide something unusual and unique that recipients wouldn't throw away.

The solution was to design an invitation that resembled an old hiking map, that guests could use to familiarise themselves with the course prior to the start of the competition.

Inside the thick, recycled paper slipcase is a tiny die-cut golf player that can be used as a bookmark or as a reminder that the

golf tournament is imminent. A small format was chosen so the guests could easily pocket the map during the tournament. The map has a handmade feel to it and was produced on waterproof paper. The amusing copy plays with the difficulties of the course.

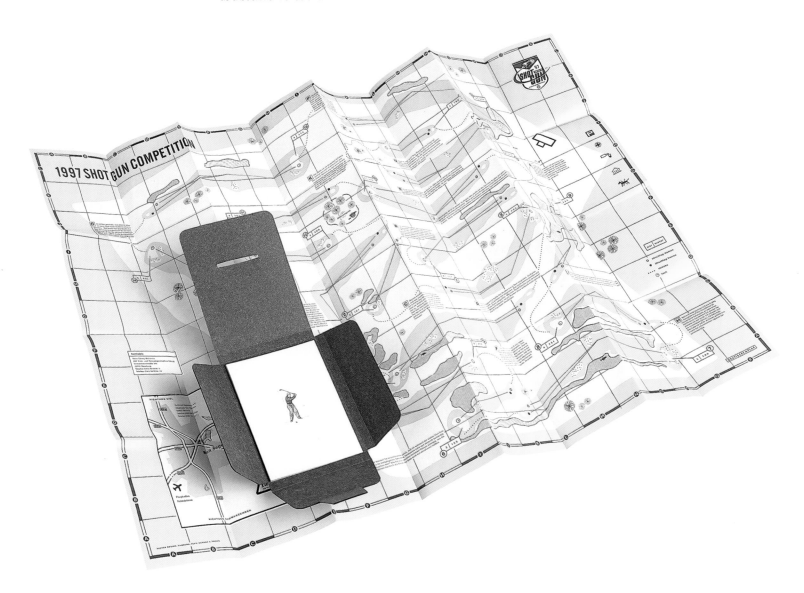

Event: International Holland Dance Festival, 1998
Designer: Studio Dumbar, Holland
Medium: Handwritten font and photography

Celebrated Dutch design group Studio Dumbar created a complete series of posters, brochures, tickets and invitations for the International Holland Dance Festival. The festival programme focused on each dancer and his or her individual qualities. Designer Bobo van Dijk tried to emphasise this personal approach by isolating high-contrast black-and-white photographs on a stark black background. Deen van Meer's photographs were cut up to create more abstract images of 'dancers' and 'sculptures'. This particular invitation was for the festival's symposium on the role of the dancer in the 20th century. The theme, 'A Dancer's Tale', and the name of the festival were set on each item in a handwrittten font.

The consistent use of the handwriting continues the personalised theme as well as recalling the fluid movements of a dancer.

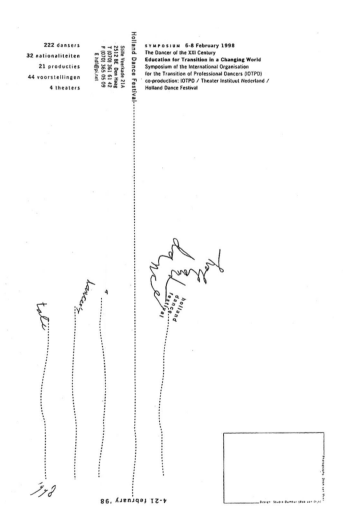

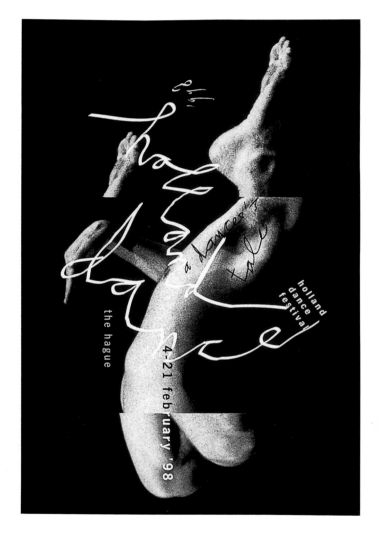

Event: Markus Lupfer Spring/Summer show at London Fashion Week, 2002
Designer: Multistorey, UK
Medium: Hot-foiled text on plastic

Design consultancy Multistorey designed a set of invitations for Markus Lupfer's Spring/Summer 2002 collection at London Fashion Week, 2001. The invitation features five different coloured credit cards printed with apparently incomprehensible text. Placing the cards next to each other in the correct order reveals the message. The colour code reflects the Markus Lupfer collection's trend towards bold colours and graphic patterns. The invitation also plays with the theme of collection and multiple pieces. The invitations were produced by Bristol Business Cards, a UK-based credit card manufacturer.

For sharpness, the text was hot-foiled rather than screen-printed. 500 sets were printed and postal tests were carried out through the UK to ensure that such a small envelope would be allowed through the mail system.

Event: Paris Fashion Week invitation, 1999
Designer: Mevis + van Deursen, Holland
Medium: Litho-printed business cards

Amsterdam-based designers Armand Mevis and Linda van Deursen created a series of invitations for the Fashion Institute, a graduate fashion programme connected to the Academy of Fine Arts in Arnhem, Holland. The students presented their work during the 1999 Paris Fashion Week. The card is large format at 42x21cm, and litho-printed in silver, green and blue with perforated tear-lines. The aim was to create an attractive, well-designed fashion invitation as an 'all-in-one' large format, which acts as a container for the smaller invitations of each student. Each participant is announced separately on the cards, so the recipient can tear off sections of the invitation and then use them as business cards for each student. The theme of each collection is also announced on the students' cards.

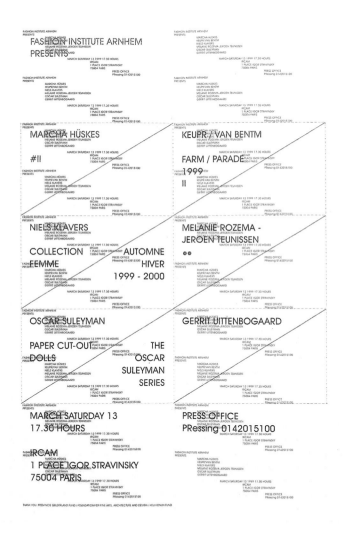

Event: Political rally for the Socialist Party during presidential elections in Catalonia, 1999
Designer: LaVista, Spain
Medium: Handwritten font on semi-transparent paper

The Spanish copy on this poster translates as 'Dialogue and creativity are the language of a country that wishes to be more a forum than a temple, a starting point more than a finishing point'. This invitation from election candidate Pasqual Maragall, mailed to Barcelona's cultural community, was one of Barcelona-based design group LaVista's various projects for the 1999 Catalan Socialist Party campaign.

Initially LaVista was asked to work with a postcard format, but once the handwritten declaration from the candidate arrived by fax, the designers felt the small size was inadequate and decided to turn it into a 59.4x42cm poster foldable to A5 size, thus giving it a dual format. The client took

little convincing to accept this. LaVista chose an inexpensive, semi-transparent paper due to budget restrictions, which allowed the mixture of handwriting, type and logos to overlap once the invitation was folded.

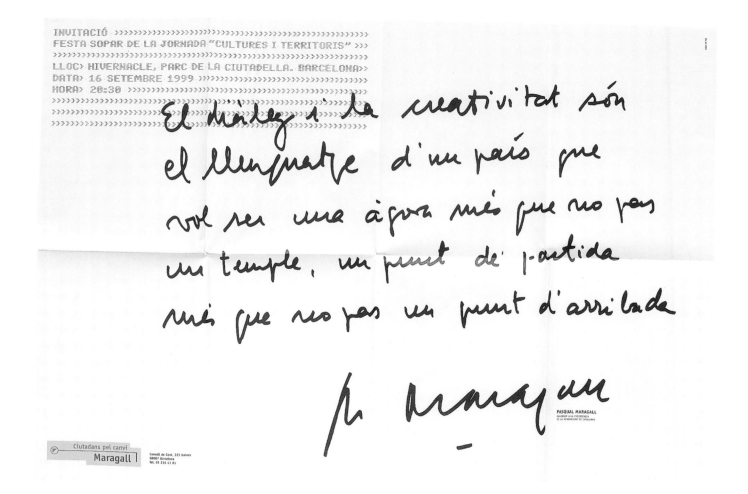

Event: Opening event for Savage
Open House, 2001
Designer: Plazm, USA
Medium: Boxboard

Portland-based design consultancy Plazm
designed the invitation to the opening of
Savage Open House, a contemporary art
gallery, as part of a brand launch that
included the naming of the gallery, livery,
marketing material and design of the
website. The aim of the design was to
emphasise community involvement through
a piece that would physically engage the
recipient with the gallery space. The die-cut
perforated invitation/mailer can be
assembled into a diagrammatic replica of
the space itself, complete with working
skylights and a floorplan. A wallet-sized
card with the entire year's event listing is
also included. All the gallery's invitations
are the same colour, size and shape.

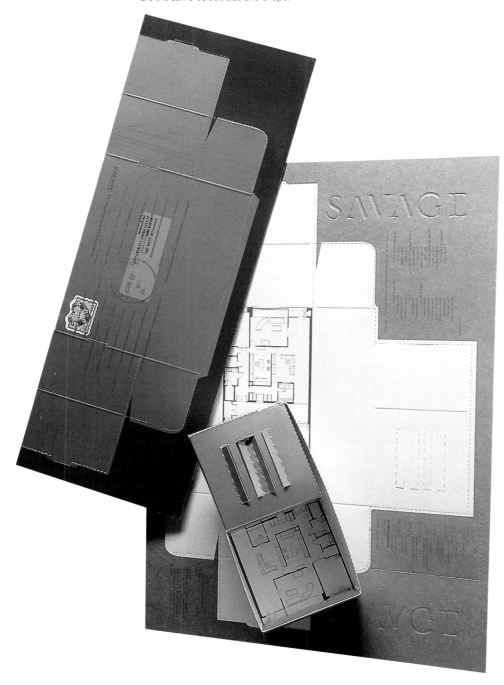

Medium

Event: American Institute of Graphic Arts lecture, 1996
Designer: Stefan Sagmeister, USA
Medium: Photograph of cow tongues and poster sheets

A precursor of Stefan Sagmeister's shocking body poster (right) is a poster depicting cow tongues, created for the American Institute of Graphic Arts (AIGA) design lecture. Like most of Sagmeister's work, it indicates a move away from digital perfection towards a more personal, hand-crafted design ethic. The two wagging tongues are an obvious symbol for the lecture's theme, 'Fresh Dialogue', a series of talks organised by the New York division of the AIGA. The initial idea was to photograph human tongues, but since their length was too short, the photographer Tom Schierlitz bought two fresh cow tongues at a local meat market and shot them with a 5x4" camera. The tongues are imposed over hand-rendered type, giving the invite a rough and organic feel. The tongues turned out to be oddly phallic, and according to Sagmeister, "We didn't mind the design but some AIGA members did." However, after trying to ask for an alternative, the AIGA sent the poster out to the other speakers for approval and it received a thumbs-up.

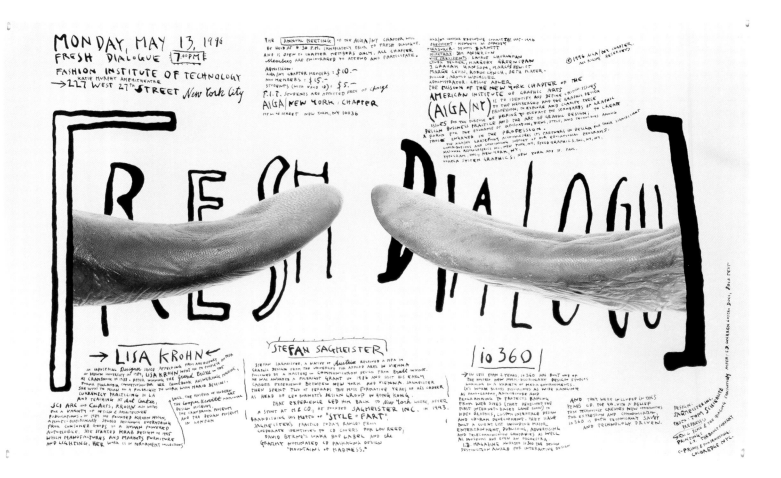

Event: American Institute of Graphic Arts lecture, 1999
Designer: Stefan Sagmeister, USA
Medium: Human body and poster sheets

Nobody has used the body more shockingly in invitation design than Sagmeister. Here his torso was used as a canvas, upon which the information was scratched into the skin as hand-drawn text. His body was then photographed, the message revealing itself as flesh wounds. According to Sagmeister, the lecture poster was intended to visualise the pain that seems to accompany most designers' projects. Ultimately the image transcends any reference to the event and becomes an engrossing example of self-mutilation. The intensity of the designer and the lengths he will go to to strengthen the message are clearly communicated here. In doing so, Sagmeister has turned the language and the medium of the invitation on its head, propelling it into a piece of graphic communication that stands alone.

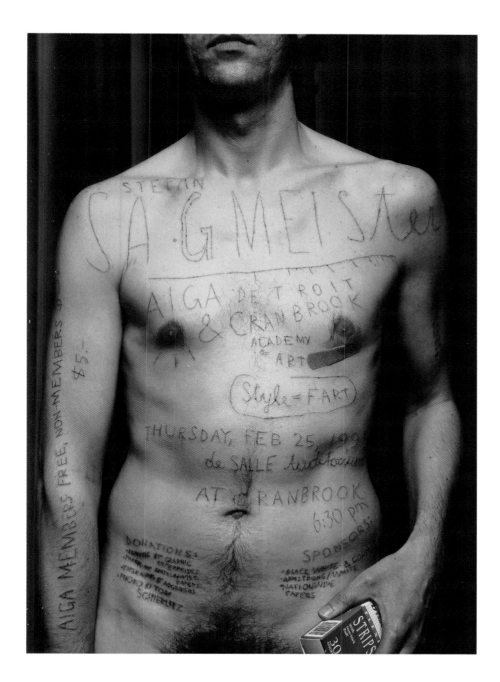

Medium

Event: A+O spring party, 1999
Designer: Factor Design, Germany
Medium: Paper, plastic and beads

The brief was to come up with a clever idea for an invitation that could be created on a low budget. Hamburg-based A+O is a public relations agency located in the same building as the design group Factor Design. The invitation for its annual spring party was created for clients and friends. The idea was to include a plastic container with 'springtime' beads which would create appropriately seasonal feelings when ingested. The advice to the guests was to swallow the beads before entering the party. The copy in the invitation plays with the springtime theme. 'Frühlingsgefühle' means spring fever, and the party was intended to celebrate the arrival of the new season after the grey and rainy winter.

FRÜHLINGS GEFÜHLE

*

* Inhalt zum Verzehr geeignet.

ANWENDUNG
Kurz vor Betreten des Frühlingsfestes auf der Zunge zergehen lassen.

WIRKUNGSWEISE
Frühlingsgefühle stellen sich unmittelbar bei Verzehr ein.

NEBENWIRKUNGEN
Prickeln in Mund- und Bauchbereich, angenehmes Herzflattern, in einigen Fällen auch Lachfältchen.

a+o

Event: The London Institute Future Map graduation show, 1999
Designer: Lucienne Roberts and Bob Wilkinson at sans+baum, UK
Medium: Invitation-catalogue, uncoated paper bag and litho-printing

Future Map is an annual show celebrating the best work of graduates from The London Institute. For the exhibition, sans+baum created uncoated paper bag invitations which were sent out shrink-wrapped. The bags listed all 50 participants on one side as well as the contributing colleges and the details of the exhibition. On the other side, it explained the rationale of the show and how to create your own catalogue. The bags were also available to visitors as they arrived. Information sheets placed next to the works could be torn off by the visitors and collected into the bag, thereby turning it into a low-tech, handmade catalogue of the show.

Essays on larger pads were also available for collection, which allowed visitors to add their own thoughts and interpretations, creating a personalised reminder of the talent on show.

Event: Craft Council exhibition, 2001
Designer: NB:Studio, UK
Medium: Perforated paper dolls

The launch of an exhibition on paper art at London's Craft Council Gallery was the theme of NB:Studio's invitation. The designers chose an ironic image by artist Charlie Thomas which shows a man and a woman dressed in hyper-realistic paper clothing. The characters were placed against a coloured background (pink for the girl and blue for the boy), and this imagery was used throughout all the printed promotional material. There is a perforation around the characters to illustrate the versatility of paper techniques. The paper bag invitation is the free entry version.

Event: Launch of Ron Arad's
Cappellone hat, 2000
Designer: Sara Fanelli, UK
Medium: Illustration

London-based illustrator Sara Fanelli
was commissioned by Italian accessories
manufacturer Alessi to create an invitation
for the launch of Cappellone, a limited
edition hat designed by Ron Arad. The
result is a foldable card illustrated with
surreal, dream-like images, which does
not give away the nature of the product.
Clues are only given on the back.
Black silhouettes derived from computer-
generated images of the hat from different
angles have been turned into animals.
The boy in the photograph is Ron Arad
as a young child. The inside text replicates
the language of a formal invitation.

Fanelli also created a surreal figure in
the centrefold, again wearing the hat.
All the illustrations were hand-drawn by
the designer and then processed by
a Mac operator.

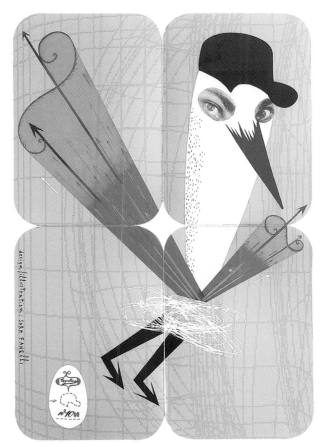

Event: Paul Smith Autumn/Winter collection, 2002
Designer: Aboud Sodano, UK
Medium: Photocopied notepaper

As a contrast to the conventional luxuriousness of most fashion invitations, Aboud Sodano created a deliberately low-tech, cheap invitation for Paul Smith's Autumn/Winter 2002 collection in Paris. The theme of the show was 'opposites', a concept the invitation also plays on. The bulk of the production budget was spent on producing bespoke tissue-lined envelopes set with an embossed Paul Smith coat of arms. For the invitation, the catwalk show details were handwritten on cheap, lined notepaper and then photocopied onto several colours of Day-Glo fluorescent paper. On the back, a hand-drawn map pinpoints the show venue.

The scribbles and corrections enhance the idea of a handmade, disposable format, and the designer also succeeds in producing an unusual contrast between envelope and invitation.

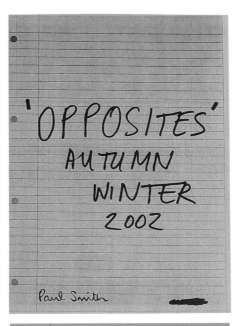

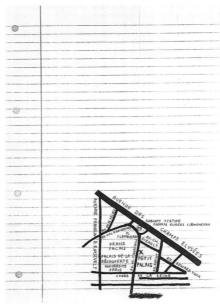

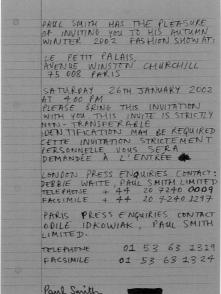

Event: Launch of the Art Directors Club book, 2001
Designer: Müller+Hess, Switzerland
Medium: Photography and poster

Swiss design group Müller+Hess was commissioned to produce an invitation for the launch of the Art Directors Club book 2001, which it also designed. Because the book's theme is about winners, Müller+Hess decided to concentrate on the iconography of losers. Having sourced over 45,000 photographs from archives all over the world, it published a selection in the book. The photograph selected for the invitation is a typical 'last man standing' figure at a party when everyone else has long gone home. The picture contains a level of tragic sadness which contrasts with the event promoted by the invitation, a fun party in a disused warehouse. The poster format was chosen because the designers felt the size added gravitas to the image.

Event: Sign Kommunikation office-warming, 2001
Designer: Sign Kommunikation GmbH, Germany
Medium: Communal illustrated puzzle

When Frankfurt-based design group Sign Kommunikation decided to have an office-warming party, it formed a special party committee with members of the studio. The initial idea was for the nine party organisers to each create an invitation as an individual design, set as a fragment of an outlined drawing of the actual office space. The illustration was also used as signage, so that recipients who only received one copy would realise the card was part of a larger puzzle. Those on more than one mail list received numerous copies, which could be assembled into the larger picture, allowing them to discover the details.

On the back of each invitation is the name of each recipient, and the appropriate checkbox is ticked to indicate who sent out the invitation.

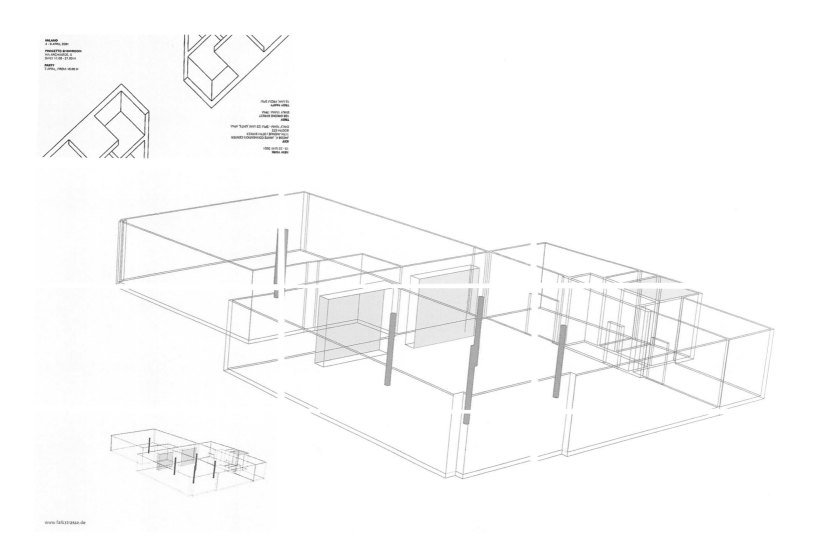

www.falkstrasse.de

Event: Takashi Murakami exhibition, 2001
Designer: Takaya Goto, USA
Medium: Die-cut and laminated paper

Created by New York-based Japanese designer Takaya Goto, this laminated mushroom-shaped invitation was for an exhibition of the work of artist Takashi Murakami. According to the designer, the bright, candy colours (including turquoise, yellow, green and white) and playful shapes (swirls, loops and flirtatious eyelashes) aim to capture the essence of Murakami's work, which is translated here as a cute and playful vision with a subtly erotic undertone. The invitation stays intentionally clear of the darker side of Murakami's work. The 8x18cm invitation was laminated to make the invitation strong enough to be used as a bookmark.

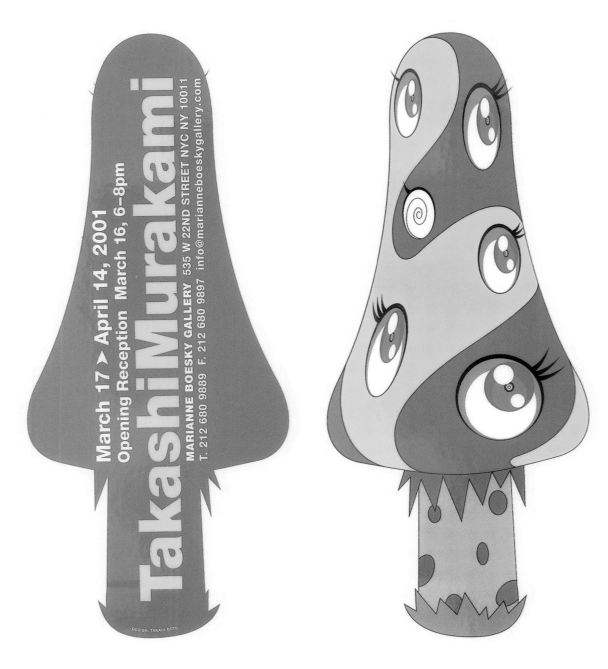

TakashiMurakami

March 17 ▶ April 14, 2001
Opening Reception March 16, 6–8pm

MARIANNE BOESKY GALLERY 535 W 22ND STREET NYC NY 10011
T. 212 680 9889 F. 212 680 9897 info@marianneboeskygallery.com

DESIGN: TAKAYA GOTO

Event: 'Men & Shapes' exhibition at The Gallery at Pentagram, 2000
Designer: Anthony Burrill, UK
Medium: Letterpress on strawboard

Designer Anthony Burrill used letterpress print for the invitation to a private view of his 'Men & Shapes' exhibition of prints held at London's Pentagram Gallery. The brutal quality of the invitation reflects the industrial imagery of the work on show. Burrill chose letterpress as a technique because of its associations with reproduction on cardboard boxes. The two-colour artwork was created as two-colour separations, which were converted into metal print plates. Strawboard, a cheap card conventionally used for backing pads, is uncoated and soaks up ink, creating a very dense black. The card accepts a heavy impression from the letterpress block. As a technique, letterpress is no longer the mainstream printing process it was. Apart from the specialised graphic design studios, printers that produce letterpress are usually local, specialising in business cards or other short-run ephemera. The letterpress printers used here are based in south Wimbledon in London.

'NO MESS LINE PAINTING'
Anthony Burrill
020 8674 3707

MEN & SHAPES

WORK BY ANTHONY BURRILL
21 AUGUST TO 29 SEPTEMBER 2000
PRIVATE VIEW WEDNESDAY 6 SEPTEMBER 6.30 TO 8PM
THE GALLERY AT PENTAGRAM DESIGN
11 NEEDHAM ROAD LONDON W11 2RP
TELEPHONE 020 7229 3477

Event: Simon Carter Menswear collection show, 2002
Designer: Multistorey, UK
Medium: Linen embossed paper, folded into a miniature shirt

Multistorey duo Harry Woodrow and Rhonda Drakeford created and folded 200 origami invitations for the launch of menswear designer Simon Carter's Spring/Summer 2002 collection. The shirt-shaped invitation is constructed from one A4 sheet printed one side only with purple gingham on the bias, a key seasonal pattern from the collection. The shirt sits in a navy blue pinstripe envelope to emphasise that tailored suits are included in the season's range. The text is displayed on the back of the shirt and is set on the bias to increase legibility and emphasise the detail of the pattern. A linen-embossed Zanders paper adds to the cloth effect, as does the Fedrigoni envelope paper, appropriately named Savile Row Pinstripe.

SIMON CARTER MENSWEAR

PRESS OPEN DAY
TO PREVIEW S/S 2002

WEDNESDAY 3 OCTOBER - 9AM TO 6PM
THURSDAY 4 OCTOBER - MIDDAY TO 6PM

SIMON CARTER SHOP AND SHOWROOM:
15 QUADRANT ARCADE
80-82 REGENT STREET
LONDON W1

RSVP TO ROSANNA TICH PR
T: 020 7729 7010 F: 020 7729 5332
E: rossana@rossanatich.co.uk

STATING THE TIME YOU WISH TO VISIT

Invitation Design: Multistorey

Event: University of Westminster fashion show, 1997
Designer: Maxine Law, UK
Medium: Telegram card and ribbon

Maxine Law used the urgent messaging tone and the quaint, old-fashioned medium of a telegram card for the University of Westminster BA Fashion catwalk show. The ribbons carrying the text were produced by Adastra labels, a manufacturer specialising in creating woven labels for garments. The designer provides the information of the event using the language of telegrams, such as stop divisions and equal signs. The text continues on the back of the invitation. The invitation bears classic telegram markings as well as faux franking, alongside the sponsors of the show. Below on the front of the card is a set of further instructions, explaining to the invitees that they can, as with real

telegrams, telephone the RSVP line for 'free repetition of doubtful words', a clever variation on response mechanisms.

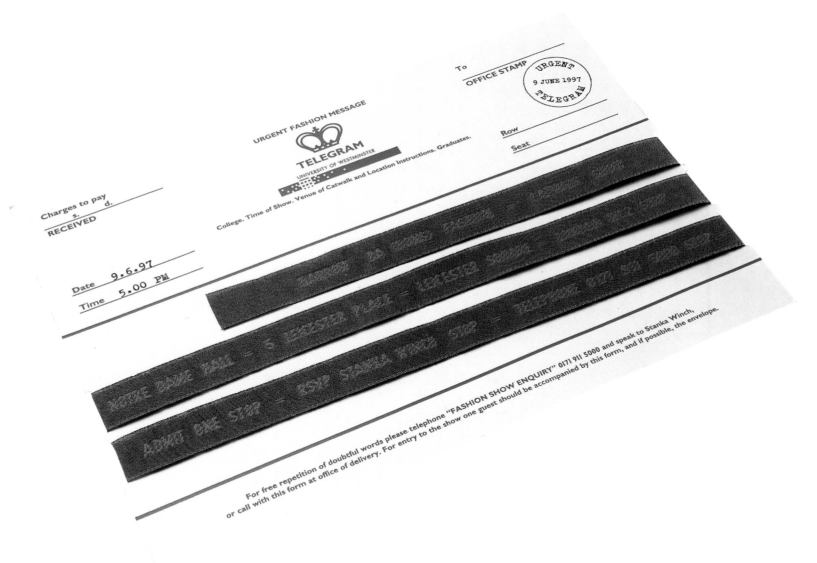

Event: British Design & Art Direction
Annual Show, 2000
Designer: SEA, UK
Medium: Cardboard and PVC

London-based design group SEA was
appointed for two years in succession to
design all the print and exhibition design
for the British Design & Art Direction Annual
Show. The show includes all the nominated
and award-winning work from the design
and advertising categories. For the 2000
edition, the idea was to centre the
exhibition around typographic
constructions spelling out the word
'annual'. MDF, perspex and steel formed
the letters of the exhibition graphics and
this idea was transferred to the invitation,
set in a cardboard slipcase with screen-
printed, malleable plastic rolled inside.
The plastic unravels and reveals
explanations of elements of the event.

In this way, the invitation became a taster
and a compact miniature example of
the show, using similar techniques,
materials and colours.

Event: Fundraising picnic for the Mecklenburger State Theatre, 1997
Designer: Eggers+Diapers, Germany
Medium: Cloth napkin and paper

A fundraising picnic event combined with the birthday of the designer's father, became the occasion for a celebration. The event involved over 100 people and took place in an idyllic lakeside setting, which included a large marquee and a live orchestra. The main concern of the brief was to include the important fundraising element within the more personal, birthday aspect. The solution was to side-step both and focus instead on the attractive nature of the event, a lakeside picnic. The napkin idea fulfils several criteria: it focuses attention on the culinary nature of the fundraiser; the witty use of an unusual object makes the invitation engaging and memorable; and it is functionally light and can be posted

without fear of wear and tear. The idea was crowned with the logical addition of a paper 'serviette ring' carrying the text. The response to the invitation was enthusiastic, both in terms of attendance and forthcoming donations.

EINLADUNG

ANLÄßLICH MEINES 60.GEBURTSTAGES LADE
ICH EIN ZU EINEM PICKNICK MIT DEM
STREICHQUARTETT DER MECKLENBURGISCHEN
STAATSKAPELLE IM FRANKENHORST 7
AM ZIEGELSEE IN SCHWERIN

Wer der Einladung folgen möchte, finde sich
am 9.8.1997 um 10.45 Uhr an der Anlegebrücke der
Weißen Flotte gegenüber dem Schweriner Schloß ein

Event: Rankin/GF Smith event, 1998
Designer: SEA, UK
Medium: Mixed materials

The Rankin/GF Smith event was the first in a series designed to help launch a range of uncoated papers by paper company GF Smith. The idea was to invite the fashion photographer Rankin to talk about his work at London eaterie East One. The audience was photographed and the result was a swatch book of the night mixed with photographs from Rankin's 'star' list. The invitation, created by London design group SEA, was only sent out to a limited guestlist, denoting the exclusivity of the event. It was designed to be immediately noticed. The plastic wrap, covering the camera-shaped box inside, suggests the shape and format of the book-to-be. The paper printed inside shows Rankin's shots with information about the event.

Event: 50th birthday party, 1997
Designer: Dotzerodesign, USA
Medium: Teaser card silkscreened on wood, with booklet and golf ball

A surprise birthday party was planned for Tom Devlin, the owner of a nearly completed world-class golf course. His wife asked Portland-based Dotzerodesign to create a teaser postcard to be sent out before the actual invitation. Since the clubhouse at the course was a timber-framed building, the designers created a teaser card silkscreened onto wood. For the invitation, a booklet was designed with an alternative copyline about the party on each right-hand page. On each left-hand side is a photograph documenting Tom's life, the first showing him as a baby in his mother's arms and the last with his wife. The entire book has a hole drilled in the middle of it to hold a golf ball, set with text denoting name

and birth date. The whole package was set in paper grass inside a box. The box was also screen-printed in one colour.

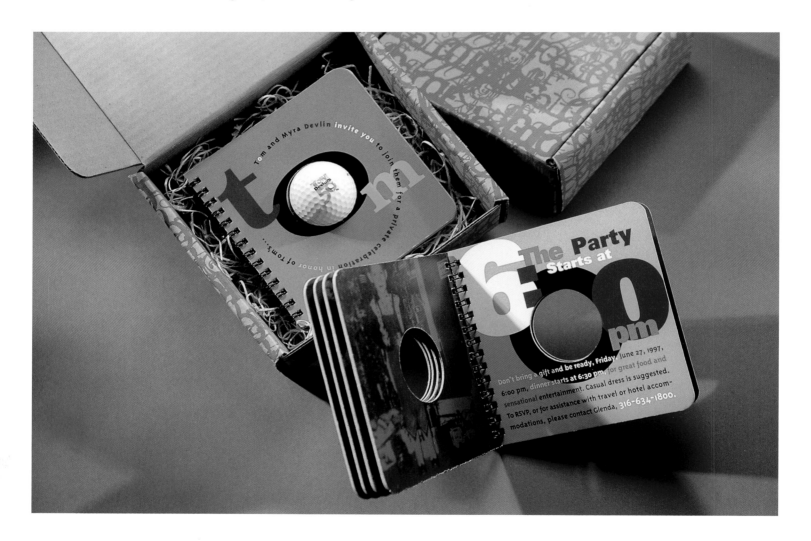

Event: 40th birthday party, 1999
Designer: David Hillman, partner at Pentagram, UK. Design assistant Liza Enebeis
Medium: 7 inch record with label

Pentagram was commissioned to design an invitation for client Alison Canning's 40th birthday party. Alison wanted an invitation that would reflect the 1960s, the era in which she grew up, as well as her enthusiasm for music. Pentagram chose a 7 inch record, sourcing over 200 decorative 1960s labels. The result is a pastiche on some of the era's best known record labels such as Decca, CBS, EMI, Phonogram, HMV, RCA and Pye.

Details of the event were printed on each side of the label; the venue and dress code featuring on the A side and the evening's programme on the B side. The label has a custom-designed record company logo and the title of the imaginary song is

'Life begins at 40'. The authenticity and vintage look are achieved through traditional printing techniques.

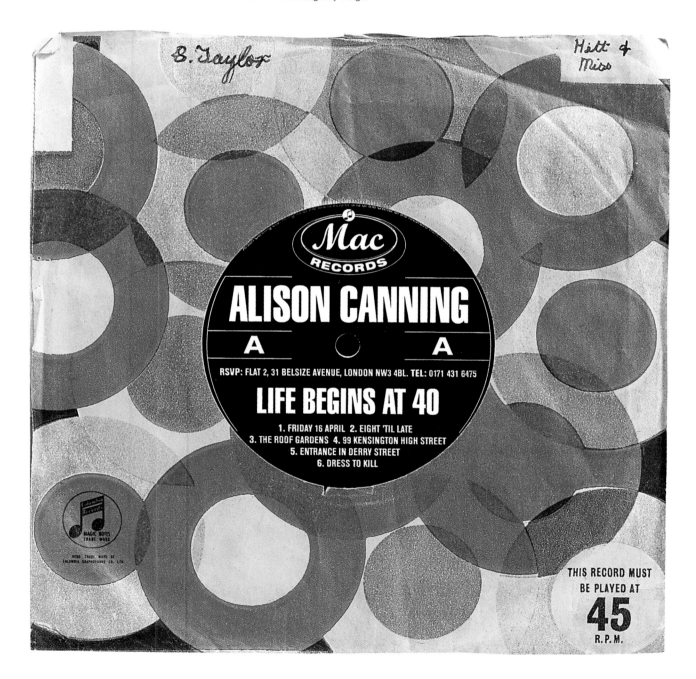

Event: Birthday party for Maya Polsky, 2001
Designer: Boxer Design, USA
Medium: Feather boa, card and box

Ms Maya Polsky, a Chicago art dealer, approached Eileen Boxer of New York-based Boxer Design to create a dark and provocative invitation for her birthday. Boxer Design had previously created an invitation for the Pierre Molinier exhibition at the Ubu Gallery which involved a black stocking. While Maya wanted a similar stocking, Boxer convinced her that they could conjure up the same feeling of seduction but with a new idea. Invitees received a gold-painted corrugated cube in the mail, the label discreetly indicating that it was an invitation. Once the box is opened, the recipient sees a simple, letterpress card, a gold cord and lots of feathers. When the card is pulled out of the box, the cord reveals a long feather boa.

The client was so thrilled with the concept, she decided to give her party a 'feather boa' dress code. Several guests wore their boas to the event. Sourcing the feathers was easy, but Boxer could not find any gold mailing boxes, so had to ask a furniture finisher to spray paint on some standard ones.

AN INVITATION

THE STAGE IS SET
PLEASE JOIN US IN CELEBRATING
MAYA'S BIRTHDAY
SATURDAY, APRIL 28, 2001
SEVEN O'CLOCK

THE CASINO
195 EAST DELAWARE PLACE
CHICAGO

RSVP: 312 440 0055
DRESS: FEATHER BOA
NO GIFTS PLEASE

Event: Launch of Fable magazine, 2001
Designer: The Farm, UK
Medium: Box, feather and pin

A delicate and slim handmade box, reminiscent of jewellery packaging, was the format chosen for an invitation to the launch of Fable magazine, an upmarket lifestyle publication for gay men and women. Inside the box, a white script on a suspended transparent film is revealed, under which lies a glossy black feather, the recipient's passport to the venue.

London design group The Farm was asked to produce an invitation that would be sensual, precious and suggest an evening of pure indulgence. The limited edition invitation was sent out to celebrities and designers. The Farm was also asked to art direct the launch evening in a

louche style. The evening featured installations, performances and a series of fables written on parchment and attached to feathers.

Medium

Event: Mulberry Autumn/Winter collection show, 2001
Designer: Four IV, UK
Medium: Screen-printed on suede

Traditionally a luxury UK leather goods brand, Mulberry went through a complete revamp in 2001, repositioning itself as a desirable fashion label. London-based retail and branding design group Four IV designed this invitation for a preview of the label's Autumn/Winter 2001 collection, attended by buyers. The invitation was intended to provide a flavour of Mulberry's new direction, reflecting the developments of a brand which had not changed since 1971.

A scroll of chocolate brown suede was screen-printed in gold with the dates, time and venue. The branding was kept minimal, with the Mulberry name appearing on the swing tag threaded onto a leather strand and bound around the rolled-up invitation. The design hints at a more contemporary future for Mulberry while reinforcing the heritage of Englishness and pure quality through its luxurious, sensuous texture.

MULBERRY AUTUMN/WINTER COLLECTION 2001

Mulberry are delighted to invite you to view the new Ladies Ready to Wear Collection at 41/42 New Bond Street London on 15/16th February. By appointment only. RSVP to Tessa Eles-Brown: tel 020 7409 3607 fax 020 7491 2518 and email Tessab@mulberry-england.co.uk

Event: Tesco business lunch, 2001
Designer: Andrew Benson at Bloomberg, UK
Medium: Lunch box, crisps, carton of orange juice and digitally printed receipt

Bloomberg's design team was asked to create an invitation for a business lunch event with guest speaker Terry Leahy, CEO of the supermarket giant Tesco. The invitation was sent out to a selected group of CEOs in the City of London and had to both be appropriate to the subject and create interest among the recipients.

The solution was to create an invitation with a theme that was common to both the speaker and the event. The actual invitation takes the format of a Tesco till receipt, splitting the wording into items and highlighting in red the more important details such as time and date.

The packaging consisted of a lunch box with a branded sticker and inside it, some Tesco food products. The lunch motif was based on the Tesco logo and the fonts used for the receipts were the ones used on actual till printouts.

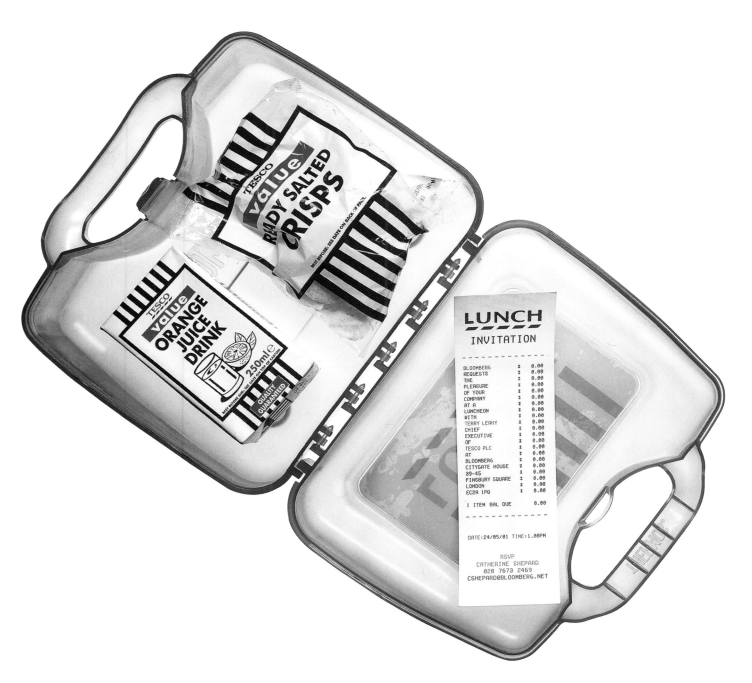

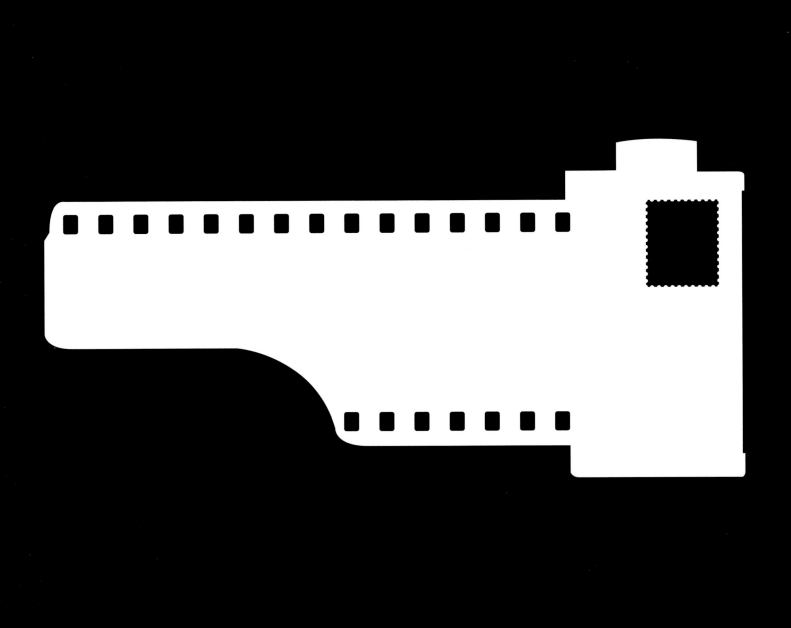

Message

Should the message contained in an invitation follow the rules of straightforward and direct communication, or is the real message between the lines? Aside from other elements such as reply requests, an invitation is founded on the factual trilogy of 'what', 'when' and 'where'. Yet the way an invitation is expressed varies according to the intent of the sender and the complex social environment in which he, she or it is operating.

A well-designed invitation employs a language that reflects the essence of the event: a dry, informative tone may be right for a business lecture or a conference, while popular culture jargon may work for clubs and concert events. Formal and diplomatic invitations are traditionally written in third person with details supplied about dress code. Here, rules are strict, and assume the recipient's prior knowledge of their convention. For informal invitations, half the pleasure is subverting the rules. Irony, wit and intrigue may all be the favoured instruments of persuasion, clever devices to attract the attention of even the most exhausted party hack. Often, an intimate and conspiratorial tone is adopted as a means to denote exclusivity. Other invitations may suggest that all are welcome by the use of a more impersonal tone.

In design terms, the adoption of certain visual metaphors or typographic styles also forms the basis of communication. It can help the recipient of the invitation to decipher the nature of the event and decide if attendance is worthy. For example, a graphic device, like the perforated grid designed by Dutch group Experimental Jetset (page 76) mirrors the gallery space of the event, while design group Blast's 1950s-style illustrations suggest a playful nostalgia (page 74). Techniques like foil-blocking or letterpress can evoke tradition or be used in a more radical way. Ultimately what is important is a certain level of correspondence between that being promised and that which is staged.

Event: The Mill Christmas party, 2000
Designer: Made Thought, UK
Message: A quirky invitation hints at a fun event

Design consultancy Made Thought produced two versions of this invitation for London-based production company The Mill. The first featured a series of snowflakes embossed on white uncoated card, with seasonal greetings set in Neue Helvetica. The second version was an invitation to the Christmas party, sent out only to a selected list. The aim was to create an amusing invitation, without it being too gimmicky. Enclosed is a cardboard insert with a bespoke detachable stainless-steel bottle opener. Rather than straightforward text, Made Thought designed three humorous diagrams depicting 'the instructions' to the party. The bottle opener is both a guest pass and an asset at the party, since all the beer bottles at the bar were served closed.

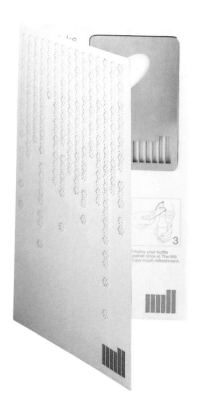

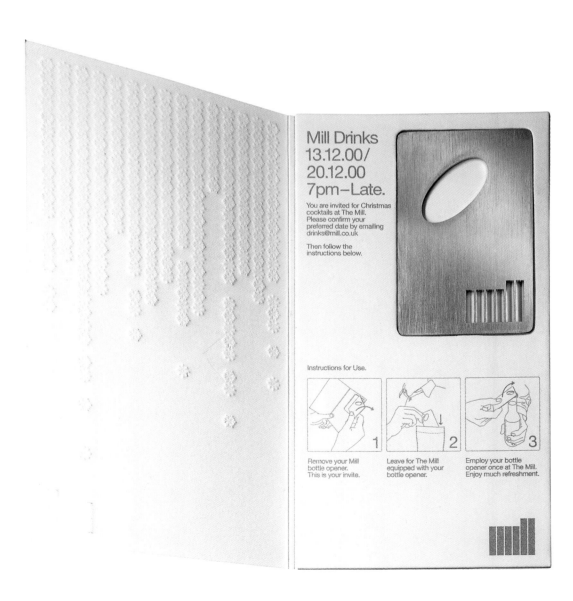

Mill Drinks
13.12.00/
20.12.00
7pm–Late.

You are invited for Christmas cocktails at The Mill. Please confirm your preferred date by emailing drinks@mill.co.uk

Then follow the instructions below.

Instructions for Use.

1 Remove your Mill bottle opener. This is your invite.

2 Leave for The Mill equipped with your bottle opener.

3 Employ your bottle opener once at The Mill. Enjoy much refreshment.

Event: 'Snapshots: The Extraordinary Ordinary' exhibition, 2000
Designer: Boxer Design, USA
Message: A chalk-written invitation

For 'Snapshots: The Extraordinary Ordinary' exhibition held at the Ubu Gallery in New York, Boxer Design sent out to each guest an original print of a snapshot photograph. Although the print gives the impression of being someone else's casual snap, further inspection reveals a carefully staged set. The writing on the blackboard in the photo is actually details of the event. The shadow seen in the picture is one of the gallery's partners, posing on the ladder used to position the camera for the shoot. Although it has the quality of a cheap camera shot, the task of lighting the blackboard in order that the chalk text could be seen proved very labour-intensive.

Boxer Design wanted to use fibre-based photograph paper with old-fashioned sculpted edges, but that was not economically viable. The final effect is still one of casual shabbiness, helped by the black-and-white print quality.

Event: A.P.C. slide show, 2002
Designer: Rik Bas Backer, France
Message: One-off invitations reflect individuality

Several invitations were created for the same event, a slide show for French fashion label A.P.C. The organisers wanted the show's theme to be a surprise for their guests, so the invitation was designed to look like a normal invitation to a catwalk show. Because the venue couldn't hold all the people invited, two separate slide show sessions were planned. A.P.C. founder and designer, Jean Touitou, communications director Emmanuel Bérard and musical director Judith Sraer attended a printer's session together for a collaborative 'ink mixing session', directly on the litho plate and printing.

The design idea came from cheap printing techniques used up until the early 1960s for poster work. But this time the idea was used to create a random, handmade effect.

The process allowed multiple colour variations for one print run on a large number of invitations. According to the designer, the number of people involved helped create an invitation that reflects a spirit of randomness. As a result, no two invitations sent out were alike, the message being that no person resembles another.

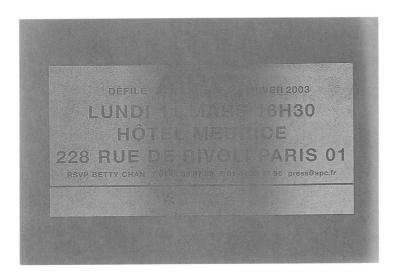 

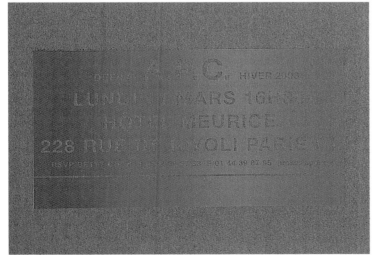

Event: Opening of Utrecht
City Hall, 2000
Designer: Anker Strijbos, Holland
Message: A formal invitation designed
for multiple events

Dutch design group Anker Strijbos
was asked to create an invitation for
the reopening of Utrecht's City Hall, after
a renovation of the building by Spanish
architect Enric Miralles. The brief required
an invitation for different groups of visitors
to various events: special guests at
the official opening by Queen Beatrix,
the personnel of the City Hall and the
inhabitants of Utrecht. Therefore, the
design of the invitation had to appeal
to all three groups and reflect the quality
and atmosphere of the renewed building.
Anker Strijbos designed three different
inlays for each of the groups. Each inlay
has a unique colour and alternative text
denoting the different days of each
group's activities for the show.

The information can be viewed by peering
through a hole in the cover of the invitation.
The language used connotes a grand
occasion, and is threaded through with
notes on the building and activities held
during the opening days. The cover is
made of rough paper, intended to express
the unfinished character of the building.
The handwritten notes on the front and
back of the invitation are remarks made
by Miralles.

Event: International Fabrica conference, 2002
Designer: Oscar Mariné at OMB, Spain
Message: A familiar Spanish catchphrase is reworded for effect

Oscar Mariné's career as a Spanish designer has always been closely associated with La Movida, the cultural and artistic movement that shook Madrid in the early 1980s. Film director Pedro Almodóvar was arguably the most successful character to emerge from La Movida, and Mariné has often collaborated with him, illustrating his film posters. In particular, Mariné was involved in the design of an underground magazine called Madrid Me Mata (Madrid Kills Me). Over the years, this catchphrase has become quite popular in Spain, and has even become a vehicle for a range of merchandising. When Mariné was invited to speak at a conference in Lisbon, organised by Fabrica, Benetton's design centre, he designed the postcard invitation on which he rephrased the familiar catchphrase into 'Lisbon Me Mata' ('Lisbon Kills Me'). The audience immediately associated the phrase, typography and the use of colour with Mariné's design legacy.

LISBOA ME MATA

(Y PESSOA TAMBIEN.)

Oscar Mariné na Fabrica Features

Event: Exhibition of Irish artists at London's Heathrow Airport, 1994
Designer: Mette Heinz at Atelier Works, UK
Message: A passport invitation mimics the language of travel

The UK Public Art Development Trust organised an exhibition by Irish artists, whose works were hung in the corridors of London's Heathrow Airport Terminal One. Everyone attending the private view needed security clearance by the airport in order to access the exhibition. Having an open brief, Atelier Works decided to turn the invitation into an old-fashioned British passport. The language – both written and typographic – mimics the old, pre-European British passports as far as possible. The invitation was produced using a dark, royal blue card for the cover, with distinctive rounded cut-out windows, and thin white paper with a specially made security pattern for the text pages.

Since there wasn't enough time or money to print the sponsor's logo with a rubber stamp, the designer had to fake the effect of a stamp using conventional offset litho-printing.

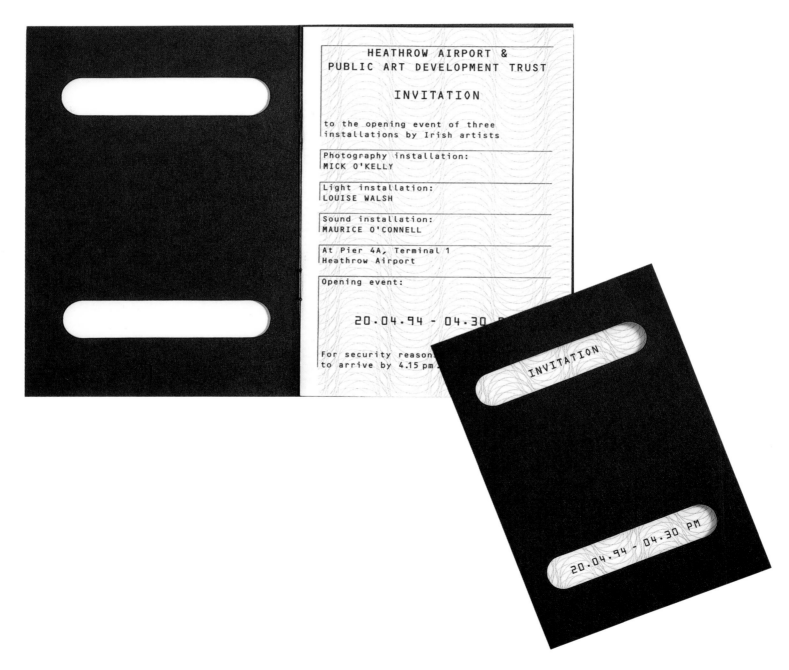

Event: Party for the EON Centre for Health and Wellbeing, 2002
Designer: Vince Frost, UK
Printer: Artomatic, UK
Message: Positive slogans for a health centre

The invitation's expensive production, including multiple die-cuts and folds, is a reflection of the client's emphasis on presenting the vision for the EON Centre for Health and Wellbeing. Designer Vince Frost wanted a Day-Glo print effect which he mocked up for the client using very fine rub-downs. Day-Glo ink is very thick and needed a coarse mesh to lay the ink down. This created a problem for the very fine text, so Frost added more weight to allow the small texts to print. The invitation has a multiple concertina fold with a set of ever-decreasing concentric circles die-cut into the centre of each fold. Each panel holds snippets of positive slogans – about peace, fulfilment, vitality – in keeping with the tone of the operation.

The last concentric circle is printed and reveals itself to be the 'O' in EON. The last concertina fold is perforated into two halves which can be torn off and used. One is the invitation card and the other an RSVP form.

Message

Event: Diesel Design fifth anniversary party, 2000
Designer: Diesel Design, USA
Message: Playing with fuel

The language and format of this party invitation is a play on the name of US design group Diesel Design and a diesel fuel theme. Diesel Design based the idea on a form issued by local American automobile shops where you would purchase your diesel. The form would usually come in triplicate. The invitation comprises pink, white and yellow carbon and even includes omnipresent greasy finger prints on the black plate. The recipient is asked to sign it like an estimate and fax it back as an RSVP. Diesel Design emphasised the interactive element of the invitation by allowing the partygoers to indicate drink, music and food preferences. The language of the automobile shop car service form is picked up on and slightly subverted. Phrases like 'please pay this amount' become 'please play this amount'. The auto shop theme was continued throughout the event, where the caterers wore mechanics' jumpsuits and served drinks such as windshield wipe fluid (blue curaçao margarita) and motor oil (black vodka martini).

Event: Book launch for Sharp, 2000
Designer: Justus Oehler at Pentagram, UK
Message: Bold graphic language replicates the tone of the book

Justus Oehler, partner at multidisciplinary design firm Pentagram, designed the invitations for the presentation of Sharp, a sumptuous volume of photographs by Nigel Parry, which he had designed for publisher Powerhouse Books. The book features black-and-white portraits of rock stars, actors, politicians and opera singers. The invitations are for two separate events, one for an exclusive dinner reception and the second for a cocktail party. Both invitations employ the same bold graphic language of the book itself, using the same colour palette of black, red and white and the same sans serif Helvetica typography.

All relevant information regarding venues and times is set upon a ground that suggests the form of an open book: a subtle but distinctive indication of the nature of the events.

Message

Event: Film preview, 2000
Designer: Haku Shoukon, Japan
Message: A British ferry ticket translated into Japanese

An odd game of translation is at play in this invitation created for the Japanese release of Atom Egoyan's film Felicia's Journey. The film's plot sees the heroine Felicia travelling across the sea to England in search of her ex-boyfriend. The language used copies that of a British Midland Ferry ticket with details such as class, issue date and port of origin inscribed in English. The client, Nihon Herald, wanted the designers to create an invitation which was 'cute and innocent' yet conveyed the sense of suspense in the story. To underline Felicia's innocent character, the designers added light pink on the Japanese and English text.

The texture of the paper also expressed the story. While the front part of the invitation depicting Felicia's face is slick and smooth, the back is rough and sandy. According to the designers, "This enhances the feeling of an innocent girl haunted by a killer, a crucial moment of the film."

 BRITISH MIDLAND FERRY

START DATE : UNVALID
PORT IRELAND TO ENGLAND

STATUS ADULT
PRICE £25.30 Q

CLASS ORDINARY
ISSUE DATE 62557854E

NO. 991130

STATUS ADULT
PRICE £25.30 Q

CLASS ORDINARY
ISSUE DATE 62557854E

NO. 991130

NOT FOR SALE

issue subject to conditions (s) (5281a) see over

拝啓、時下益々ご清栄のことと御慶び申し上げます。この度、日本ヘラルド映画では、今年のカンヌ映画祭を熱狂の渦に巻き込んだアトム・エゴヤン監督作品「フェリシアの旅」をシネマライズにて公開する運びとなりました。
本作はカンヌ映画祭国際批評家協会賞を受賞した「エキゾチカ」、そして97年カンヌ映画祭でグランプリ以下3冠受賞の快挙を成し遂げた「スウィート・ヒアアフター」で現在最も高い期待を寄せられているエゴヤン監督の待望の新作です。エゴヤン監督は原作となったウィリアム・トレヴァーの小説に童話"美女と野獣"の魅力的変形を読み取って脚本を執筆したと語り、原作者は「見事な映画化で、小説家はこれ以上何も望めない」と絶賛。テレビ番組「新ヒッチコック劇場」の手腕を操り、現在・過去・未来を自在に往き来するエゴヤンならではの見事

なストーリー展開で完成させたのが、息を呑むほど美しいサスペンス「フェリシアの旅」です。
アイルランドの17歳の少女、フェリシアは住所も告げずに去ってしまった恋人を探す為に、イギリスにやってくる。見知らぬ土地で途方にくれる彼女に親切にしたのが、大きな邸で古いテレビの料理番組に従って、ひとり豪華な料理を作る中年の男、ヒルディッチだった。しかし、優しそうな男は誰にも知られない秘密の顔を持ち、彼女を静かに、確実に追いつめていく。だが、フェリシアは彼が今まで出会った少女達の誰よりも特別な存在であり、物語は孤独な二人の心の癒しへと向かっていく・・・。
フェリシアを演じるのはアイルランド出身の新星エレーン・キャシディ。共演は「モナリザ」の名優ボブ・ホスキンス。フランス訛りの料理研究家をユーモラスに惨酷に演じるのはエゴヤン監督の公私に

わたるパートナー、アルシネ・カーンジャン。フェリシアの厳格な父には「ボクサー」「ブレイブハート」のジェラード・マクソーリー。
原作はアイルランドの作家、ウィリアム・トレヴァーの1994年のホイットブレッド賞に輝いた小説。撮影、音楽、編集のスタッフは「エキゾチカ」「スウィート・ヒアアフター」に続き本作でも名を連ね、「ベルベット・ゴールドマイン」「ほんとうのジャクリーヌ・デュ・プレ」でアカデミー賞常連の衣裳、サンディ・パウエル、「インタビュー・ウィズ・ヴァンパイア」の美術監督ジム・クレイが加わり、エゴヤン作品3部作完結編ともいえる最高傑作「フェリシアの旅」が誕生したのです。
年末が迫り、御忙しい時期ではございますが、皆様に是非ご高覧いただきたくお願い申し上げます。

敬具

日時: **11月30日 (火)**
開場13:00／開映13:30（終映15:26予定）
場所: 徳間ホール（新橋駅下車2分）
本状1枚につき、記名ご本人様のみ有効です。
上映開始後、満員の際はご入場できませんのでご了承ください。
ご来場の際は封筒をご持参ください。

監督 脚本:アトム・エゴヤン
原作:ウィリアム・トレヴァー（角川文庫刊）
撮影: ポール・サロシー、作曲: マイケル・ダンナ
衣裳: サンディ・パウエル
美術: ジム・クレイ
キャスト: ボブ・ホスキンス、エレーン・キャシディ
アルシネ・カーンジャン
提供: 日本ヘラルド映画、ポニーキャニオン
配給: 日本ヘラルド映画
お問い合わせ: 日本ヘラルド映画宣伝部 03-3248-1166

フェリシアの旅 完成披露試写会のご案内

CUT

2000年陽春 シネマライズにてロードショー

FELICIA'S JOURNEY.
フェリシアの旅
A FILM BY **ATOM EGOYAN**

Event: Talk at the London Business School, 1997
Designer: Lippa Pearce, UK
Message: Business talk with an international feel

London-based design group Lippa Pearce was asked by the London Business School (LBS) to design an invitation for Lord David Currie's talk on the European Monetary Union. The invitation needed to have an international feel about it, due to the nature of the topic and of the audience, but also because it was part of a worldwide tour. A pared-down pea green and white palette was derived from the LBS corporate identity colours. The silver icons on the front are used as universal tools for communicating across countries, like a miniature signage system. A 'business class' feel was required, hence the foil-blocking, die-cutting and unusual format of the card.

The bespoke style of binding using a rubber band enabled the invitation to be adapted for each of the countries that the tour went to.

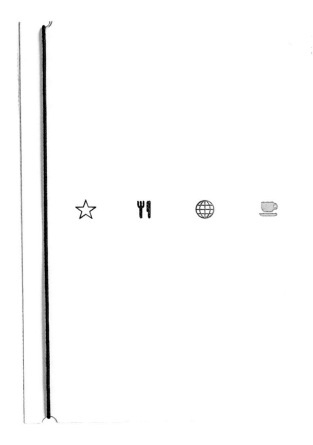

Lord David Currie, Professor of Economics and London Business School request the pleasure of the company of

_____

to a presentation on The European Monetary Union

Lord David Currie

David Currie is Professor of Economics at London Business School and Director of the Regulation Initiative. Formerly he was Deputy Principal and Director of the Centre of Economic Forecasting (1988-95). Before coming to London Business School he was Professor of Economics at Queen Mary & Westfield College, University of London.

A well-known figure in economic policy and forecasting for both the UK and international economies, Lord David Currie has held visiting appointments at the International Monetary Fund, the Bank of England (Houblon-Norman Research Fellow) and the University of Manchester. His research interests are in the field of international macro-economics and policy, in which he has published extensively, and in the field of government regulation of industry.

rsvp

London Business School
Sussex Place
Regent's Park
London NW1 4SA
United Kingdom
Telephone +44 (0)171 262 5050
Facsimile +44 (0)171 724 8433

Event: Mulligan Womenswear Spring/Summer catwalk show at London Fashion Week, 2001
Designer: Brian Griver at Imagination, UK
Message: A play on a familiar rhyme

Designer Brian Griver was asked to create an invitation which reflected one of the techniques employed in the Mulligan Womenswear Spring/Summer 2001 collection. He chose to experiment with the technique of printing patterns over closed pleats. When the pleats open, a pattern breaks across them. This effect was recreated using tactile paper and typographic information.

The message of the invitation repeats the theme of the collection: 'Something Old, Something New'. According to the collection's designers, they were inspired by the desire to use something old (familiar florals, pleating from the 20th century), that would provide the sense of security needed to embrace the new and yet unknown 21st century.

When the card breaks open over the pleats, it reveals information about the show and contact details. The invitation, spelt out in Aqua, one of the key colours of the collection, is printed on Ikono silk matt 200gsm paper, scored and then individually hand-folded.

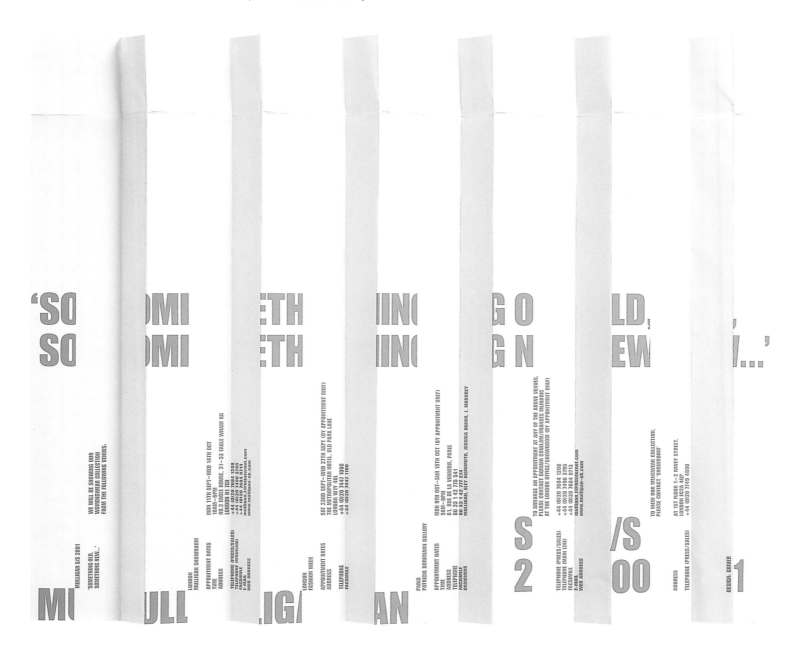

'SOMETHING OLD, SOMETHING NEW…'

MULLIGAN S/S 2001

Event: Un Poema per la Pau
book launch, 2002
Designer: Pere Alvaro at Bis, Spain
Message: Teaser for a book of poetry
by children

Spanish design group Bis created an
invitation for the launch of the book
Un Poema per la Pau, published by
The Catalonian Institute of Architects.
It is a collection of over 3,000 poems
dedicated to peace, with varied and
eclectic poems written by both children
and adults from around the globe. The
client asked Bis to use the design as a tool
to increase the interest for the publication.
Bis designed the book using pictograms,
illustration and photography to render its
own interpretation of the poems. For the
invitation, Bis simulated eight pages
of the book itself.

According to the design group, the best
way to explain the book was to reproduce
a bit of it, sending out an invitation which
anticipated the paper, format and even
the smell of the book. The final piece was
presented in the format of a colour proof,
folded twice like a form and mounted
in the book.

Event: Kylie Minogue 'Fever' tour aftershow party, 2002
Designer: Tony Hung at Adjective Noun, UK
Printer: Artomatic, UK
Message: A visual translation of sound

How to translate the effects of sound into print was the main concern behind Tony Hung's design for Kylie Minogue's 'Fever 2002' aftershow party. The solution was to design a series of sound waves which reflected light like a CD. Having worked on the whole campaign for the artist's 'Fever' album and tour, Hung wanted this invitation to be an extension of the promotional material and the concert set design. The designer used the same one-sided foil board used for the concert programme. The board was over-printed with a foil block of silver over the top of the colour foil. The non-foil side of the board is printed black and red out of white and contains all the party details and other information.

The invitation was sent out in a silver bubble wrap envelope, the idea being that it was a package out of space just like Minogue's concert entry number, which saw her riding onto the stage in a space shuttle. The typography, set in a sci-fi, data style, also echoes the tour atmosphere.

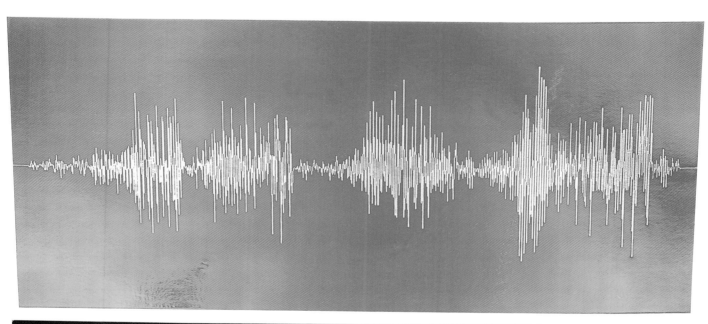

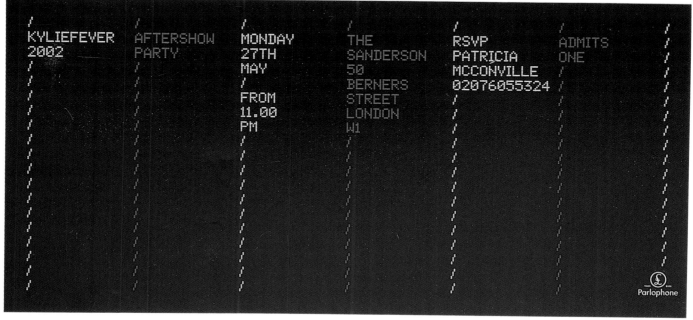

Event: Barcelona Convention
Office party, 2001
Designer: Grafica, Spain
Message: A Mediterranean tone
to promote Barcelona

Spanish design group Grafica was
appointed to design a party invitation for
the Barcelona Convention Office (BCO),
which is a branch of the Barcelona
Tourist Office. The BCO promotes
Barcelona around the world as a city to
hold international fairs, conventions and
conferences. The party was held during
an international trade fair on tourism in
London, and was aimed at the fair's
guests. As such, the graphic language of
the invitation had to convey the spirit of a
fun, exciting, Mediterranean city. On the
'cover' of the invitation, Grafica wanted to
express the style of Los Manolos, the band
that was playing at the party. The band
plays a mix of flamenco and Spanish pop
music, and its members have a 1970s

look, wearing flower-patterned shirts with
big collars and brightly coloured trousers.
The inside section of the invitation contains
all the information for those attending.

Event: Launch of BBC Radio 4 programme 'Routes of English', 2001
Designer: Blast, UK
Message: Language as a graphic device

For UK's BBC Radio 4's launch of international series 'Routes of English' by author and television critic Melvyn Bragg, design group Blast created an invitation that would be sent out to opinion-formers and literary circles. Since the radio programme celebrates and investigates the gradual changes in the use of the English language across the world, the graphic device chosen by the designers was a St George's Cross made out of quotes, verses and prose by poets, authors and writers. The design features bold, red text set in Centaur that picks out random words like 'India', 'Chinese' and 'Island'.

In addition to the print invitation, a CD containing audio extracts from contributors such as Bill Bryson and Salman Rushdie was sent out. The CD sleeve features the same typographic device as the larger invitation.

As a place which caught our interest
AUSTRALIA
ranked about level with Belarus
and Barundi. Among the general subjects which outstripped it were *balloons* and *balloonists*, the Church of Scientology, dogs (though not dog sledding), Barneys, Inc., and Pamela Harriman... Put in its crudest terms, Australia was slightly more important to us in 1997 than
BANANAS but not nearly as important as ice cream.

I MADE THIS IN YOUR HONOUR
When the Chinese when vows and affections failing
government recently took the decision to extend the teaching of English to nine-year-olds, they estimated that they would need to recruit
your soul leapt like a heron an additional one million English-teachers.
IN CRICKET MAD India
from the salt, island grass into another
HEAVEN
ubiquitous satellite TV
has made Geoffrey
Boycott one of the
greatest influences on
CONTEMPORARY INDIAN ENGLISH

Event: Wohnhaus furniture shop opening, 2002
Designer: Volker Muller, Germany
Message: Bold lettering helps to memorise a new brand

When a furniture shop changed tack with new products and collections aimed at a younger audience, it decided it needed a rebrand and name change. The owner commissioned Volker Muller, a designer based in Konigsbach-Stein, to come up with the brand name and logo. Muller came up with Wohnhaus, which in German means 'house for living'. The design – bold red type on a black background – also appeared on posters across the town, gaining more attention for the new shop. The logo on the invitation is stretched out over the length of the card, with spaced out lettering. According to the designer, "The longer it takes to read, the more it will stick in one's memory." The format also lends itself to being hung on the wall as a mnemonic device.

Event: Opening of YMC shop, 1999
Designer: Julian House, UK
Printer: Artomatic, UK
Message: A foil-blocked numeric design announces an opening

Julian House had collaborated with fashion label YMC on a number of T-shirt designs and promotional print matter. For the invitation to the opening of the YMC shop in London, he replicated a T-shirt print that was originally based on a 1960s book design. The graphic, foil-blocked collage of random numbers was then used on a number of different media. The invitation is announced by a silkscreen-printed single colour on eyeball-jarring blue plan card. The colours have been deliberately selected because they reflect the clashing, discordant colours of YMC clothing. The bright pink text is printed in a very thick silkscreen ink to allow maximum opacity of the discordant colours. The invitation was sent in a plan card envelope in the same bright blue.

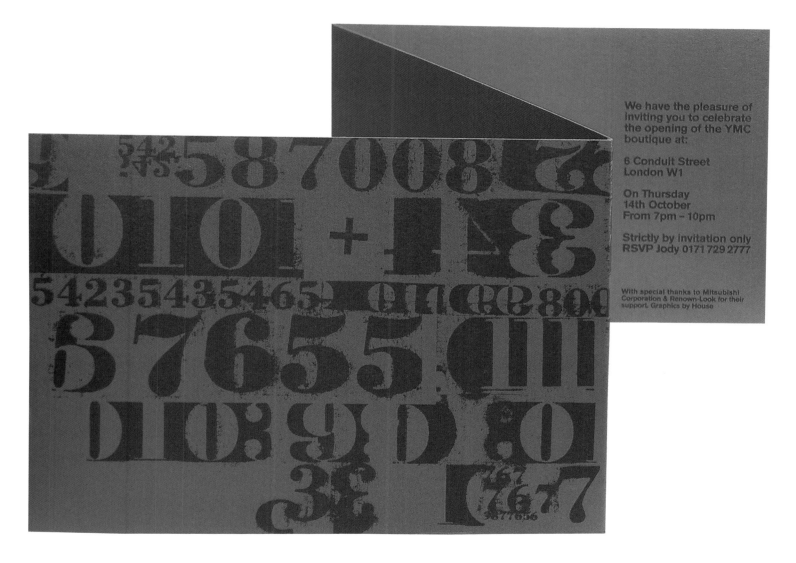

We have the pleasure of inviting you to celebrate the opening of the YMC boutique at:

6 Conduit Street
London W1

On Thursday
14th October
From 7pm – 10pm

Strictly by invitation only
RSVP Jody 0171 729 2777

With special thanks to Mitsubishi Corporation & Renown-Look for their support. Graphics by House

Event: The Serpentine Gallery
30th anniversary gala dinner, 2000
Designer: Vince Frost, UK
Message: Tradition with a
contemporary twist

Vince Frost designs all the London
Serpentine Gallery print material and
is responsible for the guidelines on the
various invitations the gallery issues.
Its annual summer party is a big event
and Frost had to work with the main
sponsor, fashion design label Emanuel
Ungaro, who decided that the invitation
should have a square format and feature its
trademark pink colour. The invitation
represents a modern take on formality. It
is split into four sections: the main invitation
carries information about the event as well
as a listing of the gala dinner committee
and the board of trustees, an admission
card, a place card and additional list of
guests, patrons and donors. Although the
terms of address use conventional

language, the Ungaro shocking pink adds
a contemporary twist. Even when working
within tight parameters, Frost believes it is
important to produce a memorable, tactile
invitation. The invitation was printed in a
two-colour litho process on Matrisse
540gsm paper.

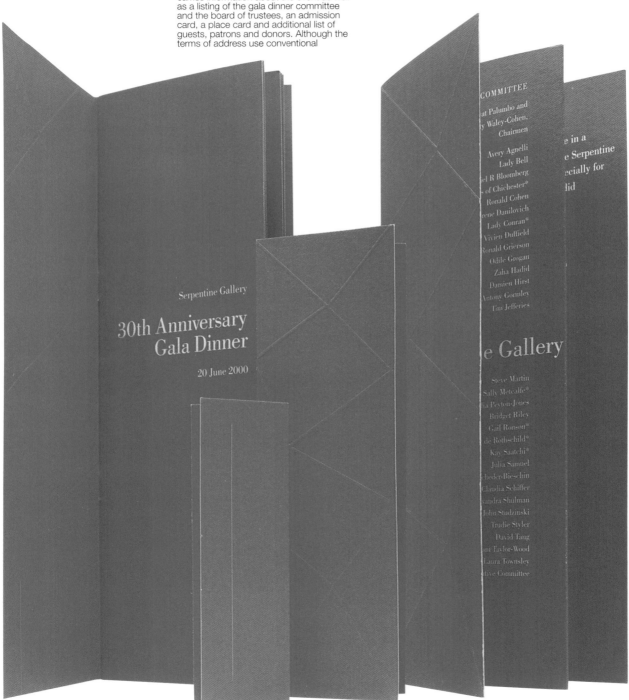

Event: Private dinner function at the Tate Modern, 2002
Designers: Zulder and Co., UK
Message: Humorous quotes from the artist

Andy Warhol's laconic wit was the theme used for the invitations to a private function dinner party at London's Tate Modern Gallery during a major Warhol retrospective. The exhibition brought together over 150 paintings, sculptures and early drawings. According to the designer Andrew Zulder, Warhol's celebrity status owes as much to his unconventional persona as to his iconic art. The party invitation, reply slips, place cards and menus were designed to express the artist's personality as well as conveying the impression that he was somehow involved in the event. Quotes by the artist were applied across the range of materials, specifically chosen to give a humorous twist or perspective to each individual item. For example, the invitation reads: 'My painting's just about entertaining people. I'm surprised it's lasted so long.' The affirmative reply slip reads: 'I have a social disease. I have to go out every night.' And the negative one reads: 'I had a lot of dates but decided to stay home and dye my eyebrows.'

Event: Launch party for the book Size isn't Everything, 1998
Designer: Milk, UK
Printer: Artomatic, UK
Message: A religious tone to invite worship

There are two versions of this invitation: one for a preview launch at the trendy Colette shop in Paris and one for the book launch and exhibition at the Open Gallery in London. The invitation plays on the concept that the book is a training shoe bible and calls for readers to worship. The quirky designs follow the spirit of the book, also designed and written by Milk. Both invitations are printed on specified Bible paper and are at first glance a facsimile of the first page of a standard Bible. Instead of psalms, the text refers to quotes from the book about the cult of the training shoe by fashion commentators such as Jil Sander and Paul Smith. The text mimics the Bible in detail, including psalm and page numbers.

The pages themselves have die-cut curved edges on one side of the paper giving the impression that the paper was torn out from an actual Bible. The invitation title 'Worship Here' is printed in gold in apt, Bible-like text. On the bottom of the page, where the Bible's printer's mark would normally be found, the sponsors, publisher Booth Clibbon's logo and the Milk logo appear. For the Colette show the title is printed offset in gold. For the London show the title is gold-blocked because more sponsorship money was available. Although similar in layout, the texts were subtly altered for the London show, deleting any mention of Nike because the sponsor for the London show was the competitor Adidas.

You are invited to the launch of *"Size isn't everything"* the trainer book. Trainers Only
Published by Booth-Clibborn Editions

WORSHIP HERE

4th November 1998
Service commences: 8pm
Open Gallery; 144-148 Charing Cross Rd

Supported by

A Milk project

Booth-Clibborn Editions

You are invited to the launch of *"Size isn't everything"* exclusive to colette
Vous êtes invité au lancement de *"Size isn't everything"* en exclusivité chez colette

WORSHIP HERE

21st September 8-10 pm
Lundi 21 Septembre 20h - 22h

DJ on the night: **Fraser Cooke** from Hit & Run, London.

chez/at:
colette 213 RUE SAINT-HONORÉ 75001 PARIS T. 01 55 35 33 90 WWW.COLETTE.TM.FR

A Milk project

346 THE majors say it is for sport and we say it is fashion, when will the right hand know what the left hand is doing and understand that sneakers are fashion whether for sport or for the street.

IN all the interviews milk did for this book, people talked so passionately about their "whatever's" that we felt we shouldn't straight-jacket their words...so we left their English as their English. Consequently, this is a book of many different voices.

The fact is trainers/sneakers/kicks/baskets, whatever you call them, function as much more than mere performance-oriented coverings for your feet! —

At the communion;

1
What's your favourite brand?
How do you say sneakers in your mother tongue?
How do you wear your laces?
Do you like white soles or dark?
What's the cheapest / most expensive pair you own?

Part 2;

2
Have you ever customised your sneakers?
What would your ideal sneaker look like?
How do you react when people step on your sneakers?
Do you remember the first pair of trainers you ever wore?

"After you try trainers you can't wear anything else...because they're so comfortable. So I make shoes like trainers, but I try to make them not look too sporty, more sophisticated, more city-like." *Jean Paul Gaultier.*

"I like trainers with the wrong things, in the wrong colours...with a suit they look fantastic." *Paul Smith.*

"Do we get described by the things we wear? I suppose we do because you make your choices don't you?" *Graham Wood.*

347 *My Adidas, RUN DMC:*

My Adidas walk through concert doors,
and roamed all over coliseum floors.
I stepped on stage at live aid,
all the people gave and the poor got paid.

And out of those speakers I did speak,
I wore my sneakers but I'm not a sneak.
My Adidas reached the sands of foreign lands,
with mike in I cold took command.

My Adidas and me, close as can be,
we make a mean team, my Adidas and me.
We get around together and get down forever,
and we won't be had when caught in bad weather.

Book Bites, milk: 02.07.96; 20.07.98 ©1998 *Booth-Clibborn Editions* ARTOMATIC
240

THIS BOOK IS MORE THAN SIMPLY A FOOT FETISHIST'S WET DREAM.

346 THE majors say it is for sport and we say it is fashion, when will the right hand know what the left hand is doing and understand that sneakers are fashion whether for sport or for the street.

IN all the interviews milk did for this book, people talked so passionately about their "whatevers" that we felt we shouldn't straight-jacket their words...so we left their English as their English. Consequently, this is a book of many different voices.

The fact is trainers/sneakers/kicks/baskets, whatever you call them, function as much more than mere performance-oriented coverings for your feet! —

At the communion;

1
Whats your favourite brand?
How do you say sneakers in your mother tongue?
How do you wear your laces?
Do you like white soles or dark?
Whats the cheapest / most expensive pair you own?

Part 2;

2
Have you ever customised your sneakers?
What would your ideal sneaker look like?
How do you react when people step on your sneakers?
Do you remember the first pair of trainers you ever wore?

"After you try trainers you can't wear anything else...because they're so comfortable. So I make shoes like trainers, but I try to make them not look too sporty, more sophisticated, more city-like." *Jean Paul Gaultier.*

"I like trainers with the wrong things, in the wrong colours...with a suit they look fantastic." Paul Smith.

"Nike...they do it in a very, let's say constructive way." *Jil Sander.*

"Do we get described by the things we wear? I suppose we do because you make your choices don't you?" *Graham Wood.*

347 *Book Bites, milk: 02.07.96; 20.07.98*

1. I bought my grandmother a pair of *Nike Air Humaras*, she wears them when she goes to walk the dog to the postbox.
2. I bought my niece some *Adidas shell-toes*, she's only two but she still points to them whenever I go round and see her.
3. I bought my mother some black *Vans Chukka boots*, they're perfect, she says, for being not too smart.
4. I bought my brother some *Nike Air Zoom Alphas*, he told me he wanted the old ones, fool.
5. I bought my girlfriend some *Air Max Totals*, she wears them in the gym.
6. I bought myself some *Shakendestrukts*, and haven't worn them yet because they look so good on the mantel piece.
7. I bought my dog two pairs of *kiddy Jordans*, he ran about the room shaking his four legs like a badly handled puppet.

240

Event: Alexander McQueen's Paris catwalk show, 2002
Designer: Katherine Doubleday at Michael Nash, UK
Message: A scribbled tongue twister

Created as a teaser for British fashion designer Alexander McQueen's main Paris show, this invitation was based upon the fictional character Mary Poppins' mantra 'Supercalifragilisticexpialidocious', and some original Tim Burton sketches sent by the film director to McQueen. In a very short time, designer Katherine Doubleday devised a series of ideas based on the sketches provided and developed an invitation resembling a school exercise book, complete with drawings, scribbles and doodles. Litho-printed stock with random ink marks helped create the effect of a childish, messy school pad. Some pages were left blank so the press, buyers and fashion pack could scribble their own notes or draw sketches.

Event: Maastricht Art Fair, 2000
Designer: Experimental Jetset, Holland
Message: Sticker sheets spell out MAF

The Maastricht Art Fair (MAF) 2000 involved a group of 20 galleries and exhibition spaces. To reflect this, Experimental Jetset (EJS) designed a logo on stickers in a group of 20 squares that spells out 'MAF'. The group also designed the catalogue, logotype and signage for the fair. The sticker sheets were sent out to the owners of galleries that were exhibiting there. They could apply the stickers onto their own invitations, correspondence and print material to advertise their presence at the fair. EJS designed the stickers in such a way that they could be used as small labels or flags.

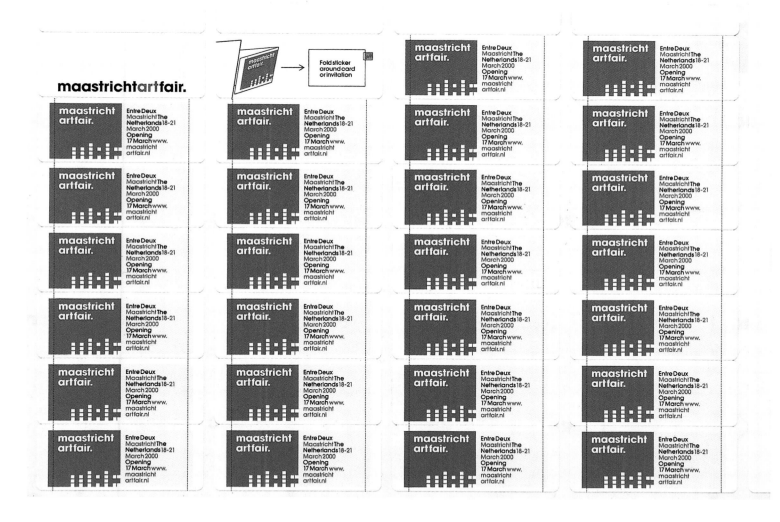

Event: Press launch for Pretty Polly and Playtex, 1996
Designer: Blast, UK
Message: 1950s glamour style

Blast was commissioned to produce an invitation for the launch of a new range of 'figure enhancing' lingerie and hosiery from women's accessories manufacturers Pretty Polly and Playtex. The design was based around the theme 'back to the age of glamour'. Blast produced illustrations in the style of 1950s Vogue magazine fashion drawings to demonstrate the product, and produced them as a 'pattern for a total body refit'. Using the language and visual style of 1950s' advertising, the invitation is printed onto pattern-cutting material with wording in the style of instructions. The admission ticket for the event is screen-printed onto silk, which is cut with pinking shears and pinned to the invitation.

This is then folded down into a brown paper envelope, printed again in a pastiche of the era. The overall concept, use of unusual stocks, and painstaking hand-finishing created a successful invitation which provoked a 90 per cent attendance rate.

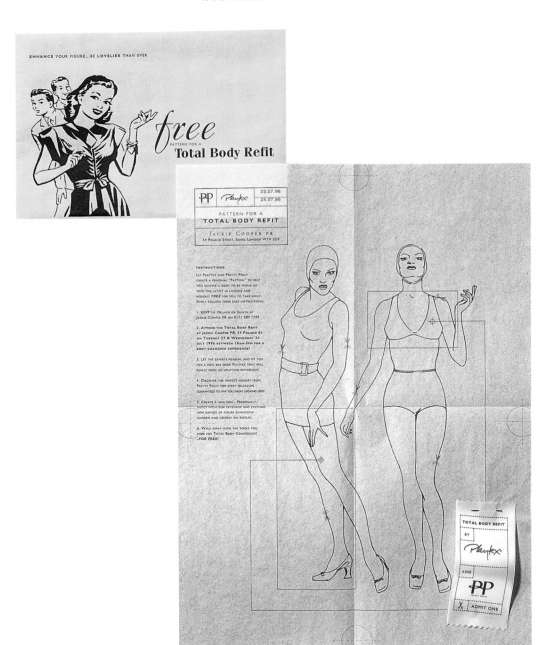

Event: Givenchy couture show, 2001
Designer: Peter Saville, UK
Printer: Artomatic, UK
Message: A formal text which exudes classic yet modern elegance

This invitation by London-based designer Peter Saville is folded twice with one inside panel silkscreen-printed on a coated white stock. The silkscreen panel is itself a rich overprint of three layers, the last layer a glossy varnish with black powder in it. This quality was specified by Saville, who required the finish to look like the paintwork of a sprayed car. Printers Artomatic originally intended to flood-coat all of one side, but tests showed the silkscreen would crack on the creases of the panels. The silkscreen colour was selected from a series of swatches supplied by Givenchy designer Julian Macdonald. The Givenchy name, logo on the front and inside invitation details are all set in gold foil-blocking.

Although the design is modern, it had to work within the conventional requirements of a couture show. Therefore the language used is straightforward and formal, with the authority of understated elegance. A reply card and a parking pass were also enclosed.

Event: Monthly exhibitions for Amsterdam gallery W139, 1999
Designer: Experimental Jetset, Holland
Message: A perforated grid gives uniformity to different events

Dutch group Experimental Jetset (EJS) was asked to design a series of invitations for Amsterdam gallery W139's monthly exhibitions. The exhibitions are always thematic group shows, so instead of concentrating on showing artists, the designers wanted to convey a strong, recognisable element that would hold the invitations together as a series. Searching for this mnemonic element, EJS visualised the exhibition space as a three-dimensional grid, with the artists' installations as a variation on that grid. As a consequence, the invitation represents the three-dimensional space as a series of perforations.

To introduce the grid, the first invitation was left completely blank, allowing the holes maximum impact. All the following invitations featured simple additions that were quick responses to both the theme of the exhibition and the layout of the invitation.

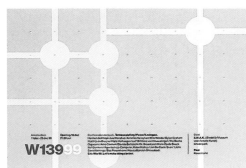

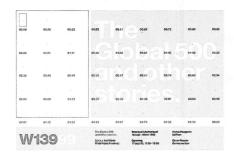

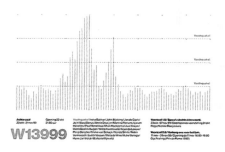

Event: Sally Scott shop opening, 2002
Designer: Atsuki Kikuchi at Bluemark, Japan
Message: An intimate scribble on a postcard

Japanese designer Atsuki Kikuchi was commissioned to design and art direct the brand image of fashion label Sally Scott. The invitation for the label's new shop is in the format of a postcard, printed on Softlight Rough paper and created to appeal to the tactile senses of the recipients, mostly buyers and clients. The language used is intimate, "like a letter written to your friends". The designer was briefed to create an object that was 'cute and sweet', a mode favoured by the Japanese; the format resembles sweets packaging. The front is a cut-out scribble of the shop's address; below, the ironic 'no dogs, two cats' line suggests the shop's door policy. On the back, the address and the shop opening times are spelt out in English and Japanese.

Postcard

Sally Scott Shimokitazawa Shop Open
1 February 2002

サリースコットの部屋には彼女の好きな
服や本や絵がたくさん並んでいます。
そんな彼女の部屋をしばらく借りて、私たちはお店をはじめます。
是非たくさんの方に訪ねていただきたいと思っています。
いつでもお時間のある時、遊びにいらして下さい。
心よりお待ちいたしております。

サリーの友人より

to Shinjuku
Yokohama Bank
Peacock
Shimokitazawa Sta.   to Shibuya

1F, 2-30-3 Kitazawa Setagaya Tokyo
Tel 03 3465 5870
Open 12:00 - 20:00 (Weekday)
11:30 - 20:00 (Sat, Sun & Holiday)

Event: Party to celebrate relocation of Pinkerton offices, 1996
Designer: SooHoo Designers, USA
Message: Investigative jargon is used for an invitation

When Pinkerton, one of the USA's oldest security services firms, decided to celebrate its move to a new office, SooHoo Designers was asked to design an invitation that would announce the move while reflecting Pinkerton's heritage. The design group opted to use investigative language in an ironic way, hinting at the nature of Pinkerton's operations. The label of the invitation spells out the fact that the guests will, from September, need to investigate where Pinkerton have moved to. Inside the box, a pen that identifies counterfeit bills is used as a metaphor for the company's security services, while Mr Pinkerton's image appears on a specially designed dollar bill with the party information on the back of it.

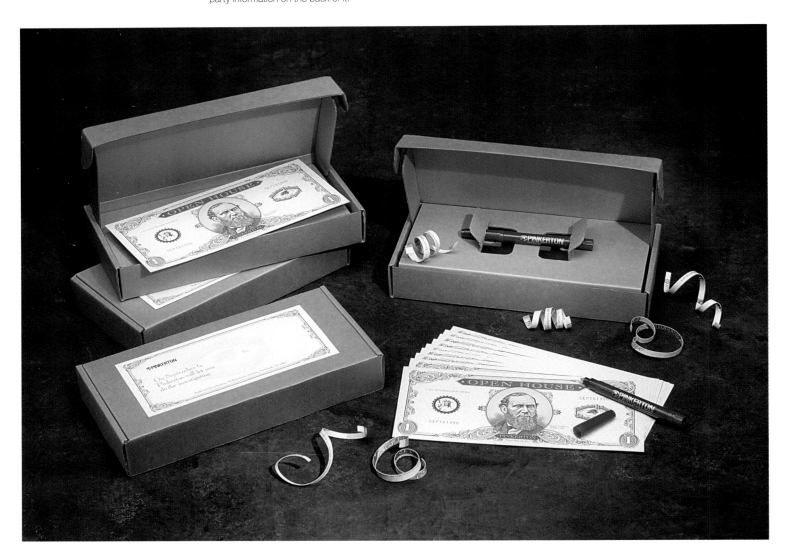

Event: Shirin Soccer film preview, 2002
Designer: Noboru Okano, Japan
Message: A soccer game suggests the film's theme

The client approached Japanese designer Noboru Okano to come up with a design that would show the frivolous aspects of the film comedy Shirin Soccer. The film, produced in Hong Kong, is a surreal comedy about six men trained to fight against a team of cyborg-like players, who use high-tech machines and muscle-building pills to win their game. As the invitations were being sent to the media, film critics and writers, Okano wanted to try and present the feeling of an epic without being tied to the taste and style of Hong Kong films. Rather than resorting to verbal expression, the invite uses the visual language of a board game, with the enclosed stickers representing the various characters.

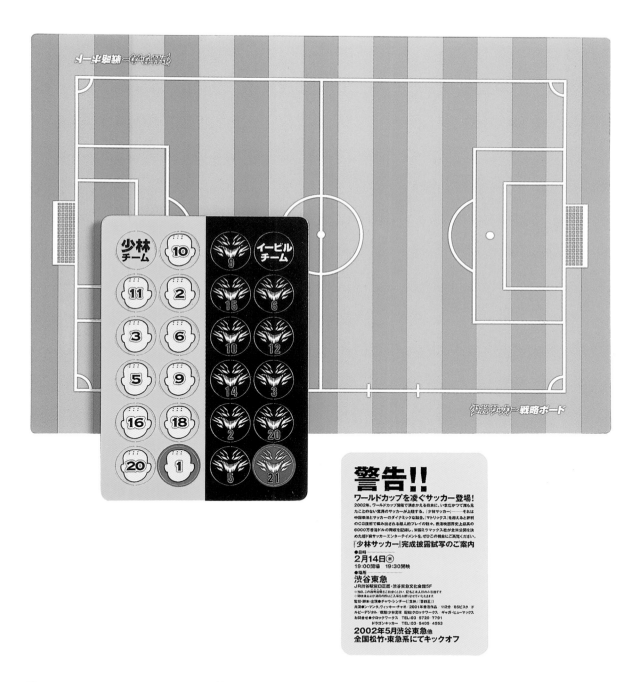

Target

Targeting a specific audience can often be a designer's preoccupation. On a large-scale project, the application of design is usually only a part of a wider scheme involving researchers, marketers and strategists. Because invitations are somewhat smaller in scale, they are a chance for designers to apply that thinking for themselves. A well-conceived invitation can be the culmination of the type of strategic thinking common to large-scale branding, advertising and point of sale, all captured in a microcosm. Invitations are instant, one-hit campaigns that need to prove their worth.

Targeting is about getting a maximum response with minimum wastage. Designers often use a series of devices that can range from subtle persuasion techniques that gradually arouse the interest of the target audience, to a complete sensory bombardment. Tactics include sending out save-the-date cards, attendance details of well-known personalities, personalisation techniques such as handwritten notes from the organisers, or even enclosing gifts. Often the methods of other strategic media are employed, such as direct mail or poster campaigns. For example, the St Luke's 'Think Print' invitations (pages 82–3) were for an in-house event which became a chance to showcase a great target strategy without any risk to a client account.

Other invitations are targeted in a more straightforward way. While when designing for the media-jaded fashion press, extreme shock tactics may have the desired effect, a simple and well-designed invitation can work wonders with an appreciative audience. In this case it is through the quality of design that you can target your market. Designers working with galleries, for example, tend to design invitations to their events as part of a general identity. Maintaining a consistent image for a gallery over time means a design that allows the recipient to recognise the institution at one glance, as soon as the envelope drops on the floor, and that also represents the uniqueness of that event.

Event: Lecture by Stefan Sagmeister, 2001
Designer: St Luke's, UK
Target: London's creative community

The London-based advertising agency St Luke's wanted to create a series of invitations that would promote their 'Think Print' talks. US-based designer Stefan Sagmeister would be the first in a series of six speakers. The aim of the invitation was to reach top advertising creatives, the design community and specialist press. The question the designers asked themselves was, 'What would grab your attention as a creative?' Conventional means of communication were dismissed in favour of a poster campaign. As part of the invitation campaign, posters would have the advantage of not only helping to ensure a big turnout, but also acting as a statement of what the agency was

doing. They needed to generate interest, create an impression and provoke respect from other agencies – St Luke's' direct competitors in the close-knit world of the London advertising industry.

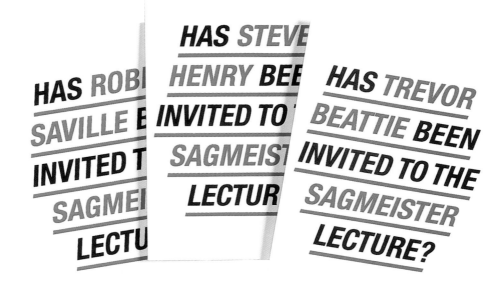

YOU *HAVE* **BEEN** *INVITED TO THE* *SAGMEISTER* **LECTURE**

1,000 standard A2 format posters were fly-postered in the areas of London with a high concentration of advertising, design and magazine publishing companies, three weeks before the event. The posters were printed as small print-run editions. Each poster was the same format of bold red, black and white-out text, except that each edition named a well-known creative who would be familiar to the advertising community. One edition asked 'Has Trevor Beattie been invited to the Sagmeister lecture?', immediately hinting at the exclusive nature of the event. Four days after they were distributed, the posters were followed by 2,000 flyers, handed out in Soho and Hoxton, two hubs of creative industry.

Finally, 300 invitations were sent out, featuring the strapline 'You have been invited to the Sagmeister lecture', and the details for the event. Having had their sense of professional rivalry stimulated, the recipients could hardly fail to attend the event – if only to see who else made the grade.

HAS PETER SOUTER BEEN INVITED TO THE SAGMEISTER LECTURE?

Event: Mina collections Spring/Summer 2000 and Autumn/Winter 2000/01
Designer: Atsuki Kikuchi at Bluemark, Japan
Target: Fashion press and buyers

Atsuki Kikuchi was commissioned to create all the graphic literature for fashion label Mina. Each season, motifs of the collection are incorporated into the graphic design. For the Spring/Summer 2000 collection, the theme was 'features of colour', duly represented as a multicoloured series of tick marks on the back of the envelope. Inside, a series of fashion shots are a substitute for text. For both invitations, the information, set in Neue Helvetica, is kept to a minimum, providing just the essential details to the knowledgeable fashion crowd.

Event: SooHoo Designers office relocation, 2002
Designer: SooHoo Designers, USA
Target: Clients

A none-too-symbolic invitation to taste a cup of coffee was the strategy adopted by California-based design group SooHoo Designers to communicate its recent relocation and new identity to clients. The move was seen as a way of getting reacquainted with old and new contacts. Based on the 'let's connect' idea, a 'join the dots' graphic reveals a coffee mug, while enclosed in the box-invitation is a pack of chocolate-covered espresso beans, a mug and the company's brochure.

A personalised, handwritten note was enclosed to invite the recipient of the box over for tea or coffee at the new offices.

Event: CAT fashion trade show, 1999
Designer: Martin Tickner, UK
Target: Buyers and retailers

Even though each of the fashion label CAT's invitations is unique in design and format, they are all linked by the singular simplistic, industrial workwear ethic of the CAT brand value. All the promotional material is conceived as part of a larger marketing campaign aimed at European buyers and retailers, to show how the American Midwest brand is managed by Overland, which holds the UK, European and South African licences for Footwear and Apparel.

The materials have therefore been designed by the UK design team to have a coherent set of brand design values to spread across Europe.

The CAT brand value is upheld in the use of coarse materials like Dutch grey-board and uncoated stock. Simple graphics are applied in single colours in silkscreen print in one of a set of CAT brand colours. The supporting items, such as postcards, swing tags, leaflets etc, are consistent with this design. Created by Martin Tickner while he was Overland's in-house art director, these items act as reminders of CAT's presence at the three main annual fashion trade shows as well as their presentation of new stock. They are usually printed in runs of up to 2,000.

Event: Virtual forum at
www.tinytaboos.nl, 2002
Designer: Mattmo Concept+Design,
Holland
Target: The young online community

An invitation to share ones' thoughts with other members of a virtual community, the tinytaboos website combines SMS and WAP cellular technology. It aims to be an arena where fragments of thoughts are clustered together and users can react and participate using their own messages. Designed by Dutch design group Mattmo, the site is aimed at a teenage audience, who, according to the designers, "might be more embarrassed at discussing feelings of love, shame and family matters with relatives and peers". The site contains thoughts from people of different cultures, visualised across an entire townscape.

The messages are always anonymous and usually sincere. Snippets of these messages are displayed as urban poetry on the windows of trams and subway trains and as signage or LED messages on buildings and stations.

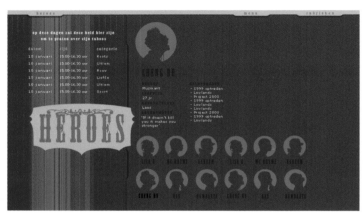

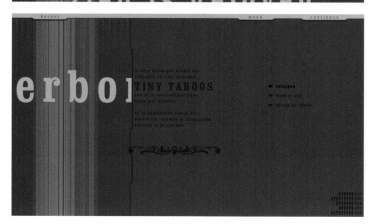

Event: Matsuda Spring/Summer show, 1996
Designer: Hideki Nakajima, Japan
Target: The fashion audience

To appeal to the fashion pack who attend New York's Fashion Week, Tokyo designer Hideki Nakajima created a slick yet minimal invitation for the Spring/Summer 1996 collection of Matsuda, a fashion label designed by Yukio Kobayashi. The card, produced on U-lite paper, unfolds into six concertina panels, each one with an image of Kobayashi's hand, photographed by Nakajima and set to a glossy black background. On the other side, silver printed text regarding the event flows underneath a photograph of a sewing needle that stretches horizontally across four panels.

The images chosen denote the globally recognisable idea of the fashion designer creating with his hands and his needle. Any hint of cliché is dispelled in the sensitive treatment, sparse tonality and glossy black mirror coating of the envelope and card.

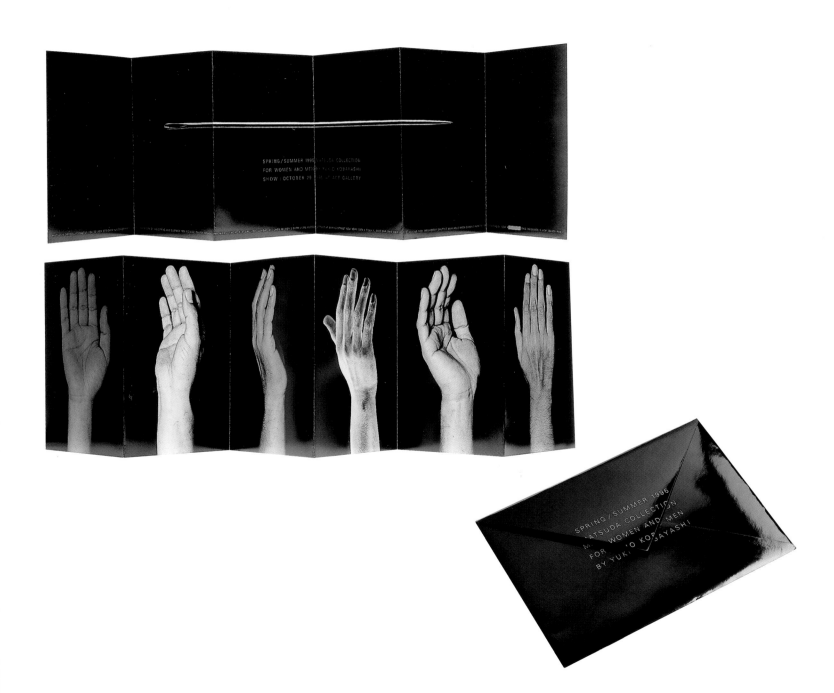

Event: Opening of + A Via Bus and Via Bus Stop 2, 2001
Designer: Hideki Nakajima, Japan
Target: The fashion audience

A white-and-grey-printed, semi-opaque acetate wrapped pack reveals invitations to the opening receptions of two Tokyo fashion shops, + A Via Bus and Via Bus Stop 2, which sell exclusive European and American fashion labels. Designed by Hideki Nakajima, each invitation is a large glossy card. The invitation for + A Via Bus displays surreal fashion photography by Naoki Tsuruta, while the one for Via Bus Stop 2 employs the minimal image of the brand as a motif pattern. Two extra cards, one blank and one featuring abstract yellow imagery, complete the package. Information is printed on the back of each invitation, which includes a stylised map of each shop. Descriptions are supplied in Japanese and English.

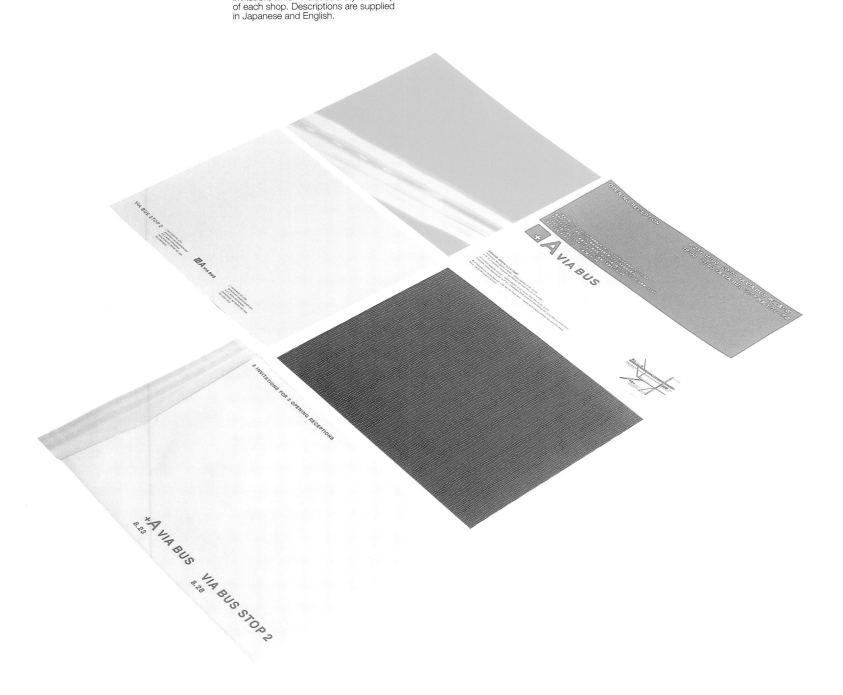

Event: Exhibitions at Centre La Première Rue, 2001
Designer: Steven Vitale, France
Target: Architects, art schools and gallery-goers

Designer Steven Vitale is the artistic director of La Première Rue, an association that promotes contemporary architecture and the plastic arts, based in a Le Corbusier-designed building in Briey-en-Fôret, France. Vitale created the association's identity and has been producing invitations and brochures for them since 1997. The idea of a brochure enclosed with the invitation was to give the public a 'mini-catalogue' of the exhibition, since the limited budget did not allow for a larger, more lavish production.

Until recently, all the Centre's print work has been produced with a low-budget in two colours. The challenge for Vitale was to make the two-colour print feel like a rich print environment. For example, the Pierre Vago invitation and brochure was created in a teal blue and a rusty red, allowing Vitale the possibility to create an overprint black. According to Vitale, printing a percentage of each colour superimposed resulted in a "new-found nuance".

The target audience for the invitations was quite diverse, as these publications find their way throughout Europe, as well as the USA, Canada and Japan. The mailing list is made up from a list of architecture and design schools, publications, collectors, individuals and all those involved in the world of contemporary architecture.

The Centre has a system in place for people interested in becoming members which entitles the recipient to receive invitations and news about the association.

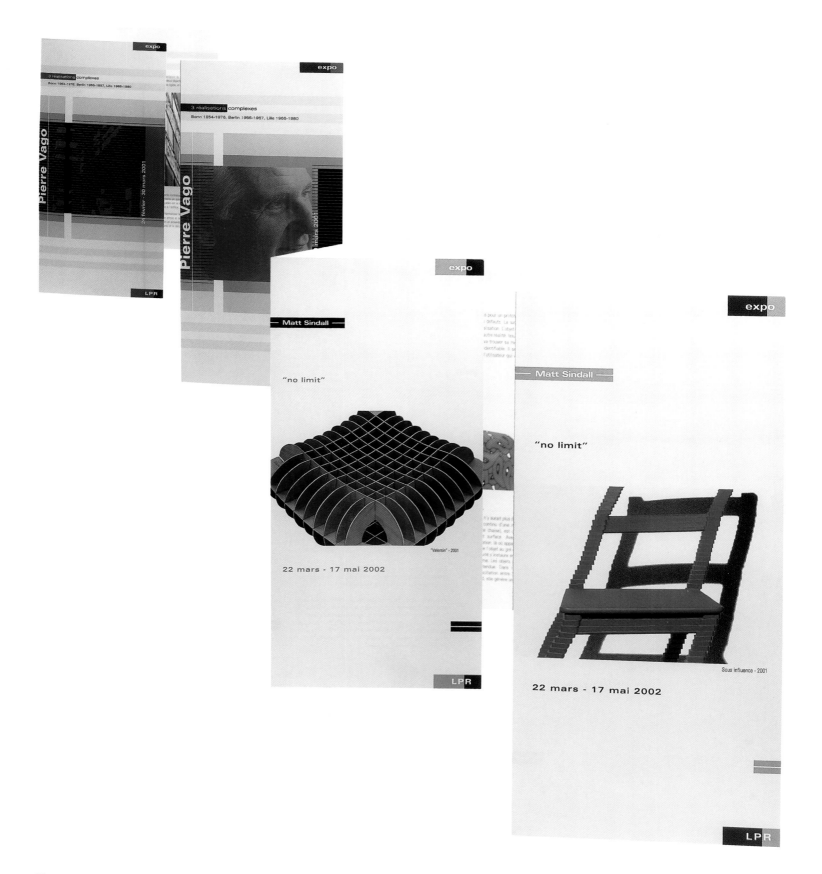

"Valentin" - 2001

Sous influence - 2001

Event: Johnson Banks' summer party, 2001
Designer: Johnson Banks, UK
Target: Clients, the creative community and friends

The persuasion tactics of direct mail were adopted by London-based group Johnson Banks when it created a staggered invitation campaign for its 2001 summer party. Five cards were sent out at different times, each depicting a person related to the company in some tenuous way, photographed by Johnson Banks designer Chris Wigan. A strapline stated each individual's reason why they didn't want anyone to attend the party. The company accountant, the local postman and even the local kebab-shop owners all had credible reasons to dissuade those invited. According to Michael Johnson at Johnson Banks, the invitations were sent out at different times to combat the lack of attendance which is typical at other design groups' parties. Johnson was determined that it wouldn't happen to them. Hence the idea of a staggered mailing campaign, since designers are notoriously forgetful. The notion that people often think up reasons not to go to parties led to the reverse psychology approach to the invite. The response to the party was good, with over 100 people attending. However, some recipients were a bit thrown by the multiple invitations. All the characters featured on the invitations were real. According to Johnson, the postman got into trouble from the sorting office for dissuading potential custom. Many people thought the characters in the photographs were staged for the invitation.

Some recipients were so intrigued by the picture of Paul that they rang just to see if he really was the Johnson Banks accountant.

This is the nice man from across the road. We're sure he won't mind about the party but he'll get ratty with us if you park in front of his garage. Park a bit further down the road, that'll keep him sweet.

This is our postman. We don't think he really cares if you come to our party or not, but he's always saying that his bag's too heavy, so do him a favour and rsvp by e-mail. Thanks very much.

This is Paul, our accountant. He can't see the point of us having a party. He doesn't want you to come. He sees drinks and canapés for 150 people as a terrible waste of money (but he would say that, wouldn't he?).

We're pretty sure that the lady next door doesn't want you to come either, you know, fun, music, laughter, mindless revelry etc. But the truth is we're not really sure – we've only seen her once in the 18 months we've been here.

These are the Gizel brothers. They can't come to the party because they'll be working but they asked us to ask you not to eat too much so you can pop in for a kebab on the way home. OK?

Response

French is traditionally the language of diplomacy. It comes as no surprise then that the universally accepted acronym RSVP found on invitations refers to the French phrase 'Répondez s'il vous plaît', meaning 'please reply'. The formality of diplomacy is comfortably mirrored in an RSVP as a means of response to a formal invitation. According to worldwide etiquette rules, one should always respond to an RSVP, even if only to decline. In more modern times, formality has been somewhat diluted, but many organisers of events still need to have an idea of turnout, and the requirement of the invitation to elicit a response remains constant. Many invitations include fill-in reply cards. These contain address details as well as the name of the person to whom the replies should be sent to. Ideally, it should be stressed whether an RSVP is essential to gain entry and the date by which the reply should happen.

A response, however, is not always demanded in such a formal fashion. Designers now use a variety of mechanisms to obtain feedback. Wearing an element of the invitation in order to gain entry is one of the mechanisms that has become increasingly popular. Bracelets, necklaces, bags and guest passes are just some of the devices which can be used as 'body language' to express acceptance. On a different level, online invitations allow organisers to record each participant with registration and entry password mechanisms, and a digital response can expand into games, community links and other interactive gimmicks. The call for response can also double as a call to radical action, as Elmwood's Yorkshire Water project shows (pages 112–3). In this case, schools from all over the country planted trees as a response to a reforesting campaign.

Event: Stars and Styles party, 2002
Designer: Work In Progress, France
Response: Bring yourself to
be photographed

Two separate invitations to Stars and Styles, a collection of photographs by the likes of Jessica Craig Martin, Terry Richardson and Asia Argento for French magazine Self Service, were designed by French group Work In Progress and distributed by Paris store Colette and fashion label Lanvin. According to Sarah, the artistic director and buyer at Colette, the idea was to create something that was both "chic and tacky". The first invite, in gold-blocked foil, was for an exclusive event on 10 July at Club Regine, where the 500 expected guests would be photographed. The RSVP required a conventional telephone or e-mail response, but a more effective response mechanism was devised by the 'Venez chic' guideline,

an invitation to look good for the photographers. The second invitation, designed in a more sombre black, was aimed at 2,000 guests for the actual exhibition at Colette, where the photographs taken on the 10 July event would be shown.

Event: Wedding of Jacqueline S. Quintanilla and Albert C. Lin, 2000
Designer: Chen Design Associates, USA
Response: A traditional RSVP card

A traditional response mechanism to a wedding invitation is given new life by the delicate and detailed treatment of San Francisco-based group Chen Design Associates. The invitation, RSVP card, map, directions card and envelope are all letterpress-printed, while the overall card bears a hand-finished rubber stamp. A twine with a Chinese bead holds everything together. According to the designer, the brief was to represent a symbolic connection between two unique yet similar individuals. The invitation theme is based on a circle and two flowers, representing the couple themselves.

JACQUELINE S. QUINTANILLA AND ALBERT C. LIN

Together with our families
Ms. Martha Quintanilla and Ms. Julia Fuentes
Mr. Wen Jiang Lin and Mrs. Mary Hwang Lin

Request the honor of your presence
at our wedding

Saturday, October 14th, 2000
Half after Four O'Clock
The Stanford University Golf Course
198 Junipero Serra Boulevard
Stanford, California

Dinner reception to follow

MAP AND DIRECTIONS

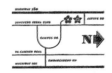

FROM HIGHWAY 101
Exit Embarcadero Road west. Enter the University. Turn right at Campus Drive and continue two miles to the Golf Course.

FROM HIGHWAY 280
Exit Alpine Road east. Turn right onto Junipero Serra Boulevard. Turn right at Campus Drive West, and continue up the hill into the Golf Course.

For travel and accommodation information, visit www.albertlin.com/wedding or call 650.701.0323

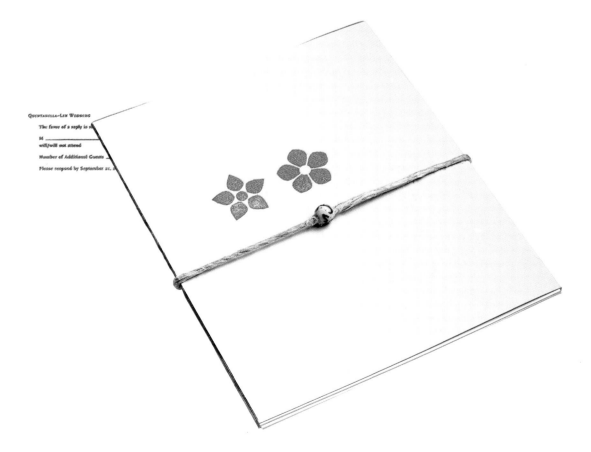

QUINTANILLA-LIN WEDDING

The favor of a reply is

M

will/will not attend

Number of Additional Guests

Please respond by September 21,

Event: Tony Kaye's 'Seaside Suicide' concert in Cannes, 2001
Designer: Kerr/Noble, UK
Response: Badges for concert-goers to wear

At the 2001 Cannes Film Festival, film-maker Tony Kaye staged a concert rather than show a film. The gig was called 'Seaside Suicide'. He presented himself as the front man of the band K, singing maniacal lyrics that portrayed fictional, autobiographical characters such as Bun Bun the rabbit. Badges bearing the characters sung about by Kaye and illustrated by Ian Wright were given to the concert-goers alongside the invitation. Each badge had lyrics around the edges. The card was printed gold on gold, using thermography to achieve the feel of an expensive, 250-dollar bill.

Event: G-Shock launch party, 1998
Designer: Experimental Jetset, Holland
Response: Textile-like flyer to stick on

A wearable die-cut sticker badge in textile-like material, personalised with each guest's name handwritten upon it, was the response mechanism for the launch of the Casio G-Shock watch. Dutch design group Experimental Jetset were aware that many of the guests were well-known DJs, artists and musicians, although their faces might not be as well known as their names. Making the entry pass a wearable sticker allowed people to put the face to the name during the event. The photograph set onto the sticker, taken by Ingmar Swalue, portrays the location of the party.

An additional RSVP request is set on the back, asking guests to confirm attendance via telephone, fax or e-mail. A G-Shock watch was given out as a gift to those attending.

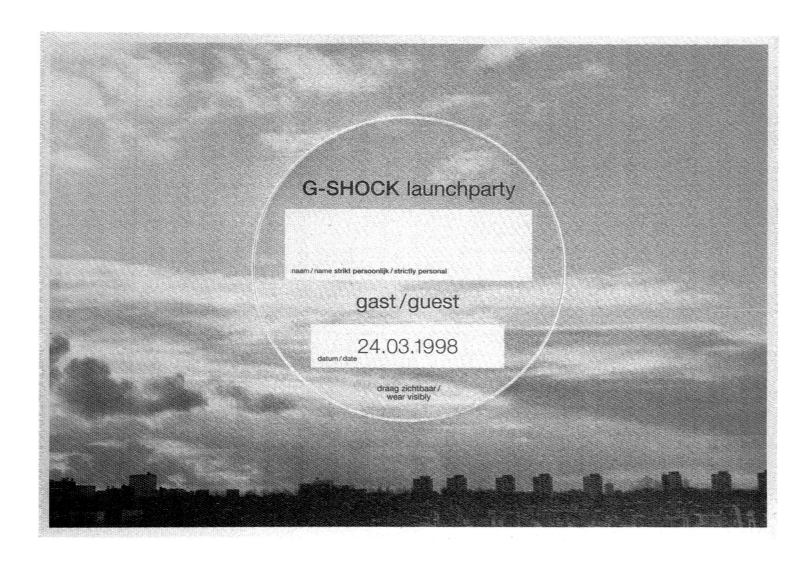

Event: Gio Ponti exhibition at the Design Museum, 2002
Designer: Kerr/Noble, UK
Response: A sketched RSVP card captures Gio Ponti's essence

An invitation to an exhibition of the work of 1950s' Italian designer Gio Ponti displays a subtle reworking of the master's distinctive style. Having created the graphics for the exhibition, London-based design duo Kerr/Noble was commissioned by the Design Museum to produce the invitation for the private view. This included an RSVP card, and both featured illustrations derived from Ponti's style of sketching and handwriting. On the RSVP card the designer doodled an image of Ponti's hand holding a pen. The card is set in Bodoni, which furnishes the invitation with a classical Italian feel and mirrors Ponti's use of thick and thin strokes in his decorative works.

For the exhibition graphics, the group reworked Bodoni and created a modern variant composed of arrows, playing with a theme of looking to both the future and the past.

Event: London Fashion Week shopping night, 2001
Designer: Claire Kinge at Bloomberg, UK
Response: Entry band to wear

The idea was to create a special invitation to an exclusive evening of shopping during London Fashion Week 2001. Over 80 top UK fashion designers were selling clothes and accessories at special prices for Bloomberg clients. The invitation needed to be alluring and convey the exclusivity of a London Fashion Week event. This was achieved by using screen-printed glitter and pearlised paper, reflecting the glamour of the evening. The barcode design on the invitation and an entry ticket tag tie in with the purchasing theme. The tag is attached to a glitter bracelet, all carrying the same look and feel. The bracelet becomes both the ticket and the RSVP.

EXCLUSIVE ENTRY

LONDON FASHION WEEK END

Event: British Council party at the
Venice Biennale, 2001
Designer: Claire Kinge at Bloomberg, UK
Response: Survival kit

A survival kit for guests was the idea
behind the invitation for a special party
organised by Bloomberg in co-operation
with the British Council in Venice. The party
was in honour of the artist Mark Wallinger,
who was representing Britain at the Venice
Biennale. The bag holds a selection of
'survival items', such as a mosquito spray
and a torch, deemed to be useful on the
deserted island of Lazzaretto Nuovo where
the party was held. The bag also includes
an entry bracelet which needed to be worn
to gain access to the island. The pattern on
the bag alludes to the water ripples formed
by the speedboat as it ferried the guests
to their destination.

The baby blue represents the colour of the
lagoon that surrounds Venice. A compass
card with the island's layout details the
event's attractions. Another card displays
a map and timetable for the pick-up boat.

Event: Design Business Association summer party, 2001
Designer: James Dicken at Designhouse, UK
Response: Sweatband and card

An entry bracelet for a sweaty summer party may not always remain a valued accessory. For this reason, Designhouse decided to opt for a sweatband, playing on the evening's theme, 'meltdown', and paving the way for a tacky, 1980s theme of sportswear used as casualwear. James Dicken of Designhouse was asked by the Design Business Association to create an invitation, tickets, banner and advertisements that would appeal to the whole range of the design community, from young junior creatives to chief executives within design consultancies. The aim was for the invitation to be clear and simple with a touch of wit.

First, a card was sent featuring a girl's arm wearing a 'meltdown' sweatband set to a beach and sun background. Upon response, guests were sent their own sweatband, to be worn to gain entry into the club.

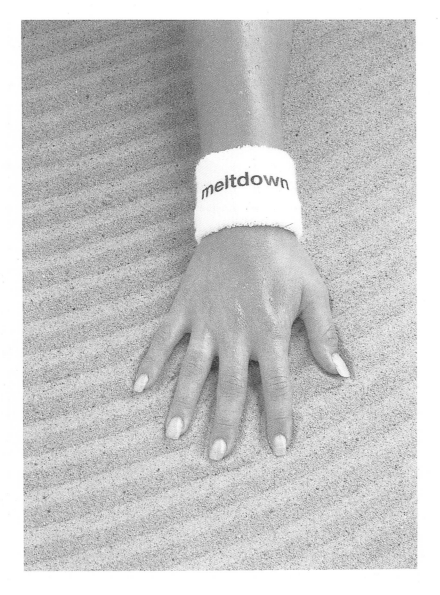

Event: Bill Feldman's surprise 70th birthday party, 2002
Designer: Margot Madison, USA
Response: A 1950s-style RSVP card and request to send photos

This invitation was designed to get guests in the dancing mood with a special-release 45rpm record. Old friends and family got a dose of birthday nostalgia when they went to the 1950s-themed surprise birthday party dressed in poodle skirts and leather jackets. The invitation included a record packaged in a facsimile vintage slip and an RSVP card designed and written in a 1950s style and tone.

An additional response request came in the form of an extra card, an invitation to stroll down memory lane and requesting guests to bring an old photo of Bill to add to a special book.

Event: Opening of the Mayor of London's European Office, 2001
Designer: Hem Patel at Bloomberg, UK
Response: A London bus pass to secure entry

A bus pass that would represent London and allow entry to those invited to the opening of the European Office of the Mayor of London was the idea devised by designer Hem Patel at Bloomberg. The brief required the design to continue a theme set by a previous invitation enveloped by another agency, something identifiable with London without being stereotypical. At the opening, food and drink was served on a double decker bus, so the location became the inspiration at the same time.

An envelope, simply printed with the Mayor of London's logo, contained the invitation. The pass was designed to look as realistic as possible while incorporating details such as the location and map.

MAYOR OF LONDON

Event: Film screening of Beloved, 1998
Designer: No 17, USA
Response: RSVP by telephone

An invitation to the screening of Beloved, the film adaptation of Toni Morrison's novel set in the 19th century, sparked off this assorted typographic treatment, which included Sabon, Linotext, Garamond, Garamond Italic and Engravers Gothic fonts. The invitations were letterpress-printed and sent out to cast, crew and friends. RSVP was essential for admission, and required a response by 21st-century telephone.

YOU & A GUEST

ARE CORDIALLY INVITED

to attend

an extremely special screening

of

BELOVED

at

THE ZIEGFELD THEATER

141 WEST 54TH STREET

between 6TH AND 7TH AVENUES

IN NEW YORK CITY

at four o'clock in the afternoon
Sunday, the 13th of September, 1998.

———————————

AN **RSVP** IS

REQUIRED FOR ADMISSION

kindly CALL 212 807 6800
IF YOU WISH TO ATTEND.

———————————

Event: Dentist studio's anniversary party, 2002
Designer: Simon Gallus and Barbara Bättig at Fons Hickmann m23, Germany
Response: Vampire teeth to wear

A plastic set of Dracula-style teeth was the response mechanism for an invitation to a dentist studio's cocktail party. The client, Fassbender Zahngestaltung, commissioned Berlin-based design studio Fons Hickmann m23 to design an invitation which would celebrate the studio's 25th anniversary. The vampire theme was inspired by the dentist studio's corporate design, based on symbols depicting teeth. Its website features a drilling sound in its introduction, and its greeting card shows the teeth of celebrities such as Brigitte Bardot. According to the designers, "The design of a vampire's dentures is so special, that it is the perfect symbol for the anniversary of the studio, which designs teeth."

The invitation calls the victims to the tomb, hence the macabre tone. The party took place in the cellar of the studio; all guests wore the vampire teeth and bloody marys were served as drinks.

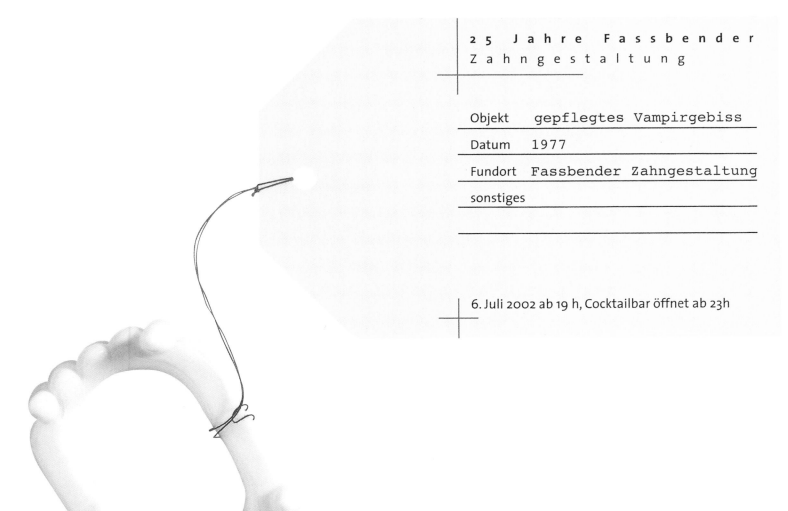

2 5   J a h r e   F a s s b e n d e r   Z a h n g e s t a l t u n g

Objekt   gepflegtes Vampirgebiss

Datum   1977

Fundort   Fassbender Zahngestaltung

sonstiges

6. Juli 2002 ab 19 h, Cocktailbar öffnet ab 23h

Event: Colette's New Year's Eve party, 2000
Designer: Groovevisions, Japan
Printer: Artomatic, UK
Response: Pass card printed in water-reactive ink to lick

For a New Year's Eve party called Tokyo Paris, trendy Parisian 'concept store' Colette commissioned Japanese designers and musicians Groovevisions to design the invitation. As part of the celebrations, the group was also showcasing its work at Colette with the exhibition 'Groovevisions GRV 1529'. A corrugated cardboard box contains a combination of items for the event. Inside, the invitation is printed onto a roll of yellow packing tape while a pass card is printed in water-reactive ink. The card looks like a simple black-and-white print job but adding water makes the print smear into a range of colours. Licking the card to reveal the printed colours proves authenticity and secures entry. Also enclosed is a colour litho-printed card

showing two of Groovevisions' cult Chappie characters, who sport the words 'Paris Tokyo' on their shirts. Normally, Colette uses standard postcard-format invitations, but Groovevisions' New Year's Eve event was deemed important enough for larger expenditure. The Chappie theme is reiterated on the paper address label of the cardboard box with a further ten characters, each with one letter on their shirts spelling out 'Paris Tokyo'.

The invitation was inspired by a visit to London-based printer and retailer Artomatic when Sarah, the artistic director and buyer at Colette, saw the printwork on packing tape and was impressed by the idea. However, according to Sarah, most people

did not understand that they could put water on the paper invitation to make the colour appear, allowing the idea to pass somewhat unnoticed.

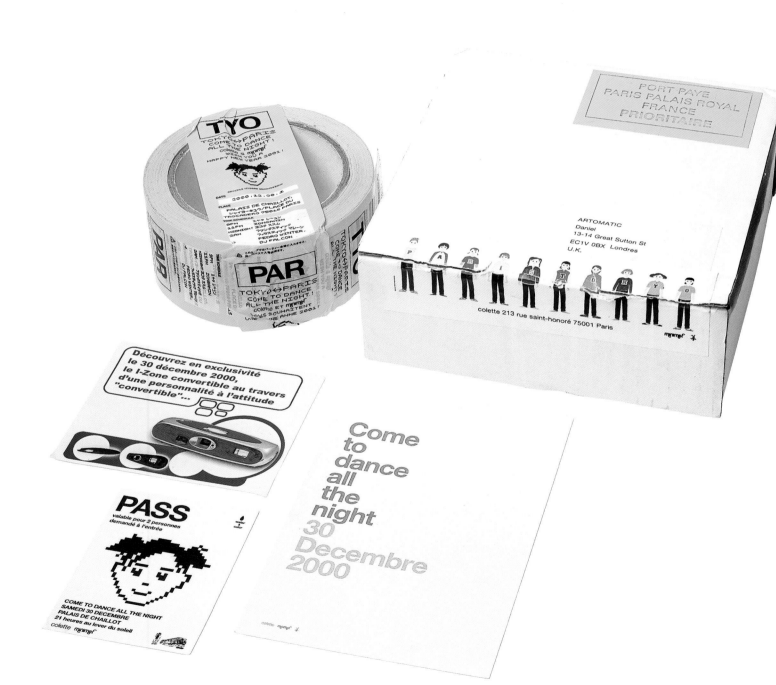

Response

Event: Yorkshire Water's 'The Children's Forest' project, 1999
Designer: Elmwood, UK
Response: The creation of a forest

UK design group Elmwood was asked by the UK water supplier Yorkshire Water to develop a regional campaign as part of a national tree-planting millennium project called 'Trees of Time and Place'. This involved major industry sponsors, environmental bodies and local children. The campaign highlighted the creation of a 'Children's Forest' on land owned by Yorkshire Water, along with the launch of an award-winning website for the benefit of schools, the community and the environment. It was also aimed at positioning Yorkshire Water as a community-conscious business.

The campaign was divided into two main phases. First, as a PR launch, a mailer was sent to the national and regional press, Members of Parliament, television personalities, VIPs, environmentalists and various opinion-formers. The mailer consisted of a tree sapling that guests could personally plant in the forest. Details of the event and a response mechanism were also enclosed.

Secondly, all head teachers of schools in the Yorkshire region were sent a mailer which included a leaflet, explaining the scheme as well as introducing the website and the educational potential of the project. Also included was an introduction to the 'Future Kids' (virtual friends) component, posters, merchandise, a T-shirt you add water to to make it expand and a CD with the software required to browse www.childrensforest.com. Where possible, uncoated natural paper stocks were used.

The response from the target audience was overwhelming. An estimated 47 per cent of the schools that received the packs subsequently asked to join the campaign. Yorkshire Water's Educational Department estimated a response rate of about 23 per cent. On the actual event day, children and the media planted the first trees, including oak and ash, in the Children's Forest. Today, the Children's Forest continues to grow. Each tree will outgrow each child, leaving a legacy for future generations to enjoy.

Response

Event: Launch event for BBC's children's television series 'I Was a Rat', 2001
Designer: Blast, UK
Response: A die-cut rat mask to wear

The UK television channel BBC1 wanted to produce an invitation which would be mailed to an adult audience, comprising the press and opinion-formers, but which would also appeal to the children attending the launch of a new television series.

The invitation had to reflect the programme's theme, be fun and, if possible, allow those invited to interact with it. Design group Blast came up with the idea of making the invitation a mask of a character from the storyline of the programme, where a boy had been turned into a rat. The children, whose ages ranged from six to ten, wore the masks to the launch event, thus paralleling the story. An illustrator was commissioned to create the mask in the

style of a children's book illustration. The invitation was litho-printed and die-cut to the shape of the rat's face. Finally, elastic was attached to hold the mask in place.

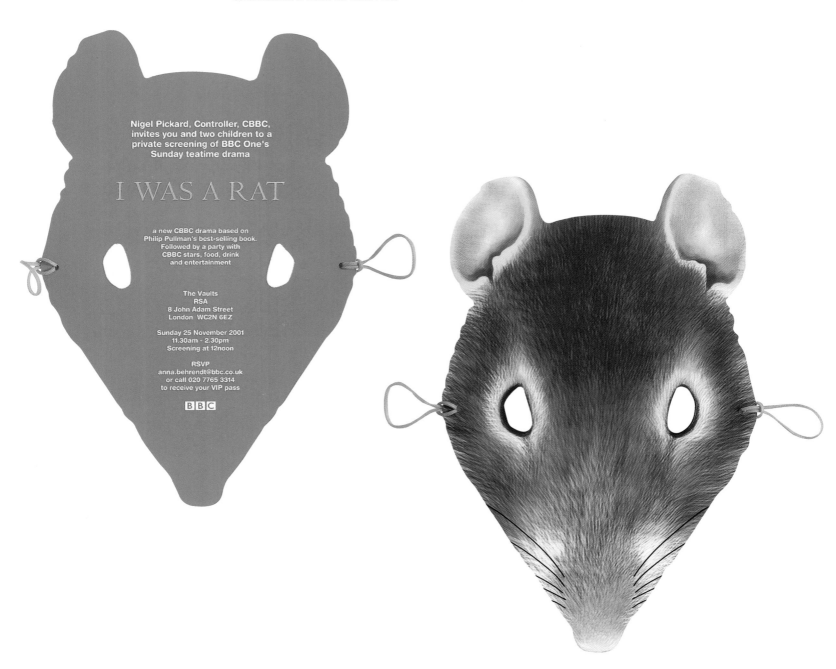

Nigel Pickard, Controller, CBBC, invites you and two children to a private screening of BBC One's Sunday teatime drama

I WAS A RAT

a new CBBC drama based on Philip Pullman's best-selling book. Followed by a party with CBBC stars, food, drink and entertainment

The Vaults
RSA
8 John Adam Street
London WC2N 6EZ

Sunday 25 November 2001
11.30am - 2.30pm
Screening at 12noon

RSVP
anna.behrendt@bbc.co.uk
or call 020 7765 3314
to receive your VIP pass

BBC

Event: Beck aftershow party, 2000
Designer: Orla Quirke at Polydor, UK
Printer: Artomatic, UK
Response: Luminescent bracelet to wear

A screen-printed Day-Glo green card bearing a luminescent bracelet was designed by Orla Quirke, head creative at music label Polydor's design department, for American singer Beck's aftershow party. The invitation was sent out to the media, fans and assorted celebrities. The card's colours reflect the artwork on Beck's then current album, Midnight Vultures. The party location, London's Cobden Club, was also decorated in similar fluorescent colours. The glowing bracelets, sourced by printer Artomatic, were originally made as emergency kit for lifeboats but have more recently been associated with rave music fans, who wave them as glo-sticks. Quirke wanted to create a device that would act as a memento of the party once the card

had been thrown away; an entry mechanism to appeal to both male and female guests. The bracelet works once the plastic is bent and shaken. Instruction details and a safety warning are printed on the back of the card.

Event: Alexander Gelman's Green Card party, 1998
Designer: Design Machine, USA
Response: The person identified by the card is allowed entry

A postcard-format invitation promotes a Green Card party for Alexander Gelman, the founder and creative director of New York design group Design Machine. The back of the card is a play on the real immigration Green Card and uses the language of the US Department of Justice/Immigration and Naturalisation Service. It plays on the idea of officious formality, stating 'Obscure Objects Magazine, 555 Gallery and Design Machine Co., LLC cordially invite you to Alexander Gelman's Green Card Party'. The person identified by the card is authorised to 'enter and re-enter the party, drink alcoholic beverages, and smoke cigarettes'. The fluorescent green card bears a barcode printed one-colour offset and was sent out to friends and clients of Design Machine.

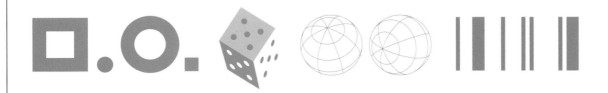

U.S. Department of Justice / Immigration and Naturalization Service
Obscure Objects Magazine, 555 Gallery and Design Machine Co.,LLC
Cordially invite you to Alexander Gelman's Green Card Party.

The person identified by this card is authorized to enter and re-enter
the party, drink alcoholic beverages, and smoke cigarettes.

Please join us in Void at 16 Mercer Street on Thursday, August 20th
There will be open bar from 8:00 to 9:30 and cash bar thereafter
DJ Code scratches from 10:30.

© 1998 Design Machine, 648 Broadway, New York NY 10012; phone: 212 982 4289; fax: 212 982 1260

Event: Coley Porter Bell office relocation, 2000
Designer: Roy Davison at Coley Porter Bell, UK
Response: Pop-up disc to send off

To inform Coley Porter Bell's clients, suppliers and friends of the design group's relocation to new offices, an invitation was sent inviting guests to pop in for a few drinks. The RSVP message is a play on the meaning of 'pop'. It is a call to action – 'Please pop round for drinks' – but it also requires the invitee to pop out a disc. The RSVP section is a pop-up part die-cut window, cut into 300gsm Dutchman Smooth paper. This was cut, form-creased and roll-folded to create an opening mechanism. The reply mechanism required guests to fill in the options, spelt out in a witty style, and send it off in a pre-paid envelope. Four special colours were used on both sides of the invitation, using a palette that reflected the new Coley Porter Bell brand colourway.

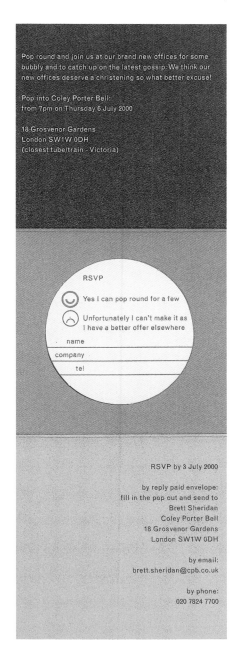

Pop round and join us at our brand new offices for some bubbly and to catch up on the latest gossip. We think our new offices deserve a christening so what better excuse!

Pop into Coley Porter Bell:
from 7pm on Thursday 6 July 2000

18 Grosvenor Gardens
London SW1W 0DH
(closest tube/train - Victoria)

RSVP

☺ Yes I can pop round for a few

☹ Unfortunately I can't make it as I have a better offer elsewhere

name

company

tel

RSVP by 3 July 2000

by reply paid envelope:
fill in the pop out and send to
Brett Sheridan
Coley Porter Bell
18 Grosvenor Gardens
London SW1W 0DH

by email:
brett.sheridan@cpb.co.uk

by phone:
020 7824 7700

please pop round for drinks

Event: New York and London launch
of NoiseFour, 2001
Designer: Attik, USA
Response: Digital invitation with URL links

The New York office of design group
Attik produced this online invitation to
showcase their book, NoiseFour, launched
in December 2001 and published by
HarperCollins. The online invitation was
sent out at the same time as a traditional
print card. Because the group has a
presence both in London and New York,
it created a double invitation valid for both
cities. The invitation uses Flash and HTML
and takes the user across a series of the
book's tableaux. The choice of a digital
format was motivated by the ability to
produce it quickly and cheaply in-house,
and because it afforded an effective
response mechanism. Most people –
around 95 per cent – chose to respond
by e-mail rather than postal (slow) mail.

Image from NoiseFour.
©2001ATTIK.

You are invited to the London
launch of NoiseFour.

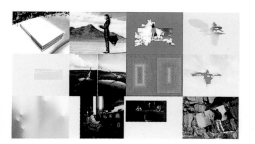

Date:
Monday 10
December 2001
Place:
Magma Bookstore
117-119 Clerkenwell Road
London EC1
Time:
6.30pm – 9.30pm

Private Invitation Only
R.S.V.P. Required
BiancaN@ATTIK.com
+44 (0)20 7674 3000

For information and
previews of NoiseFour
visit ATTIK.com

For directions and downloadable map
please visit www.magmabooks.com

NoiseFour. Five Studios. Synergy.
504 pages devoted to creativity, passion and vision.

ATTIKLondon, 3rd Floor, Elsley Court, 20-22 Great Titchfield Street London, W1W 8BE.

Event: Gallery clubsandwich.com launch, 2002
Designer: Benoit Poulain, France
Response: Submission of digital pictures

An invitation to an interactive, non-profit-making gallery called clubsandwich.com was e-mailed to creatives and designers internationally. Each recipient was cordially invited to submit a picture to display on the website. This could be a pre-formatted image file, perhaps of a photograph or illustration. The selected images would be assembled into a gallery on the website. A different image loads onto the homepage each time the page is loaded or refreshed. No specific theme for the entrants was required, so all spontaneous entries were accepted. The aim of the gallery is to make clubsandwich.com a personal space for talented designers while nurturing the notion of a club in which to share ideas.

Designed by Paris-based Benoit Poulain, clubsandwich.com is a personal project. www.studio.clubsandwich.com

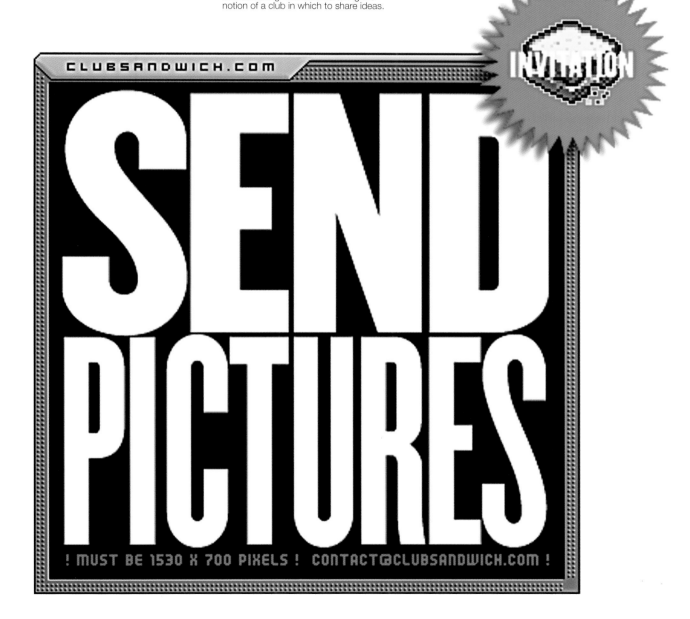

CLUBSANDWICH.COM

INVITATION

SEND PICTURES

! MUST BE 1530 X 700 PIXELS ! CONTACT@CLUBSANDWICH.COM !

Event: American Institute of Graphic Arts National Design Conference, 2002
Designer: Flat, USA
Response: An interactive game produces thoughts about design

For the American Institute of Graphic Arts (AIGA)'s ninth biennial design conference, 1,200 designers were invited to Washington DC to talk about passion, power and design's effect on politics. To aid the enormous task of inviting this scale of audience, Flat created an electronic invitation delivered by e-mail with links to a supporting website.

Following a theme of public service announcements, the invitation posed the topic 'What is design good for anyway?'. By using simple techniques, the invitation manages to engage those invited, arouse awareness about the conference, and also discuss subjects that would hopefully emerge at the conference itself.

With game-like interactivity featuring animation and sound, invitees can select a series of statements on design which connect to other statements and links, allowing them to build what Flat call "a web of thoughts about design". Statements often have clickable stars next to them which launch new browser windows with related links. Sometimes the links are directly related to the topic and sometimes they are more whimsical and funny in nature. One related link, an article on the CNN internet site about ballot design, guides the invitee into prompt discussion about the most significant design debate in the US the previous year, ie how the design of the ballot papers in the US Presidential election nearly led to

the breakdown in the democratic voting system. All interactions with the invitation eventually lead to a 'get involved' button that takes those interested to a voice-activated site to register for the conference itself.

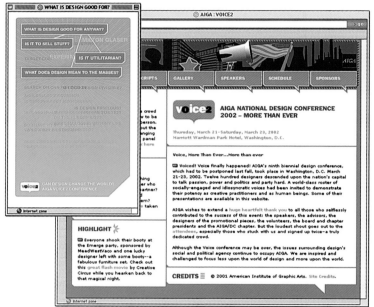

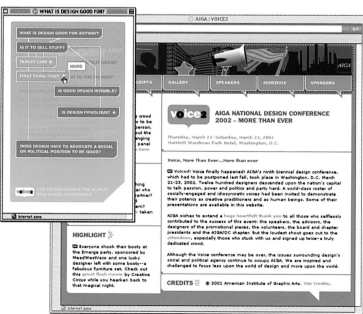

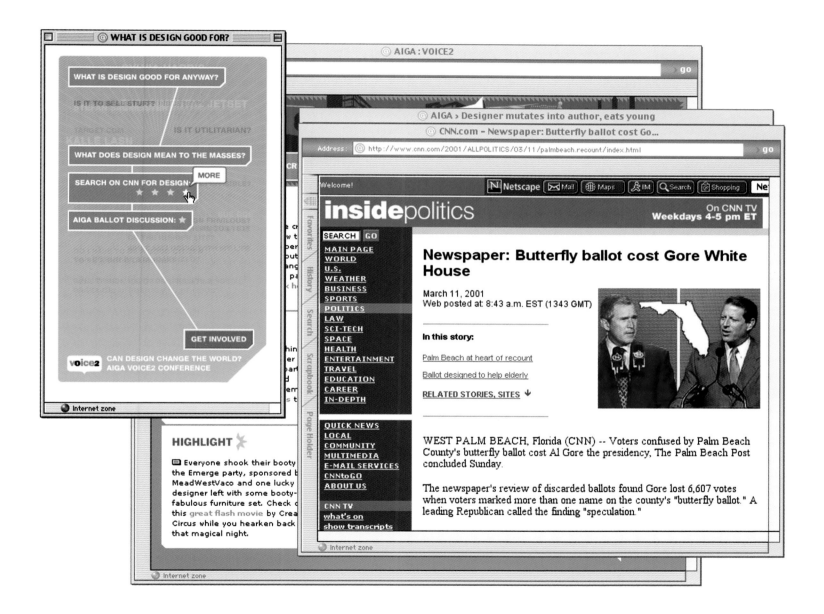

WHAT IS DESIGN GOOD FOR?

WHAT IS DESIGN GOOD FOR ANYWAY?

IS IT TO SELL STUFF?

IS IT UTILITARIAN?

WHAT DOES DESIGN MEAN TO THE MASSES?

SEARCH ON CNN FOR DESIGN   MORE
★ ★ ★ ★

AIGA BALLOT DISCUSSION: ★

GET INVOLVED

voice2 CAN DESIGN CHANGE THE WORLD?
AIGA VOICE2 CONFERENCE

Internet zone

AIGA : VOICE2

go

AIGA > Designer mutates into author, eats young

CNN.com – Newspaper: Butterfly ballot cost Go...

Address: http://www.cnn.com/2001/ALLPOLITICS/03/11/palmbeach.recount/index.html   go

Welcome!   Netscape Mail Maps IM Search Shopping Net

insidepolitics   On CNN TV
Weekdays 4-5 pm ET

SEARCH GO
MAIN PAGE
WORLD
U.S.
WEATHER
BUSINESS
SPORTS
POLITICS
LAW
SCI-TECH
SPACE
HEALTH
ENTERTAINMENT
TRAVEL
EDUCATION
CAREER
IN-DEPTH

QUICK NEWS
LOCAL
COMMUNITY
MULTIMEDIA
E-MAIL SERVICES
CNNtoGO
ABOUT US

CNN TV
what's on
show transcripts

Newspaper: Butterfly ballot cost Gore White House

March 11, 2001
Web posted at: 8:43 a.m. EST (1343 GMT)

In this story:

Palm Beach at heart of recount

Ballot designed to help elderly

RELATED STORIES, SITES ↓

WEST PALM BEACH, Florida (CNN) -- Voters confused by Palm Beach County's butterfly ballot cost Al Gore the presidency, The Palm Beach Post concluded Sunday.

The newspaper's review of discarded ballots found Gore lost 6,607 votes when voters marked more than one name on the county's "butterfly ballot." A leading Republican called the finding "speculation."

Internet zone

HIGHLIGHT ✕

▢ Everyone shook their booty
the Emerge party, sponsored b
MeadWestVaco and one lucky
designer left with some booty-
fabulous furniture set. Check
this great flash movie by Crea
Circus while you hearken back
that magical night.

Internet zone

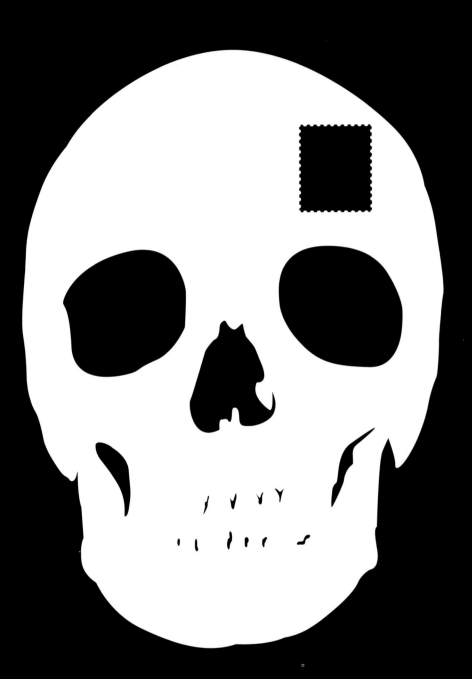

Lifecycle

Birth, marriage and death are three of life's milestones, marked by celebration and ritual. In a literate Western society, these events are often announced by invitation cards, a subliminal attempt to make permanent a transient, yet defining moment. In past centuries, the production of invitations was a sideline work for engravers. It eventually switched to the hands of typographers, who had a more specialised approach to the task (page 6). Today, invitations to christenings, birthdays, weddings and funerals may not follow the strict formal rules of the past, but they continue to represent deep-seated rites of passage. As a consequence, their design not only has to rise to the occasion but include the cultural considerations of etiquette, status and hierarchy.

Yet some invitations manage to avoid social clichés and test the boundaries of convention, adopting a language that best represents the sender's beliefs. A paperback trash novel, a photographic booklet or a tongue-in-cheek typographic treatment are all examples featured here that turn a common event into a unique one. This chapter offers a subjective and by no means exhaustive selection of formats and design languages used to deal with personal and special occasions. It as an arena where designers are at their most free to create, since they are usually commissioned by friends and relatives, and not constrained by a conventional client relationship.

Event: First birthday and godparenting celebration, 2001
Designer: Johnson Turnbull, UK
Lifecycle: Birthday of Rose Green

A corporate client asked designers Johnson Turnbull to create an invitation for her daughter's godparenting and first birthday. She wanted a personal, hand-crafted approach and asked for her daughter Rose's name to be incorporated visually. A playful use of type and a simple, graphic, hand-drawn flower combined with collage give immediate impact.

The materials used give textural as well as visual importance to the invitation. The small print run of 80 allowed the designers to produce the cards in-house, printing the type on tracing paper via laser printer to keep costs to the minimum.

The paper stock used was Fenner Pecunia, appropriately containing pieces of real banknotes inside to wish the child a happy and prosperous future. The square format was chosen to fit the envelopes the client had provided.

Event: Play-themed birthday party, 1999
Designer: Lana Le at Woolypear, USA
Lifecycle: Lana Le's 30th birthday

For her 30th birthday, designer Lana Le of Woolypear wanted to throw a kiddie party where guests played games and won prizes. To reflect the playful theme of the party, the designer created a childlike character of herself, Little Lana, and asked the guests to help dress her for her big day. (There was a prize offered for the best creation.) The invitation and colouring book designed for the party were based upon children's colouring and activity books, set in black and white. This allowed the designer to laserprint them and save costs. The colouring book was included in the goodie bag as a souvenir of the party.

The illustrations brought out a childish sense of excitement in the guests with a great response to the dress contest; one guest even fashioned a dress out of marshmallows. The copywriter Ransome Bruce helped the designer compose the playful tone of the invitation.

Event: An Italian-British wedding calls for a double typographic treatment, 2001
Designer: Paul Neale at Graphic Thought Facility, UK
Lifecycle: Marriage of Cristina Betto and Philip Hunt

As a favour to a friend, Paul Neale of design group Graphic Thought Facility created this bilingual wedding invitation. The brief suggested that the invite should not be over-the-top or ostentatious but as simple as possible. The solution was to create a black text-only invitation, with both sides worked up together and printed as a double-sided job, which was very economical. The pattern on the card was the groom's suggestion. While providing ornament to the invitation, it also recalls the decorative paving of Michelangelo's Campidoglio Square in Rome, where the registry office was located.

Plenty of blank space was left for the unapologetically handwritten names of the guests. The choices of type play with archetypes and are slightly tongue-in-cheek: Bodoni for the Italian and Gill for the English.

CRISTINA BETTO E PHILIP HUNT
HANNO IL PIACERE DI INVITARVI AL LORO MATRIMONIO
SABATO 15 SETTEMBRE ALLE ORE 16.50
COMUNE DI ROMA,
PIAZZA DEL CAMPIDOGLIO, ROMA

IL RICEVIMENTO SI TERRA' A VILLA SOSPISIO
VIA SAN FRANCESCO DI SALES, 20–23.
TRASTEVERE, ROMA

RSVP
CRISTINA BETTO E PHILIP HUNT
VIALE DELLE MILIZIE, 11/A
00193 ROMA
+39 063720284
CBETTO@ATLAS.CO.UK

CRISTINA BETTO AND PHILIP HUNT
REQUEST THE PLEASURE OF YOUR COMPANY AT THEIR MARRIAGE
ON SATURDAY 15TH SEPTEMBER 2001, 4.50PM
COMUNE DI ROMA,
PIAZZA DEL CAMPIDOGLIO, ROME, ITALY

AFTERWARDS AT VILLA SOSPISIO
VIA SAN FRANCESCO DI SALES, 20–23.
TRASTEVERE, ROME

RSVP
CRISTINA BETTO AND PHILIP HUNT
FLAT 3.1, PATTERN HOUSE, 223–227 ST JOHN STREET
CLERKENWELL, LONDON EC1V 4LY
+44 20 7251 3878
CBETTO@ATLAS.CO.UK

Event: A garden wedding in Santa Barbara, 2000
Designer: Margot Madison and Cindy Loon at Margot Madison, USA
Lifecycle: Marriage of Adi Kabatchnik and Jerry Greenberg

Cincinnati-based Margot Madison specialises in handmade custom invitation design for weddings and birthdays for celebrity showbusiness clients. A precursor to a garden wedding, this is a save-the-date card which anticipates both the event (with invitation to follow) and the style of the ceremony. Different hues of green – in the pea-green cardboard background, the dark green of the typography and mint green of the stationery – form the theme of the overall design. A semi-transparent slip on paper holding a tiny green leaf is delicately wrapped up in white ribbon. The recipient can remove the ribbon and vellum to find the recommended hotel accommodation inside the card.

Event: Wedding in a novel style, 2001
Designer: Love, UK
Lifecycle: Marriage of Catherine Armstrong and Dave Simpson

A torrid Mills & Boon-style paperback novel is the unlikely vehicle for inviting guests to Catherine Armstrong and Dave Simpson's wedding. But this Mills & Boon novel is a facsimile where the pages are left blank and a footnote announces that the happy couple's story is yet to be written. The foreword narrates the biography of the couple and a summary of how they met. The contents page lists the wedding day celebrations, from the church ceremony to the evening reception.

RSVP

The novel then reads that the couple will go on to an exotic honeymoon before returning home to begin experiencing the events that will eventually fill the pages. The back page reviews extracts from the best man's and the mother of the bride's speeches. Apart from fulfilling the obligation of inviting people to the wedding, design group Love had an open brief. Once the idea was conceived, the most important consideration was the production. The use of stocks was of paramount importance to recreate the authentic 1960s' Mills & Boon feel. The stock for the text pages was the most difficult to source – Bleached Episode IV from Fenner Paper. It had the toothy texture and colour of the original books.

A bookmark doubles up as the RSVP slip. The attention to detail shown even resulted in one guest not making it to the wedding because he threw the invitation away thinking it was a Mills & Boon book.

RSVP
WEDDING
INVITATION

I/We would love to attend your Wedding at St. James' Church, Sutton and afterwards at The Belgrade Hotel, Bollington on Saturday 30th June 2001 at 1.00pm

Please write your name and address on the reverse of this rsvp and return to:

**Mr & Mrs H.L.Armstrong
Star Lane Farm,
London Rd, Macclesfield,
Cheshire SK11 0JT.**

Issued by Mr & Mrs H.L.Armstrong Star Lane Farm, London Road, Macclesfield, Cheshire SK11 0JT. Tel 01625 431813

Copyright © Simpson 2001
All rights completely ignored

Printed and bound in Great Britain by Highlight Digital Imaging and Print, Warrington

Set in Adobe Granjon

The names of all characters and events in this book are no similarity between these names and those of actual persons, planned but could not be avoided.

This invite is issued subject to the condition that it shall not, b or otherwise, be lent, re-issued, hired out, sold on the black market or otherwise circulated to anyone who the issuers do not wish to attend their wedding. It was intended for you and we hope you can oblige.

The authors would like to express their indebtedness to the people who made this day a reality. From parents who raised us the way we have been raised, through friends who have influenced the way we have been influenced and the people who have made such an effort to make this the best day of our lives. Thank You.

CONTENTS

Following these events, the newly-weds will take a well deserved break in an exotic location (budgets determining exactly how long and how exotic), before returning home - hopefully to some modicum of normality - to begin experiencing the events of their lives that will eventually fill these pages.

Event: A summer wedding in Positano, 1999
Designer: Neil Churcher, UK
Lifecycle: Marriage of Sara Manuelli and Neil Churcher

Neil Churcher designed this invitation for his own wedding. He wanted the design to be simple and very informal, although he felt that a traditional 300mg white ivory card format was still appropriate. The invitation had to be written in both English and Italian, so Churcher used different colours to represent each language. Both texts are set formally side by side, but in garish pink and orange. The two-colour theme is reiterated in the illustration of the outline portraits of the couple. The portraits are set to a stylised illustration of the wedding venue in Italy, which looks down from the mountain over the town and sea below. Churcher used the white space to give a similar sense of distance to the real panoramic view.

Neil Churcher e Sara Manuelli
Hanno il piacere di invitarvi al loro matrimonio che si terrá al Comune di Positano, Via G. Marconi, Positano sabato 17 Luglio 1999 alle ore 18.30 e al ricevimento a Casa San Matteo, Positano.
RSVP Sara Manuelli,
Via dei Cappellari 35, 00186 Roma.

Neil Churcher and Sara Manuelli
request the pleasure of your company at their marriage at the Comune di Positano, Via G. Marconi, Positano on Saturday 17th July 1999 at 6.30pm and afterwards at Casa San Matteo, Positano.
RSVP Neil Churcher, 8 Wells House,
Spa Green, London, EC1R 4TR.

Event: A poetic wedding, 1997
Designer: Eggers+Diaper, Germany
Lifecycle: Marriage of Carol Parkin and Charles Diaper

In this invitation, Mark Diaper's brother Charles and Carol Parkin wanted to communicate the notion that they complemented each other perfectly. Their idea involved the reproduction of a poem on the invitation. According to Diaper, traditional wedding invitations tend to be factual statements, listing persons, times, dates and places presented in a style that generally promises a certain grandeur to the upcoming events; modern wedding invitations often balance the traditional approach with a style more suitable to the couple involved. This invitation falls in the latter category.

Printing the couple's names on opposite sides of a transparent Bible paper allowed the overlapping of the 'C' of Charles and the 'C' of Carol to form a perfect circle on the front cover. One line of the poem is just visible in the middle of the circle on the card underneath the Bible paper.

Event: A Japanese wedding with a Western style, 2001
Designer: Noboru Okano, Japan
Lifecycle: Marriage of a motorcycle magazine editor

The bridegroom is a Japanese motorcycle magazine editor who owns several Harley Davidsons. The bride loves driving, and wanted to portray the feeling of speed and excitement in the invitation. They commissioned designer Noboru Okano to produce a foldable invitation with simple yet bold lettering. The result is unconventional, resembling the imagery of pop culture rather than Japanese tradition. Most of Okano's work is for film, ranging from European and American international releases to small independent ones. His work includes flyers, posters and pamphlets for films commissioned by their distributing agencies, so he is well versed in Western iconography.

The invitation was sent out to the couple's relatives, close friends and colleagues. While the couple's family loved it, others failed to pick up the spirit of it, taking the visual image seriously and not comprehending that it had been staged.

Event: A Russian-Spanish
celebration, 2000
Designer: Oscar Mariné at OMB, Spain
Lifecycle: Marriage of Natasha Ivanova
and Jorge Brandi

Madrid-based designer Oscar Mariné
created his brother Jorge's wedding
invitation to Russian fiancée Natasha
Ivanova. The idea was to produce a formal
bilingual invitation presented in Mariné's
trademark cartoon-like style. The hard
slip envelope is made of minimal black
stiff card in handmade paper. On the front,
a red band in Cyrillic, set in Soviet era-style
typography, spells out 'We are getting
married'. Inside, a silkscreen-print
illustration of the couple is rendered with
Mariné's typical vibrantly coloured hues.
A semi-transparent slip in Spanish gives
the details of the wedding celebration.

Event: A modern American wedding, 2001
Designer: Stiletto, USA
Lifecycle: Marriage of Julie Hirschfeld and Bennett Killmer

New York-based design consultancy Stiletto wanted to design something simple, modern and unexpected for an invitation to an American wedding. The idea was to create a wedding invitation like a flyer for party events; a series of three simple, yet colourful postcards. The 'flyer' can be read from both sides – each with its own design. On one side there is the flower pattern, while the other features a more minimal design with lines and the information details. Emphasis was put on the techniques and materials, with high-quality paper and silkscreen-printing.

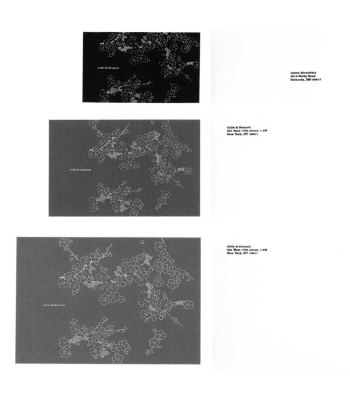

Event: An early-1960s themed wedding, 2003
Designer: Graceland Creative, USA
Lifecycle: Marriage of Grace Montemar and Antonio Garcia

Designer Grace Montemar of US design consultancy Graceland Creative created two versions of invitations for her own wedding. Because it was an early 1960s-themed wedding, a retro-inspired fabric was used as a top layer on the invitation to help set the tone of the event while piquing the guests' curiosity.

Each invitation was assembled by hand. An alternative, double-sided invitation features an organza ribbon tied towards the side playing on the 'tie the knot' expression. The reverse side displays names of the guests in the wedding party.

We've been **married** for so long, it's about time we ...

tied the *knot!*

PLEASE JOIN US AS WE CELEBRATE
OUR 10TH ANNIVERSARY
WITH THE WEDDING WE NEVER HAD.

Anthony and *Grace's* *Wedding*

Monday, the nineteenth of May
Two thousand and three
at ten o'clock in the morning

Saint Ita Catholic Church
5500 North Broadway Avenue
Chicago, Illinois

Luncheon cruise reception
following the ceremony
aboard The Odyssey at Navy Pier

Be there or be square.

Anthony and *Grace's* *Wedding*

WE'VE BEEN MARRIED FOR SO LONG,
IT'S ABOUT TIME WE ...

tied the *knot!*

PLEASE JOIN US AS WE CELEBRATE
OUR 10TH ANNIVERSARY
WITH THE WEDDING WE NEVER HAD.

Monday, the nineteenth of August
Two thousand and two
at ten o'clock in the morning

Saint Ita Catholic Church
5500 North Broadway Avenue
Chicago, Illinois

Luncheon cruise reception
following the ceremony
aboard The Odyssey at Navy Pier

Be there or be square.

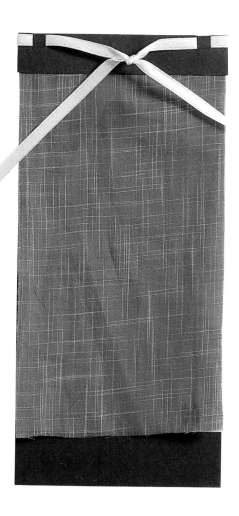

Event: An Op Art celebration, 2001
Designer: Margot Madison and
Cindy Loon at Margot Madison, USA
Lifecycle: Tammy Gustavson's 40th
birthday

This invitation is a play on Tammy 'turning' 40 years old. The birthday card plays with 1950s-style wallpaper and material pattern effects printed in gold, brown and strong pink. A small square of stiff card is set inside a square cut-out in the invitation, which twirls around when it is removed from the envelope. It is held together by a delicate thread of gold that allows the square to rotate freely. Set on the card are the invitation details on one side with a large number 40 on the other. Although employing bright, pop-ish colours, the quality of reproduction has produced a delicate effect, complemented by a crisp, tissue-like envelope of translucent gold.

Event: A Western-style anniversary celebration, 2000
Designer: Jon and Karen Wippich at Dotzerodesign, USA
Lifecycle: 50th wedding anniversary

Dotzerodesign often creates projects for family and friends. This 50th wedding anniversary for the parents of Jon and Karen Wippich is no exception. Since they live in Kansas, the sunflower state in the 'Old West' where farming and ranching are still going strong, the designers wanted to recreate an old Western look, but without going overboard.

They found some old engravings, used a screened backshot of the marriage certificate, a photograph of the parents as the background and Wild West-style fonts for the copy.

JOIN OUR PARENTS
FRED & ETHEL WIPPICH
AND US IN CELEBRATING THEIR
GOLDEN WEDDING ANNIVERSARY
Fifty 50 Years
An open house will be held on December 31, 2000
from 2 - 4pm at Trinity Lutheran Church, Winfield, Kansas
No gifts, please. Congratulatory cards are most welcome.
DEC. 23 1950   DEC. 23 2000
THE HAPPY COUPLE NOW RESIDE AT
N⁰. 18 FLEETWOOD DRIVE · WINFIELD, KANSAS 67156

Event: Memorial for actor father, 1999
Designer: Quentin Newark at Atelier Works, UK
Lifecycle: Commemorative wake for Derek Newark

Derek Newark, an actor, died in 1999. His sons, Rohan and Quentin, spread his ashes in the River Thames in London and held a wake for him outside the National Theatre. Rather than a simple invitation, they decided to design and print a small book that strived to capture and celebrate their father's life. The aim was to give those invited something permanent to remember him by.

Like many actors, Derek collected paraphernalia about his career like press cuttings, publicity photographs, programmes and letters. He also collected pictures of all the high points in his life, from his passing out parade at Sandhurst military academy to his first house.

According to Quentin Newark, the idea was to make the book the same way his father might have made it, ie with no design tricks, no fooling with the material to 'enhance' it and no words, since these would have been banal. His sons gathered all the pictures and made a narrative that concentrated on these high points that would be meaningful to anyone that knew their father, and would have made him proud. The book was printed on a simple, light, uncoated paper, and sent out with handwritten invitations to about 500 people. The wake was attended by some of British theatre's luminaries: Harold Pinter, Paul Schofield and Bill Bryden. As Quentin Newark explains, everyone loved the book, not because they were overwhelmed by

the design, in fact the opposite. They saw Derek Newark's life in the pictures; him being silly, playing roles, leading parades, winning accolades and being with friends.

Event: A Sri Lankan wedding looks at the stars, 2000
Designer: Kerr/Noble, UK
Lifecycle: Marriage of Kasunchana Wijeyawardena and Sujan Kapilasena

A Sri Lankan Buddhist marriage would traditionally look at the stars for the most auspicious date for a wedding. The bride and groom's star alignment is particularly important. In this case, the best moment for the couple was predicted at 6.44pm on 9 November 2000. Design group Kerr/Noble was commissioned by the London-based bride to create an invitation that would appeal cross-culturally – both to the British guests and the Sri Lankan relatives. Using the stars as a leitmotiv, the designers sourced an astrological map from Greenwich Observatory and replicated the wedding day's constellation arrangement in litho-printing, gold on gold, on the invitation.

Rosy & Kantha Wijeyawardena
REQUEST THE PLEASURE OF THE COMPANY OF

AT THE MARRIAGE OF THEIR DAUGHTER
Kasunchana TO Sujan
SON OF
Kamala & Upali Kapilasena
ON THURSDAY
9th NOVEMBER
2000

AT 6.30 PM, THE BALLROOM, THE BLUE WATER, WADDUWA
Poruwa at 6.44pm

FOLLOWED BY DINNER ...

R.S.V.P
Kmbuka
7A St.Dunstan's Drive
Gravesend
Kent DA12 4BH
United Kingdom
Telephone : 01474 334 969

54 Bullers Lane
Colombo 7
Sri Lanka
Telephone : 584932

Event: A wedding after 30 years, 2001
Designer: Chen Design Associates, USA
Lifecycle: Marriage of Maya and
Barry Spector

Drawing upon a myriad of aesthetic
styles and cultural references, from
Celtic, Hawaiian and Greek, the personal
influences of the couple are explored
in this wedding invitation created by
San Francisco-based Chen Design
Associates. The collection of wraps and
cards refers to the richness and complexity
of a relationship begun 30 years prior to
the actual ceremony. The materials used,
such as handmade and Japanese paper,
as well as the craft-like quality of the
letterpress printing and metallic silver
hand-stamps, reinforce the notion
of a special moment of celebration.

Max and Alex Spector invite you
to the wedding of their parents,
Barry and Maya

Saturday, September 8, 4:00 PM
At the home of Freyja Anderson and Paul Feder
19 Irving Avenue, Atherton

Reception immediately following the ceremony
RSVP regrets only by August 20: 650-329-1415

Casual dress
Bring low chairs or blankets
You are welcome to bring a swim suit
No presents please, but offerings of songs,
poems or flowers are welcome

MARSH ROAD
19 IRVING AVENUE
JAMES AVENUE

The Distance Between us
Is Holy ground
To be traversed feet bare,
Arms raised in joyous dance,
So that when it is crossed
The tracks of our pilgrimage
Will shine in the darkness
To light our coming together
In a bright and steady light.

From Highway 101, exit onto Marsh Road, heading west
Turn left onto Middlefield Road (where Marsh dead-ends)
Take the first left onto James Avenue
Take the first left again onto Heather Drive
Turn right on Irving Avenue
19 Irving Avenue is the first house on the left

Event: A magnetic wedding to remember, 1995
Designer: No 17, USA
Lifecycle: Marriage of Wesley Weissberg and David Goldberg

According to New York-based design group No 17, most people stick wedding invitations to their refrigerator with a magnet so as to be reminded of both the date and the event. No 17 decided to eliminate the middle man (the magnet) by printing a traditional wedding invitation on a two-ply magnet. The RSVP card and envelope were printed on conventional paper. When stuffing the envelopes, the designers had to be very careful to pack the RSVP card and the reply envelope behind the magnet, so that the package wouldn't stick to the side of the mailboxes. Years later, this invitation is still on refrigerators throughout the tri-state area, holding up invitations to other events.

Four years on, the couple had a baby and No 17 designed a miniature magnetic announcement for the birth of their little girl Elinor.

Event: A baby envelope announces a new life, 2000
Designer: No 17, USA
Lifecycle: Announcement of the birth of Owen August Scher

Although not exactly an invitation, this birth announcement follows, at first glance, the rules of formal invitations. No 17 felt that Owen, the son of Bonnie Siegler, one of the design group's founders, should have an appropriately scaled envelope and card announcing his arrival. No 17 believed there is a special feeling about pulling a tiny card out of a tiny envelope that makes one aware that a small and fragile life has entered the world.

The smaller card containing Owen's name and birth date is embraced by the larger card with Bonnie and the father Jeff's names, underlining how he is actually a part of the two of them. The font used is called, appropriately, Asswipe Deluxe.

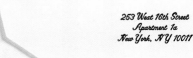

Practical tips

Producing an invitation is a precise art. What could be considered a small, manageable task can sometimes require thought and effort out of proportion to its scale. Clients often underestimate the importance of invitation design to a project, adding it as an afterthought with little budget and tight timescales. But it is important, as the invitation has to attract those invited to the event, or face failure. There is pressure on the designer to succeed: success requires a skilful approach to using all the range of practical elements and production techniques to communicate and attract in as economical a way as possible.

This chapter discusses most of the elements to consider when designing and sending out an invitation. It specifically focuses on commercial events such as those organised by public relations (PR) consultancies and organisations, for whom specific guidelines can help to increase the turnout of the event.

What to say, and how to say it

"An invitation must state the obvious," says Julian Vogel of Modus Publicity, a London-based public relations company which deals with fashion, beauty, lifestyle, press and events. "It has to convey simple information that is neither boring nor alienating. As a sender of an invitation you must make the recipients realise what 'type' of event they will be attending – whether it is an exclusive presentation for the press or a public event for a customer." A well-thought-out invitation should be an ambassador of the event, so evoking the essence of it is fundamental. Vogel recalls turning up late and dishevelled to an event at a major London art museum only to find out it was a sit-down breakfast for 20 and not, as he had thought, a general programme presentation. The tone of the invitation had obviously not conveyed the exclusivity of the event.

According to Vogel, both the medium and the message of the invitation need to be simple. An invitation should be both beautiful and elegant. Gimmicky objects and unconventional formats can work according to the type of audience and event, but a design can backfire if it slips beyond irony into the realm of bad taste. Vogel has found that even for fashion shows, a domain where invitation design is traditionally free to conjure up the deluxe and the desirable, the press tend to be familiar with the designer already, so most invitations in effect function like a cinema ticket, specifying date, time and seat number, rather than enticing them with the idea of the collection.

1

2

1, 2, 3)
Invitations created by in-house design team at Bloomberg, the financial news provider.

4)
Invitation designed by fashion label Fake London's in-house team.

Commissioning the design
Ideally the design of an invitation should be commissioned four weeks before the event. "Invitations are usually a low-budget job. They are a great opportunity to try out new people," says Vogel.

While some clients will suggest a graphic design company to Modus, Vogel prefers to commission new designers or photographers for different jobs, finding out who suits his needs best. For clients who have a design group already curating their identity and print material, invitations become an extension of that particular relationship.

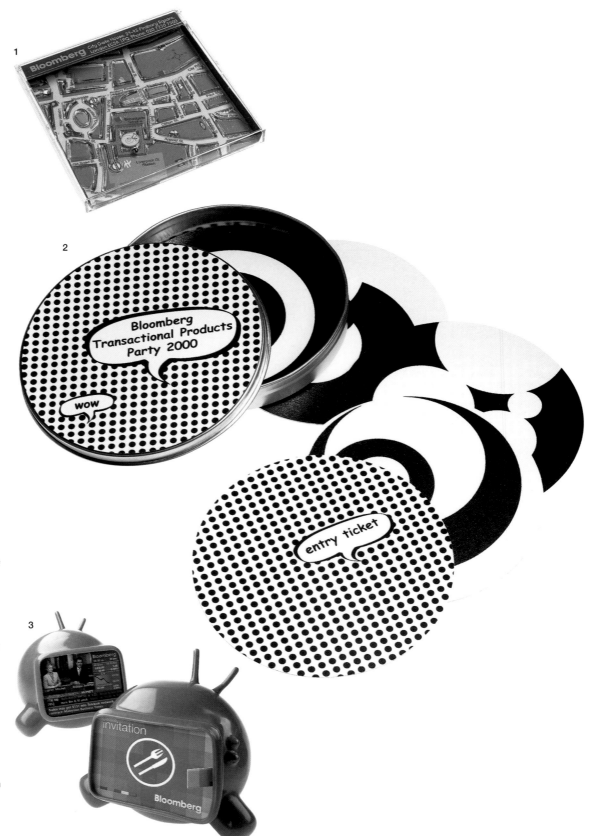

How many will attend?

Response mechanisms are more of a guessing game than a precise science. "We obviously send out RSVP cards, but invariably I've found that a third of the invitees turn up," says Vogel. For occasions such as press days, when one needs an idea of how many people will be coming, the invitation should strongly imply the need to RSVP. Formal seated dinners and very popular exclusive events also require a strict monitoring of who is attending, first by post or e-mail, and then by telephone. Response mechanisms are usually allowed until the very last minute. The number of invitations to send out is closely connected to the nature of the event; for example restaurant, club and bar openings, where the flow of people is bound to fluctuate during the evening, require considered number guessing. "If the capacity of a restaurant is 200 you can probably allow yourself to send out 700 invitations," says Vogel.

When to send invitations out

When to send an invitation is also a subtle art. "There is a fine balance between sending them so early that people forget and sending them out enough in advance so people can make the date," says Vogel. "To ensure that we have the right turnout, we sometimes send out save-the-date cards, to flag the event and the date in people's diaries – it also starts people talking about the event."

Ideally invitations should be sent out two weeks in advance but often, either because the client's brief or the printing job is late, they are sent out later. Since work-related events usually happen midweek, the last feasible day to receive an invitation becomes the Monday of the week before. Postal (snail) mail rather than e-mail is still the preferred way of sending invitations, a custom that may have a short future, with desktop calendars and electronic diary management becoming more available.

1, 2, 3, 4, 5)
Invitations created by in-house design team at Bloomberg.

How to send invitations out

The effective invitation works hard from the moment it drops through the letterbox. A poor design gives little attention to the envelope format or its tactile quality. Ultimately the sender wants the practicality of a size and weight which won't incur extra postal charges. Most will opt for a standard A5 envelope since much of the budget has already been spent on the invitation inside. There is an argument, however, that a jaded audience of press and opinion-formers responds better to unconventional or precious formats. When the budget and the occasion allow it, the envelope should be considered as important as the invitation.

A sense of expectation and mystery when opening an envelope is an important element that designers should incorporate. Leading the customer to realise it's an invitation and not a bill is a first step. Some art galleries tend to send out invitations in larger than average envelopes, immediately differentiating them from more tedious mail. An embossed or printed mark of the gallery or promoter adds the expectation without revealing the precise nature of the event.

Some design groups choose diamond-shaped envelopes, traditionally associated with parties, birthdays and intimate occasions to create a sense of anticipation. Just as Manilla envelopes speak of bills and officialdom, envelopes with internal 'noise' patterns suggest secrecy and confidentiality. All envelopes are markers for their contents. Handwritten invitations are also subject to taste, although there is little doubt about the aesthetic allure of a carefully conceived calligraphic invitation.

According to Vogel, when sending out a large quantity of invitations, it is essential to limit the amount of work it takes to send them out. On these occasions, handwritten names might be too time-consuming. Correct spelling of names is essential, and all doubts concerning postal addresses need to be checked beforehand.

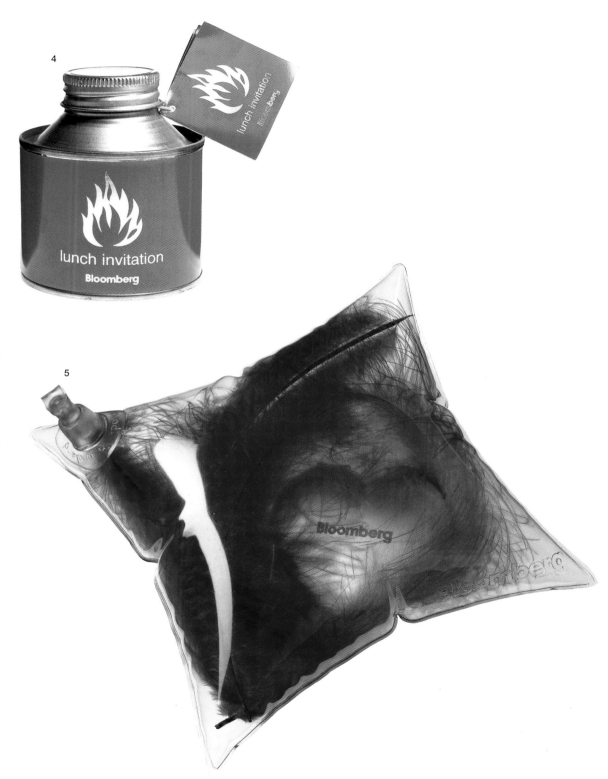

4

5

Case studies

In this section we look at the work in progress of invitation projects by three different design groups. Each project is illustrated by a series of preliminary sketches or ideas, from the initial presentation to final solution. Issues such as budget, time and technical constraints are analysed – all factors that can influence the final outcome.

British Design & Art Direction awards, 2001
Designed by SEA, UK

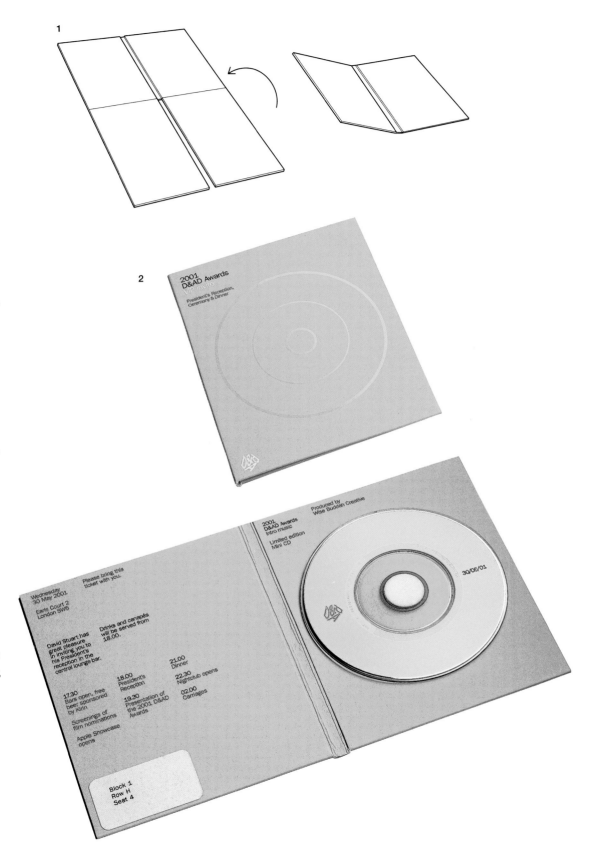

Initial brief
On the back of a long-term collaboration with British Design & Art Direction (D&AD), the London-based design group SEA was asked to design an invitation for its annual award gala ceremony and dinner. This is the design and advertising industry's most important annual event and a great chance for networking and catching up with clients. SEA was asked to produce three versions, one for the press, one for designers and one for VIPs. The invitation brief required the design to be elegant yet intriguing.

Research
SEA decided to focus on the map of the evening's layout as a theme. The event, staged at Earls Court Two in London, was arranged around three concentric circles. The idea of the circle was then realised as an audio CD. Musical collective Wise Buddha was brought on board to create a special audio identity for the evening. The pop singer Boy George was also scheduled in to DJ at the after-dinner party.

1)
SEA's initial idea was to create a CD box. A card sheet was folded into a four-sided panel, which in turn was folded into a slab of boxboard. A recess was embossed over the surface deep enough to hold the CD. The design was printed with a sparse setting of information text. The invitation would then be vacuum-packed, the idea being that the invitee would unwrap the invitation, take the CD and keep the boxboard as a pass for the night. SEA designed three versions: grey for designers, yellow for VIPs and white for the press.

This first solution was rejected for practical reasons. D&AD found the type too minimal and was worried that there was nothing to hold the CD once the cellophane had been unwrapped. Also, the size of the invitation proved too big to put in an average pocket, impairing its function as an entry ticket. The design needed to be a package that would hold the CD, be transportable, sit on the dinner table and read well. As a compromise, SEA decided to use a smaller sized CD. A 2 inch CD was specially produced in Holland and printed in two colours, grey and yellow. The white version was dropped.

2)
The final solution comprises two invitations:
yellow for VIPs and grey for designers and
press. The invitation was produced on A4
Scancote 270gsm paper and then double
folded to appear like a mini book with
a coloured spine. On the cover, a spot
UV varnish circle recalls the original idea
of the map of the show. Because the audio
identity on the CD was substituted by
a promotional jingle at the last minute,
the invitation changed its message from
a sampler of the evening to a more
conventional ticket entry format.

Check list
– Consider type size carefully. Minimal fonts
  might not work for large-scale events.
– If the invitation relies on the collaboration
  of other sponsors, make sure their
  presence does not affect your design
  too closely. In the event of their pulling
  out or changing their intentions, you will
  have to modify the layout at short notice.

2

Flowerstore opening, 2001
Designed by Multistorey, UK

Initial brief
Flowerstore owners Anita and Amala Shah and their public relations (PR) company Rossana Tich, wanted an invitation for the opening of a new shop in London's Oxo Tower Wharf Complex. The clients were familiar with London-based design group Multistorey's work. Budget-wise, they wanted to evaluate the costs once they had seen the proposals.

Research
Multistorey visited the shop to assess the atmosphere that needed to be conveyed. The moody and atmospheric interiors are filled with rich-coloured mosaics and dark wooden furniture. The plants sold are unusual, almost architectural in their form. Multistorey focused on the variety of textures available and on the relationship between the natural organic forms and their designed habitat.

1)
Multistorey's initial idea was to photograph plants in a more natural setting, such as the botanical gardens at Kew, and to over-print the resulting prints with letterpress text. Each invitation would be in effect a one-off, mirroring, in some small way, an individuality like that found in nature. The slightly indented letterpress text gives textural contrast to the gloss finish of the photographic print. For the presentation, Multistorey mocked up images on the computer using archive photographs of plants.

2)
The second proposal focused on plant leaves and their sheer size. Multistorey first wanted to apply the text to the leaves themselves by stencilling with paint, but that was soon deemed too artificial. Eventually the designers decided to cut the text from the body of the leaf itself and photograph it backlit, emphasising the text as well as the texture of the leaf. For the presentation, it chose a selection of interesting leaves and scanned them in a variety of arrangements, manipulating them in Photoshop to show text cut crudely from them.

2

　　　RSVP

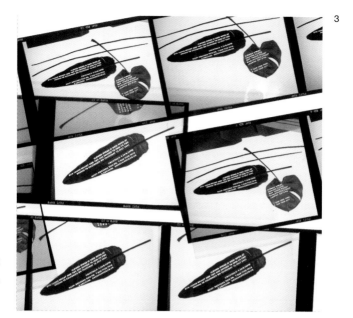

3

3)
The client overwhelmingly preferred the leaf idea. Multistorey wanted to show the leaves at life size so needed an A3 format. The printer test-printed on samples of Ikono Colour Paper. The test print showed that the ink appeared to sit on the surface of the paper, creating a contrast in surface quality. This brought out the lifelike quality of the leaves. Text was overlaid on the scans. The text was then over-printed in black as a guide for cutting.

4)
The print cost was quite high as a print run of 750 invitations was printed full colour on A3. The client decided it wanted to maximise value by trimming down any leftover invitations to re-use for the contact details of the shop. This influenced the composition of the invitation, which had to be trimmed in half. The amount of copy initially anticipated increased, limiting Multistorey to use particular sizes and shapes of leaves. On the day of the shoot, there was a race against time to photograph the leaves before they deteriorated. A specific person was allocated to cut out letters, using the text layout as a guide to keep the positioning neat. Letters were cut out using a scalpel, the process taking several hours.

Check list
– If the invitation refers to a venue or a place, don't forget to visit the location.
– Try to present your idea as closely as you can to the ideal finished product.
– Account for changes in copy when thinking about size and format.
– If you are composing the invitation during the photographic studio session, make sure you know exactly the amount of time it will take to proceed with the more laborious manual tasks.

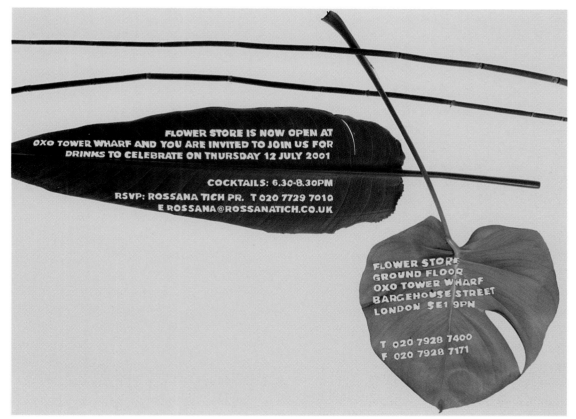

4

Case studies

Surrealism Unbound party at the
Tate Modern, 2001
Designed by Stephane Caudron at
Bloomberg, UK

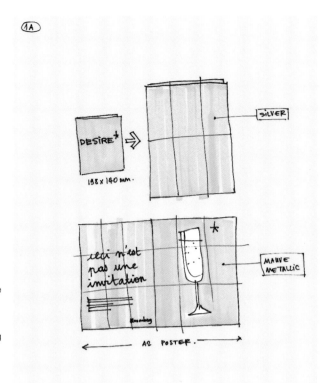

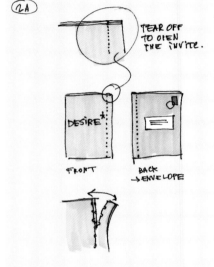

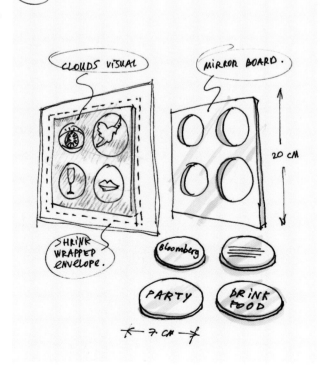

Initial brief
Bloomberg was hosting a VIP party at
the Tate Modern gallery on 14 November
2001, during the same time as the gallery's
'Surrealism: Desire Unbound' exhibition.
Various heads of department across the
company were asked to invite their key
contacts and clients. The design of the
invitation had to reflect the surrealism of the
show, and emphasise the unique, highly
desirable and eye-catching content.

Research
For the invitation to work, an understanding
of the exhibition was needed. It was the
first major exhibition of international
surrealism to be held in London for over
20 years. The exhibition was centred
around one of the defining themes of
the movement: desire, which permeated
much of the art and poetry produced
by the surrealists. The designers wanted
to reproduce the concept of desire within
the contemporary, fun context of a party.

1)
This sketch for an invitation refers loosely
to Belgian artist René Magritte's painting
'La Trahison des Images' ('The Betrayal of
Images'). By using the glass of champagne
instead of the pipe, the invitation would
reveal the fact that it is a stylish party and
reinforce the word 'desire'. The A2 format
when opened would give the invitation the
illusion of a painting.

2)
The idea behind the second sketch
was to reveal the theme of the party
(and the exhibition) in a playful way. A glass
of champagne was added to three other
major inspirational icons of the movement
(an eye, a bird and lips). These visuals
would be printed black and white on
a cloud background, and die-cut.
On the back of each piece, information
would be printed referring to each visual
(bloomberg logo > eye / address > bird /
party > glass of champagne / food > lips).

3)
Sketches of the envelope were also drawn
to show how the invitation should be
accessed by tearing along a perforation
in the envelope.

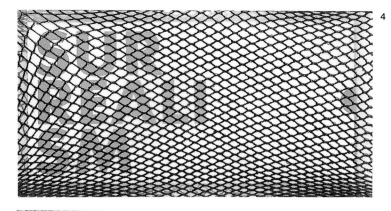

4

4)
After the initial concepts, two ideas were decided upon and mocked up. The first mock-up was a design involving 'fishnet' stocking material as a wrap around the invitation. This conveys the idea of desire and plays on the fact that the recipient would have to unwrap the invitation. This invitation was to be shrink-wrapped to enclose the contents within a kind of second skin. The actual invitation was designed using black and bright pink to convey both sensuality and desire. Each word was separated to give a playful, almost surreal, feeling to the design. The choice of the paper stock for the card was a heavy gloss-board to convey a sense of quality. The client rejected the design as its sexual overtones were deemed too controversial.

5)
The second and final design played with surrealist elements such as the use of embossed text on the front instead of printed text and the use of mirrors, common to the art of the surrealist movement. The word 'unbound' was die-cut to add a further dimension to the invitation and create a window through the card. A pink bra-strap was placed around the card to suggest desire and sexuality. This also helped to reinforce the idea of the 'unbound' title on the front. The VAG font was chosen because of its rounded and soft feel, which again picked up on the theme of the party, as did the decision to die-cut rounded corners on the invitation. The envelope was printed using the same colours as the invitation card, but they were inverted. The metallic film envelope has a rubbery texture which enhances the sensual feeling of the invitation. The total production time was two weeks.

Check list
– If the invitation refers to an exhibition, conduct accurate historical and visual research about the period to find iconic and textual inspiration for your design.
– Remember who you are targeting. An invitation may need to be watered down if it's a corporate business audience, or spiced up if it's a media-aware one.
– Choose materials that reflect the essence of the event.

5

Acknowledgements

A special thank you goes to Neil Churcher for his constant support, insight and criticism.

Many thanks to all those who provided advice and help for this book, especially: Michael Alcock, Rhonda Drakeford at Multistorey, Bryan Edmondson at SEA, Chris Foges, Peter Hall, Kanae Hasegawa, Daniel Mason at Artomatic, Paul Neale and Andy Stevens at Graphic Thought Facility, Quentin Newark at Atelier Works, Lynda Relph-Knight, Adrian Shaughnessy at Intro, Stefan Sagmeister, Kirsten Schellenberg at Bloomberg, Julian Vogel at Modus Publicity.

Another thank you goes to all those designers who submitted material and provided information about their work.

Last but not least, a big thank you to my RotoVision editor Erica ffrench, and to Mummy for babysitting.